"In 2019, the Holy Father said in ar
gift . . . not a monster . . . we must talk about it.' If we taught kids to drive
a vehicle the same way we taught them about sex, we'd throw a manual
at them and say, 'Let me know if you have any questions.' Adults are
scared to speak about sex mostly because we didn't receive 'the talk' well.
This book holds the trembling hands of parents and gives them assurance
that sex is good and that teaching their children about this powerful gift
is as imperative as sitting in the passenger seat for driving lessons."

**Rev. Daniel Ciucci**
Pastor in the Archdiocese of Denver

"In this extraordinarily practical book, Dr. Julia Sadusky wades into
the very difficult topic of helping parents talk to teens today about sex.
I remember as a teenager my father taking me to a class (probably my
mother asked him to) and speaking to me about sex. Most of it went over
my head at the time, but the fact that he had the courage and wisdom
to speak to me, or at least to go with me to a class—which, by the way,
was offered by a secular community college—left me so very grateful
and also so very respectful of human love and sexuality. Dr. Sadusky
does her best to present a reasonable Catholic approach to this important
topic, as faithful as possible to the Church's magisterium. This is a good
read for parents."

**Bishop Gregory John Mansour**
Eparchy of Saint Maron of Brooklyn

"Dr. Sadusky's treatment of this critical topic matters to us on so many
levels. As parents of adult children and now young grandchildren,
we wish we had read this book when our children were younger! The
book breaks down difficult questions about sexuality into bite-size por-
tions and offers real-world examples of how they might be answered.
Even more, the book offers lots of hope and encouragement for parents
and teens who might not have gotten things right the first time. As a
Catholic theologian, I (Michael) appreciate the book's accessible way
of sharing the Church's teaching on the goodness of marriage and
sexuality, all within an age-appropriate understanding of child development and human psychology. As a therapist, I (Nancy) recommend
this book as an important tool for parents to build better relationships
with their teens through open and honest communication. Ultimately,

this book is essential reading for every parent, teacher, pastor, minister, and clinician."

**Michael Dauphinais and Nancy Dauphinais**
Professor and chair of theology at Ave Maria University; licensed mental health counselor and certified addiction professional

"Here is a book that translates with precision and prudence the truth and the beauty of St. John Paul II's theology of the body for the practical life of the family and the healthy education of your teens. This is a book that can break the spell that has bound so many parents and rendered them mute regarding conversations about the beauty of their children's embodied life and God's glorious design for them. Dr. Sadusky equips parents and empowers them to enter into essential conversations in this essential book. With a host of very practical guiding points, conversation starters, and visual aids, all guided and inspired by the anthropology of St. John Paul II, Dr. Sadusky has given a great gift to the domestic life of the Church."

**Bill Donaghy**
Senior lecturer and content specialist at the Theology of the Body Institute

"This book is an incredible resource! As a school nurse, educator, and parent, I found *Talking with Your Teen about Sex* an insightful, practical, and extremely helpful tool to help teach children from a young age about sexual health in a holistic manner grounded in solid Catholic teaching. This should be on the bookshelf of every parent and educator."

**Michele Faehnle**
Author, speaker, and school nurse advisor in the Diocese of Columbus Office of Catholic Schools

"In my work accompanying women through recovery from addictions to pornography and other unwanted sexual behaviors, I regularly encounter the pain and shame that can come from a lack of loving education on sexuality in our upbringing. The manner in which parents speak to their children about sex can have lifelong effects, for good or ill—as a faithful parent, that knowledge can be a heavy weight. Dr. Sadusky offers a thoughtful, comprehensive, and sound guide to this crucial conversation. I will be wholeheartedly recommending this book to parents looking for direction."

**Rachael Killackey**
Founder of Magdala Ministries and author of *Love in Recovery*

# TALKING
## with your
# TEEN
## about
# SEX

## A PRACTICAL GUIDE
## FOR CATHOLICS

# JULIA SADUSKY

AVE MARIA PRESS AVE  Notre Dame, Indiana

Scripture quotations are from the *Revised Standard Version of the Bible—Second Catholic Edition (Ignatius Edition)*, copyright © 2006 National Council of the Churches of Christ in the United States of America. Used by permission. All rights reserved.

*Nihil Obstat*:     Reverend Monsignor Michael Heintz, PhD
             *Censor Librorum*

*Imprimatur*:     Most Reverend Kevin C. Rhoades
             Bishop of Fort Wayne–South Bend
             *Given at*: Fort Wayne, Indiana, on November 14, 2023

---

© 2024 by Julia Sadusky

All rights reserved. No part of this book may be used or reproduced in any manner whatsoever, except in the case of reprints in the context of reviews, without written permission from Ave Maria Press®, Inc., P.O. Box 428, Notre Dame, IN 46556, 1-800-282-1865.

Founded in 1865, Ave Maria Press is a ministry of the United States Province of Holy Cross.

www.avemariapress.com

Paperback: ISBN-13 978-1-64680-224-1

E-book: ISBN-13 978-1-64680-225-8

Cover image © Gettyimages.com.

Cover and text design by Christopher D. Tobin.

Printed and bound in the United States of America.

*Library of Congress Cataloging-in-Publication Data is available.*

TO MY DAD:
THANK YOU FOR TEACHING ME A CATHOLIC VISION
OF SEXUALITY AND FOR EMBODYING IT WITH JOY
FOR MANY YEARS. THANK YOU FOR LOVING ME. NEI-
THER LIFE NOR DEATH CAN SEPARATE ME FROM YOUR
LOVE AND GOD'S LOVE. THIS ONE'S FOR YOU.

WHEN ONE TEACHES, TWO LEARN.

—ROBERT HEINLEIN

I WISH SOMEONE HAD REMINDED ME EARLIER ON TO PARENT OUT OF LOVE, NOT FEAR.

—CINDY MORGAN

# CONTENTS

# INTRODUCTION

As a psychologist who has spent many years working with teenagers and their families, I often feel sad when I hear how many adults dread being around teens. Some of my most rewarding moments in therapy have been with a teen who gradually learns to validate and speak about their emotions, discovers answers to deep spiritual questions, and comes to experience themselves as good, capable, and lovable. These moments and opportunities to build a relationship with a teen are precious, to be sure. In fact, some of the most edifying witnesses of Christian faith, hope, and charity are teens I have had the privilege to walk with. They remind me of the great saints who, even as teens, boldly lived the Gospel!

Lest we sugarcoat things, I also want to acknowledge that building and maintaining an open and honest relationship with a teenager is *not* easy. There are valid reasons why parenting a teenager feels hard—maybe even harder today than it has been in previous generations. Developmentally, teens lack the neurodevelopment that will help them more effectively identify, name, and manage their emotions as adults. Teens' gradual developmental process can lead to intense emotional volatility from some teens, emotional suppression and disconnection from others, poor planning and anticipation of the long-term consequences of choices, and increasing resistance against sources of authority, including parents and teachers. On top of everything else, youth (and you as their parents) are seemingly busier and more distracted than ever before.

With so many distractions competing for everyone's attention, sexuality-related conversations often happen poorly or not at all. By the time most Christian parents start broaching the topic of sexuality, teens have been educated by other sources—sources that don't share a Christian vision for personhood, sexuality, and what it means to be a sexual being. Despite the Catholic emphasis that parents ought to be primary educators of their children, many teens in Christian homes are primarily influenced by friends and social media influencers.[1] Amid these competing voices, when parents don't build trust with their teens to participate in their education and formation, it's no wonder so many Christian youth are leaving the faith in college and beyond.[2]

Remember, you are not done parenting when a teen begins to communicate that they have no need of you. Teens are known to push away relationships with trusted adults more and more at this stage of development. Peers matter most—at least, that's what teens often seem to believe. This reality makes it more difficult for you to remember that, though they might admit it only begrudgingly, teens desperately need their parents as a secure base, a source of wisdom and unconditional love. In fact, the quality of your relationship with your teenager and your investment into that relationship—no matter how difficult it might be—will bear more fruit than you realize for years to come.

All too often, a crisis is what initiates conversations about sexuality with teens. Once a parent finds out about a teen's pornography use, sexual behaviors, secret relationships, or the like, most parents will reactively make the time to talk about sex. But proactive conversations are few and far between. I hope this book will help change that, especially in Catholic families and schools. The book you're holding is meant to help parents and teachers have proactive conversations about sex and sexuality. It's meant to help you nimbly, calmly, and directly shape the minds of teens toward an integrated and distinctively Christian understanding of their sexuality, as well as the goodness, beauty, and divine purposes therein.

Is this just another book to help you teach your kids about sex? To be sure, we'll spend a whole chapter helping you more effectively talk with your teen about sexual intercourse, including specific principles for the "sex talk" as we know it. There are other books, Catholic and otherwise, that have done this as well, and some of these will spell out a Catholic sexual ethic in greater detail than this one.

However, this book also goes beyond the typical "sex talk," equipping you to talk *with* your teens about bodily changes, physical boundaries, sexual ethics, technology use, pornography, masturbation, and the like with greater comfort. Once your teen knows the practical aspects of genitalia, their functions, and sexual intercourse, there is so much more for them to understand about relationships, healthy intimacy, and a robust understanding of their own embodiment. This book is meant to be proactive, practical, graceful, and responsive to the questions of your children as they enter puberty and beyond. It will challenge you in ways that, at times, will be uncomfortable. It will also equip you to face challenging moments with compassion, grace, and courage.

If you have younger children aged zero to nine or haven't yet laid a foundation for the "sex talk," start by reading *Start Talking to Your Kids about Sex: A Practical Guide for Catholics*, the first book in this series. That book is meant to lay a foundation where your children see you as a trusted resource, asset, and necessary support in discovering their own embodiment and learning what it means to steward their sexuality. It's never too late to begin these conversations, even if you feel as if you're playing catch-up.

Whereas book 1 is meant to help parents talk *to* kids, book 2, the one in your hands now, is meant to help you talk *with* your youth, ultimately so that they can be well formed to understand sexuality for themselves. If you're preparing for or currently raising or educating preteens and teens, this book is for you. While we are talking about those aged ten to eighteen here, which includes both preteens (typically ages eight to twelve) and teens (typically ages thirteen to seventeen), I will use "teens" more generally in the book to describe this entire age group when specificity is less relevant to the content. Whenever possible, I will clarify distinctions between my approach with a preteen and a teen, since there are times when there will need to be significant differences between a conversation with a ten-year-old and one with an eighteen-year-old.

Just as in the previous book, *Start Talking to Your Kids about Sex*, you will find in these pages concrete scripts you can use as a parent or educator. You'll also find psychologically grounded and accessible principles to incorporate into your own parenting approach. To be clear, I'm not prescribing a one-size-fits-all approach to these conversations. You do not have to have all these conversations exactly the way I model them. What I'm offering is simply *one* concrete model so you can begin to visualize how you want to use or adapt what I'm recommending. I encourage you to follow your own discernment, especially in conversations that this book doesn't fully account for. My hope is that you'll feel more ready to engage holistically with your child's sexual and spiritual development.

Christians who address teenage sexuality often focus on harm reduction: protecting teens from early sexual activity, sexual assault, abusive relationship dynamics, pornography, and so on. While these are important aims, we can't stop at harm-reduction approaches. Christian resources on sexuality should also help you feel confident to talk about sexuality-related topics in more winsome and effective ways. The tone and content we offer is incomplete if it doesn't communicate the beauty, goodness, and deep spiritual truths to be discovered in and through knowledge of ourselves and others in light of Christ's plan for our lives. By learning how to enter into open and ongoing conversations about sexuality—despite the ongoing difficulty of these conversations—we can help our teens embody greater sexual wholeness and freedom as they mature.

"Man . . . cannot fully find himself except through a sincere gift of himself" (*Gaudium et Spes*, no. 24).[3] I will never forget reading these words for the first time as a freshman in college. Though I'd been a lifelong Catholic, these words caused Catholic teaching on sexuality to resonate with me in a way it never had before. When we frame sexuality as a gift to be discovered, known, and found anew in relationship with ourselves, others, and God, we can begin to develop a sustainable and beautiful vision for our sexual embodiment. This vision beckons each of us to acknowledge and explore the deep longing we feel to be molded like clay in the hands of the Potter for a particular purpose. It stirs the desire to find the particular ways God calls each of us to be a gift to the world and receive the love of others and the love of God as a gift. It invites us to notice the wounds and barriers to self-gift and bring those spaces to God and trusted supports. It simplifies the meaning of our sexuality, distinguishes it from reductive approaches, and orients it toward the purpose of radiantly offering our bodies and souls as a gift to God.

My hope is that this book will help you help your teens fully find themselves through the sincere gift of themselves. I pray that they can discover, with your help, what it means to be a beloved child of God and to relate to other image bearers and themselves with gratitude, peace, and delight. Ultimately, my hope is that this book will help your teen identify *you* as one of the best resources to turn to in moments when they have important questions about sexuality, their body, sexual ethics, and anything along the way that challenges their sense of dignity and worth.

Perhaps you, like me, believe that Christians can do better in helping youth become Christian adults who freely and joyfully respond to the call God places on their lives. Perhaps you share my dream of Christian teens experiencing sexual formation that aligns with a path toward holiness. We can become the trusted adults we needed in our own lives when we were teens, learning from both the wisdom and the mistakes of those who raised us. In doing so, I trust we will find healing and hope for discovering anew our own belovedness in the Father's eyes.

# CHAPTER 1

# "WHY AM I HAVING SUCH A HARD TIME STARTING THE CONVERSATION?"

## OVERCOMING BARRIERS TO DISCUSSING SEXUALITY

Healthy teen sexual development helps to set a trajectory toward healthier adult lives. Most of us want this trajectory for our teens—and for ourselves. Unfortunately, we can *want* healthy sexual development for ourselves and our teens without ever having the kinds of conversations that foster this healthy development. Despite our best intentions, all kinds of barriers can keep us from discussing sexuality with our teens.

This is why we want to begin by taking these conversational barriers seriously. If you can identify these barriers, develop strategies for facing your own fears and challenges, and step confidently into this space, it will clear the way for necessary conversations, bearing fruit in years to come.

Maybe you feel totally behind. Maybe no one modeled for you how to have gradual, proactive conversations about sexuality. Maybe your teen has already hit puberty, and you have either stumbled through a basic "sex talk" or avoided it at all costs. Or maybe you feel confident in your own sex education and you've started talking proactively about sexuality with your kids and teens, but you still want to supplement your current knowledge and approach with new ideas. No matter how many conversations you have or haven't had yet about sex, and no matter how well-equipped or ill-equipped you may feel, this book is for you.

This chapter will offer significant space for reflection on the messaging and experiences around sexuality that you faced as a child and teen. The goal of this reflective deep dive is to help you better identify and overcome any of your personal barriers to discussing sex calmly with your teen.

## IDENTIFYING BARRIERS

If you avoided early conversations about sexuality with your kids, you probably didn't do so because you think sexuality is unimportant. You, like me, probably have a sense of the importance of sexuality and Christian sexual values, as well as the negative impacts of not being able to talk openly about sexuality with trusted adults in your own teen years.

Many parents I talk with—especially those who begin therapy due to a "crisis event," such as discovering their teen's pornography use or sexual behavior—share that one of their greatest regrets is not creating space for their teen to talk about sexuality sooner. Yet most of these parents, if they are honest, aren't exactly sure why it's been so difficult for them to start the conversation, and they don't know where to even begin in building confidence.

You also may be wondering, If we all agree these are important conversations, why is it *so* hard for many of us to talk with teens about sexuality?

Here are four questions that can help you begin to explore your own relationship with this topic. Before you continue reading, take some time to sit with and possibly journal with these questions:

1. What are three hopes you have for your family as you grow in your ability to discuss sexuality effectively with your teen? (In other words, what's motivating you to read this book?)

2. What are three concerns or fears you have about what could happen when you do talk with your teen about topics related to sexuality?

3. What are three personal barriers that could impact (or may have already impacted) your ability to talk effectively with your teen?

4. What are three concrete things that you think you'll need in place to help you feel more effective with your teen?

As you read this book, keep in mind the barriers you've identified above, and look for ways to overcome them through the guidance you find in the following pages.

## ENGAGING YOUR OWN SEXUAL DEVELOPMENT

To effectively engage in conversations about our teens' sexual development, we need to reckon with our own. This is intensive work, but it's essential to confronting our own barriers. It helps us understand and hold compassion for ourselves as well as our teens, creating the possibility of engaging conversations about sexuality fully and freely.

Adam Young, a Christian trauma therapist, talks in his podcast, *The Place We Find Ourselves*, about the importance of engaging our stories.[1] Jay Stringer, a Christian therapist who specializes in sexuality, applies this concept to his work with clients when he discusses the importance of engaging our "sexual stories."[2] This "story work" is often done in the context of counseling, where I may invite a client to outline their life in a series of chapters. The client gives each chapter a title, identifies the important "characters," and so on.[3] This kind of narrative approach can help us integrate our stories, reduce shame, and process more freely and fully the nuanced and unique aspects of our lives. It allows us to bear witness to the many twists and turns of our sexual development, building insight and awareness.

Here's the catch: Insight and self-awareness, in and of themselves, don't change the reality of our experiences or how we respond in light of those experiences. So, what's the point in engaging our sexual development and education, since we can't change them? Here's what I remind many of my clients: Our past experiences will impact us with or without our awareness. The more awareness we can bring to the stories of our past experiences and their impact on us, the more we can learn, gain wisdom, and break patterns that don't serve us. This story work can be an important step toward identifying and removing barriers to meaningful conversations with your teen.

While you could certainly do this story work alone, it's best to find ways to reflect on your story in the context of your relationships with others. Invite trusted support people into this reflection process with you. After all, we aren't made to do life alone or make sense of it in an echo chamber. God is Trinitarian, a communion of Persons, and an eternal exchange of Love. This reminds us that we, too, are made for communion and love, with God and one another, both in this life and in the life to come. Whether you talk with a safe friend, therapist, spouse, or spiritual director, having an audience to witness your story work is of great value.

## YOUR CHAPTERS

I want to give you some space now to list out the "chapters" of your sexual development. If you are in a season of life where you feel under water with the demands of your day, or you are aware that doing this work will trigger traumas you aren't ready to process, or you don't have mental or emotional space to do this reflection, that's okay. Come back to it later, gradually, with a therapist, and when you can.

If you are in a position to engage in this reflection, follow along below. If not, skip to the end of this section.

You can break your sexual development up any way you'd like, but begin at birth and work up to the present day. Title the "chapters" of your journey of understanding sexuality and yourself as a sexual being. Some may feel that the early years don't matter, but try to label them anyway. Others may find that the early childhood years actually had a significant impact on their understanding of sexuality, even when sex was not acknowledged at that time. Sometimes the most significant sex education is the absence of it.

List in a journal the chapters of your story, title each one, and list your age. Fill in as many chapters as you feel are needed to adequately account for your life, like this:

Chapter 1: _____ Age range:_____
Chapter 2: _____ Age range:_____
Chapter 3: _____ Age range:_____

## KEY CHARACTERS

Let's look now at the key characters in your own sexual development. If possible, dig deep here. As always, if you find yourself opening up Pandora's box, seek out the support of a therapist or other guide so that you are not left to spin out in this alone. If it gets to be overwhelming, pause, put the book away or move to another section, and come back to it later.

Who were the key characters in your sexual development? This could be concrete people, including parents, teachers, mentors, priests and religious, youth ministers, peers, bullies, perpetrators of harm, celebrities, siblings, books, movies, television, podcasts, speakers, and social media influencers or portrayals. Keep in mind that we are seeking to understand who spoke into your understanding of sexuality. This "speaking into" your sexuality could have occurred either by the presence of certain things or the absence of them. It's usually easier to identify and point to what was there, but I also want to invite you to identify what wasn't there that you may have needed or benefited from.

Some characters could have had an impact on you by their active modeling, by conversations they explicitly had with you or around you, or by their own sexual behavior. Other characters could have had an equally powerful impact by what they *didn't* model or conversations they *didn't* have. For example, maybe your parents never showed healthy physical affection toward you or toward each other. Maybe you were sexually abused and told your parents, but they never brought it up with you again. Or maybe your family never talked about sex at all.

## KEY TAKEAWAYS

Now that you have a list of chapters and a list of key characters, we are going to look at the key messages or takeaways from these experiences. You may be surprised that you have more takeaways than you would have expected.

Chapter by chapter, create bullet points of key messages that were communicated to you through the presence or absence of different factors in your own sexual story.

Here are a few examples of how this exercise can look in real-life stories.

---

## STORYING YOUR SEXUAL DEVELOPMENT

Chapter 1: _____ Age range:_____

Key Characters:_____

Key Themes/Takeaways:_____

Chapter 2: _____ Age range:_____

Key Characters:_____

Key Themes/Takeaways:_____

Chapter 3: _____ Age range:_____

Key Characters:_____

Key Themes/Takeaways:_____

---

### KAYLA'S STORY

Kayla (pseudonym) grew up in a home where she never saw her parents kiss, hold hands, or even express gentleness or kindness, as far back as she could remember.[4] Because of this, she titled her chapter 1 "Void of Affection" (ages zero to six). In chapter 2 (ages six to eight), titled "Home Isn't Enough," Kayla began to notice that her mom was flirting with her teachers and her friends' parents. Kayla remembers being confused by this, especially because she never saw her mom light up at home. She remembers wondering why her mom was happiest when she wasn't with her dad. In chapter 3 (ages eight to ten), "Exposure," Kayla remembers her parents' divorce, moving out with her mom, and witnessing her mom's new boyfriend come through the home. She remembers hearing noises that she now knows were sexual encounters happening between her mom and this boyfriend. This was scary and curious to her at the time, and Kayla marks this as the time when, by age ten, she was really becoming curious about romance. Her dad always seemed agitated and distant when she would visit him, and her mom seemed caught up in making ends meet, so Kayla's chapter 4, "Venturing into the Unknown to Figure It Out," meant starting to kiss boys, masturbating, reading *Cosmo* magazine, and talking with friends about what they knew about sex (ages eleven to fourteen). Chapter 5 (ages fifteen to eighteen), Kayla titled "Feeling like the Expert in the Room," because she felt confident in all she knew about sex and romance and was seen by her friends as an expert. At the same time, she looks back on this time and recognizes how upset she was that she had to learn about sex on her own. She would've liked for a person, not a magazine, to teach her. In her story's later chapters, Kayla was baptized Catholic in college and started dating a cradle Catholic whom she fell in love with. She broke up with him three times before they eventually got engaged, out of fear that she didn't know how to have a happy marriage. In some ways, she really didn't know what a happy marriage could look like, given what she had witnessed. Once she started having children, Kayla noticed her fears increasing that she wouldn't be able to teach her kids a different message than the one she was taught.

Bullet-point messages from Kayla's first five chapters include these:

- Marital love is bland and empty.
- Flings are exciting and make you come alive.
- The best you can expect from a man is intense passion at the start and distance later.
- Sex is something you figure out alone.
- If you don't feign confidence about sex, you won't have anything to offer.

Even though Kayla, at least in her mind, didn't believe these messages, commitment filled her with fear. As a married woman, she sometimes found herself fantasizing about men other than her husband, wondering if she was missing out on an electric feeling in the stability of her life with him. It terrified her, as a mom of two daughters, to imagine talking with her daughters about sexuality: "How can I teach them about this when I don't feel like I know how to be a woman in the world?"

As her oldest daughter entered puberty, Kayla sat down with her, once again feeling as if she had to be the expert in the room, and said: "We don't date in high school in our family. Guys will take advantage of you if you let them, and masturbation and porn are sins, so stay away from them." This conversation, rooted in Kayla's fears that her daughter would get swept up in unhealthy dating culture and behaviors, did little to help her daughter know *what to do* in high school. Even though she wasn't passing on the same messaging she was taught, Kayla needed help knowing how to teach her daughters in a way that would protect them from harm and help them discover what it means to be young women in the world. She needed to learn to challenge the idea that sexuality is something we are each left to figure out alone.

## HANK'S STORY

Hank remembers chapter 3 of his story all too well. He titled it, "Sex Is Scary." His dad, who was a practicing Catholic, a member of the Knights of Columbus, and a successful business executive, was his model of confidence. Hank had never seen his dad show anxiety, even in the face of many stressful circumstances—not until his thirteenth birthday, that is. Hank remembers that his dad, typically light and jovial, came up to him and said, "We need to have a talk." His dad sat him down, and it was the first time Hank saw fear in his dad's eyes. He remembers thinking, "What could this be that makes my dad so afraid?"

Hank's dad proceeded to tell him about sex. "If you ever have sex with a girl and get her pregnant," Hank's dad told him, "it will break your mother's heart." When Hank got older and did become sexually active, he kept it a secret, carried great shame, and concluded that sex was only something bad and hidden. To this day, married with three kids, Hank feels anxious when people talk about sex around him: "It just feels wrong." He wants to talk about it with his son, who is turning thirteen in a few months, but he doesn't want to do what his dad did and has no clue where to begin.

Bullet-point messages Hank received were these:

- Sex is scary and makes people uncomfortable, so you only talk about it if you absolutely have to.

- Sexual desire is dangerous and not to be trusted. It can lead to pregnancy and harm to parents.

- Sex isn't something you talk about, especially not with the people closest to you.

## GIANNA'S STORY

Gianna had a really hard time writing out her chapters. She didn't want to revisit some of those memories ever again. At the age of seven, Gianna had been asked by an older neighbor boy, age fourteen, to touch his penis in exchange for some of his Halloween candy. She did it, confused and scared, and felt some pride when he seemed pleased. At the same time, she felt disgusted and ashamed. He told her not to tell anyone because she would get in trouble, and she swore to secrecy. Because of how disgusted she felt after this experience, Gianna believed she herself was damaged. She often told people, "I am called to be a nun." She now understands that she believed she was damaged goods and would harm a "good Catholic man." Eventually, Gianna did get married and had four children. She carried with her messages like "sex is a necessary evil" and "a woman's job is to make a man feel good, even if it makes her uncomfortable." When she felt used in her own marital relationship, she thought, "I deserved it after what I did all those years ago." Sometimes her kids would hear her joke to friends, "Most men, even good men, only want one thing."

Gianna's takeaway themes were these:

- Sex exists to give guys pleasure.

- If you feel uncomfortable with something, pretend you like it anyway.

- If you have had any sexual encounter (wanted or unwanted), you are not pure.

Kayla, Hank, and Gianna's reflections give us a window into the challenges we can face when trying to educate our teens. Sometimes, like in Kayla's story, we are so afraid of teaching our teens the harmful messages we received as young people that we simply say no to "bad behaviors" and leave it at that. Other times, like in Hank's story, we internalize the idea that our desires are bad, and we live in shame about our desires even when we are trying to channel them in healthy ways. Still other times, like in Gianna's story, beliefs rooted in abuse trickle down to our children, who can come to believe that sexual acts are for pleasing others, even when we are uncomfortable, and that any past sexual activity robs us of innocence.

These stories offer models of how, when parents become more aware of their own history, that awareness can impact their parenting. My prayer is that these stories will stoke in you a curiosity to understand your own sexual story better. As you bring these experiences and wounds into the light, processing them with God and with other trusted people like a therapist, spiritual director, or spouse, you will have more power to identify and leave behind harmful messages and identify new messages that are healthier for both you and your teens. When we live as "children of light," the light will bear "all that is good and right and true" (Ephesians 5:8–9).

Living in the light in our own lives allows us to invite our children with us into that light, especially as they begin to face their own darkness. Becoming the kind of parents we needed when we were children and teens is one of the ultimate tasks and healing gifts of parenting.

Doing this work can also help you grow in your self-understanding and compassion for the particular challenges you face as you venture into these conversations with your teen. You are not alone in feeling overwhelmed by it all. You are not alone in discovering the barriers that make it difficult to have these conversations. As you hold your story with tenderness and grace and allow God to meet you there, you can move forward toward greater confidence and effectiveness.

## MESSAGES I DON'T WANT TO SEND

Whether you have stepped into the last section or not, this part is for you. First, identify at least one unhelpful message you may have learned about sexuality that you don't want to pass on. Second, identify how to move forward and overcome barriers to challenging this message and modeling something different with your teen. In your journal, respond to the following questions:

- What is one unhelpful message that I learned about sexuality that I do not want to pass on to the next generation?

- What is one thing I can do to actively challenge an unhelpful message around sexuality that I received and don't want to pass on?
- What is one barrier that may make it difficult for me to actively challenge the above message, and what is one concrete thing I could do to help me overcome this barrier?
- What are the implications of my journey, as I understand it, on my approach to engaging the topic of sexuality with my children?

## MESSAGES I WANT TO SEND

As we conclude this chapter, I want to invite you, and your spouse if you are married, to list the top messages you want your teen to understand about sexuality. This list will help you establish goals as you prepare for future conversations with your teen in the rest of this book. Remember, these messages are meant to present a positive vision for sexuality, not merely a list of do's and don'ts.

### SAMPLE MESSAGES ABOUT SEXUALITY

- Humans are made by God with a body, soul, and mind.
- The desires and longings of our hearts remind us of the call to be united with God and others in communion.
- The human body, sexual desire, and human relationships are gifts to be stewarded by us. We can speak and act in response to our desires and not merely react to them. This sets us apart from animals.
- The desire for relationship, including a sexual relationship, is a good and beautiful longing of the heart for communion. This desire points to the capacity for our relationships to be unitive and life-giving.
- Marital love is a specific call on the hearts of some people. Marriage is one of the ways God invites people to become holy. It involves opening our hearts to unity with another, embracing the opportunity and responsibility of raising children if God provides

them, and making a permanent vow that reflects God's covenant with people.

- Humans have desires, including sexual desires, that can draw us into virtue or draw us into vice. The same desires can lead us to honor ourselves and others or lead us to use and be used in relationships.

- Sin means that some people will try to use us, and we will be tempted to use others. We are not responsible for the moments when another person uses us, and we can also take steps to protect ourselves from being used or harmed when possible.

- We are responsible for protecting those around us from being used by ourselves or others, including and especially those we have sexual feelings for.

- When we feel desire, if we are honest about it and invite those we trust to help us understand it, we can learn to steward that desire in healthy ways.

- Sexual sin doesn't ultimately have the last say. When we fall short of God's best for human sexuality, we can always return to Christ, who makes all things new.

- Honesty is key to sexual health. If we keep secrets about our sexuality, we will struggle to live chastely.

- Singleness is a pathway for self-gift in the world. Many people will spend at least some significant portion of their sexual development single, and some will live as single people their whole lives. Single people's sexuality is able to glorify God and build up the Church, just as is true for those who marry. The sexuality of single people opens up vistas for freedom to be single-hearted to serve the Church and others in the world.

- Priesthood is a way to channel human desire toward Christ's bride, the Church, and to love others fully and freely without the same exclusivity as marriage. The priest embodies Christ by being "someone for everyone, but not everything for someone."[5]

- Religious orders, open both to men and women, offer a pathway for reflecting a single-heartedness for the Lord and living in the reality of heaven, where we will neither marry nor be given in

marriage. The consecrated person reflects our ultimate fulfill-
ment, union with God.

- Genitalia are a gift from God. Knowing about our bodies as they develop is important for sexual education and building self-mastery.
- All questions about sexuality are welcome to parents. Nothing is off-limits.

---

## WHAT IF I AM PLAYING CATCH-UP?

I expect that some of you have been avoiding having any conversations (or at least any substantial conversations) about sex with your teen, even though you know it's long past time to start having these conversations. If that's you, you may need to have an initial conversation with your teen before you start implementing many of the tips you encounter in future chapters. However, this initial conversation doesn't need to be as scary as you might have feared.

It's natural to feel pressure to say everything in your first conversation, and in doing so overwhelm your teen (and yourself). Instead, I'd encourage you to start by acknowledging that this conversation is new, and give yourself permission to take it slow. There is no rush. Important conversations take time to co-create. Here are a few sample scripts for ways to ease into conversations around sexuality if you've been avoiding them:

> "I am realizing that, for much of your life, we never talked about anything related to sexuality/bodies/physical boundaries. If I'm being honest, that was probably because of [list a few *general* barriers to conversation: not being taught by my parents how to do it, not knowing where to start, fears, discomfort]. It was a mistake for me to wait this long to talk with you. I am sorry for the impact of that, and I want to work on it now.
>
> "I am learning that it's actually really important for us to have sexuality-related conversations, so you aren't left to handle such important pieces of life alone. I want to be intentional about gradually starting to have these conversations

with you. It might feel uncomfortable or strange for us to talk about this at first, but I know we can build trust about natural parts of life as time goes on."

While the above script is designed for a situation where you've had no conversation at all with your teen, maybe your situation is different; maybe you've had some conversations, but you've realized in hindsight that they were characterized by reactivity or shame. If so, here's one way you could try to push the "reset" button and begin working toward a different posture in the future:

> "I know we've had some conversations about sexuality before, but they've been responding to things that came up suddenly, not calm and proactive. I am sorry for the impact that has had on you. I want you to know that I am working on talking about things when it doesn't feel urgent, which means we are going to start having more conversations more naturally. I am looking forward to that, since we want to have open communication about sexuality in our home."

It's never too late to do what you wish you did years ago. None of us is perfect, and modeling humility and compassion for yourself when you have made mistakes or fallen short of what you hoped for as a parent is a bigger gift than you realize. After all, how will our teens learn to reflect and take responsibility for their own stories and challenges if we don't teach them?

You are already well on your way in taking this first step. Now let's take another step together, as we turn to chapters 2 and 3 and prepare for conversations about bodily changes at puberty.

# CHAPTER 2

# "WHAT IS HAPPENING TO MY SON'S BODY?"

## EXPLAINING PUBERTY TO BOYS

THE BODY, IN FACT, AND ONLY THE BODY, IS CAPABLE OF MAKING VISIBLE WHAT IS INVISIBLE: THE SPIRITUAL AND THE DIVINE. IT HAS BEEN CREATED TO TRANSFER INTO THE VISIBLE REALITY OF THE WORLD, THE MYSTERY HIDDEN FROM ETERNITY IN GOD, AND THUS BE A SIGN OF IT.

**—ST. JOHN PAUL II**

As Catholics, we understand the body is fundamentally good because it is created by God as a sign of his love for us and all creation. One of the most effective ways we can communicate this truth to children and teens is to discuss openly and comfortably the facts of their anatomy, using simple terminology shared by medical professionals.

## EDUCATING AROUND GENITALIA

As your teen boy enters puberty, you will want him to understand certain aspects of his body. Using a diagram like the one below can keep the conversation medical, simple, and unmysterious.[1]

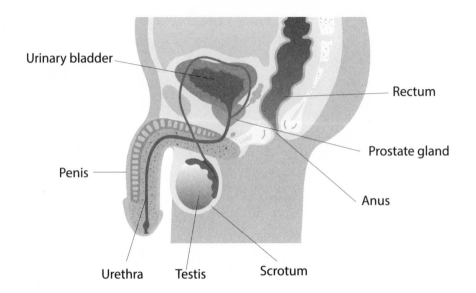

Urinary bladder

Rectum

Prostate gland

Penis

Anus

Urethra    Testis    Scrotum

"As you get older, it's good to make sure you know the right names for your genitalia and what they do, just like you've learned about other parts of your body over the years. 'Genitalia' is a long word for the sex organs or reproductive organs. These are the organs in your body that are located between your legs and below your abdomen. They are called reproductive organs because they point to the human call to be a gift to God and others and bear fruit in our lives. For some people, this will include becoming a parent to physical children; for all of us, it means being invited into spiritual fruitfulness. God designed this area of our bodies intentionally. Knowing the names of those body parts and what they do can be really helpful, both to identify if there is ever something not working right and to simply know more about your body.

"Your bladder holds urine before it passes through your prostate along your urethra and out of your body through your penis. [Point out these parts on the diagram as you go.]

"Your prostate is also important in releasing a fluid that protects your sperm anytime it leaves your body through your penis as you get older. It's important in your overall health and your ability to have kids one day if God calls you to that.

"Your rectum is the holder of your stool, or poop, before it passes out of your body through your anus.

"Your testes are two oval-shaped organs in your body that sit in a sac, called the scrotum, which hangs outside your body between your legs. Your testes are what create the sperm that are protected by fluid made by your prostate as they leave the body.

"All of these body parts are designed by God to work together in a pretty incredible way. They are what allow you to offer the sperm that can create a baby one day if you are called to be a father. Whether you become a father or not, this part of your body is a sign of the capacity you have to be a gift to the world and all those you meet through your particular body as a young man. The way we take care of our body and treat others matters, because it prepares us to be the gift we were created to be and to receive others as the gift they are too!"

## IDENTIFYING AND NORMALIZING BODILY CHANGES

### STEPS TO DISCUSSING BODILY CHANGES

1. Bring up the topic of bodily changes.
2. Ask what a child already knows about bodily changes.
3. Validate accurate information.
4. Correct inaccurate information.
5. List medical knowledge briefly.
6. Check for questions and invite follow-up.

Since this book is meant for parents of teens, all of whom are entering or have entered puberty, one of the most foundational conversations is to help a child identify and understand their own bodily changes as they are happening. It's ideal to have these conversations with your child ahead of time when possible, so that they aren't taken by surprise. Your child will probably begin to notice bodily development in themselves and others at around age nine or ten. This means that your fourth grader will benefit from your initiating this first conversation right around that age. Here's a way of starting the conversation:

"Now that you are getting older, your body is going to start to prepare for adulthood more and more. This means you will grow more in height, for one, and your weight will fluctuate more as you are growing. These are normal changes that happen to every kid at different times. Have you noticed those changes in yourself or other people?

"Height and weight aren't the only changes that will happen. You will start to notice you might sweat more (and smell stinky more easily)! In the next couple of weeks, I can take you to pick out some deodorant that smells good to you to use when you start to notice that you smell different. If you don't seem to notice, I'll also let you know if I notice. Every person does this at around your age, so even if your friends aren't talking about it at school, it's very normal!"

"It's good to know what's coming, so I wanted to talk about some of the other things you can expect. We've talked before about your genitals, like your penis, and that part of your body will start to change as well. You may start to notice more hair growing in different places, around your pubic area—which is below your belly button and between your hips—in your armpits, and on your face. When you start to notice changes, know that it's normal, and it's exactly what God made your body to do! There are really good reasons why our bodies change, and we can talk about those more as time goes on, whenever you want to understand what is happening and why. What questions do you have about that?"

## CHANGES IN BOYS[2]

- Height changes
- Body hair and facial hair growth
- Sweating and body odor increase
- Erections increase in frequency
- Ejaculations occur

- Voice deepening
- Testicle and penis growth
- Muscle growth
- Acne
- Mood changes

## WET DREAMS

Beginning around age nine, boys will start to notice nocturnal emissions (sometimes called "wet dreams"). Wet dreams will happen more frequently around ages thirteen to seventeen, particularly if a child is not self-stimulating to ejaculation. Many young boys do not realize what is happening if they wake up in the morning and their pants are wet from a nocturnal emission. Nocturnal emissions can lead to embarrassment, guilt, and shame, as well as confusion. It is important for your preteen boys to know what is happening and why, so that they don't become too confused or ashamed or disgusted with the amazing things their body can do.

Here's a surprisingly common scenario that can happen if people don't learn as teens how their bodies work: A young adult named Kathy was sitting at a gas station with her older brother, James, on a long road trip. He woke up from a nap and said, "Did I pee in my pants?" James was immediately embarrassed, his face turned beet red, and he seemed confused. Kathy, a medical student at the time, calmly responded, "Maybe you had a wet dream." He said, "That's not it. I wasn't dreaming about anything sexual!" and got out of the car to go change. Even as an adult, he didn't really understand what wet dreams are, why they occur, and that they're not something to be ashamed of.

Here are a couple of practical ways of addressing this topic early on, so that your child doesn't grow up to be an adult who doesn't understand this aspect of their body. You might notice a nocturnal emission has happened when you see a child's wet pajamas or a stain on the sheets. If you notice this, it might be a good time to introduce the concept. It's not an emergency, so finding a calm, casual moment to bring it up will be your best bet. It's not absolutely necessary for a same-sex parent to have the conversation, but when possible, a same-sex parent can certainly speak to the normalcy of this from personal experience.

> "I wanted to give you a heads up about something that will start to happen around this time of your life. It happens to every boy becoming a man and is very normal. When a boy start to get older, your body starts to make something called testosterone. Testosterone is a hormone that helps your body develop into an adult body and gain strength. Sometimes, as this happens, your penis will fill with a liquid called semen. Have you ever heard that word? Okay, it's a word to describe the liquid that contains sperm, which, as we've talked about before, is there to help you have a child one day if you get married! Before you are ready to start your own family, the semen will simply release from your penis every so often, and it will do it naturally, without you having to do anything! It's like your body knows how to release it when it needs to. For a lot of boys, this happens in your sleep. You might wake up with liquid on your sheets or your pajamas—that liquid is semen. It's nothing to worry about and nothing to be embarrassed of. Have you noticed this yet?"

Whether your son has or hasn't noticed it, you can still teach them what to do when the day comes:

> "When you notice that your penis has released semen, you can wash your clothes and sheets, just like you would if anything else spilled on them. It's also important to use soap and water to clean your penis and testicles—and if you're not circumcised, it's important to clean underneath your foreskin too. Do you have any questions about that for now? If not, you can always ask later. If you don't have time to clean your sheets, you can always let Mom or Dad know you need help, and we can throw them in the wash as well."

## ERECTIONS

It is normal for young boys to have erections even before they are born. Of course, as boys prepare for puberty, these erections will take on a different meaning, as they will be tied more often to sexual arousal of some kind.

Just as we've pointed out in earlier prompts, it's ideal to try initiating this conversation when a child is not having an erection, so that it doesn't feel urgent or reactive:

> "I know we've been talking recently about bodily changes because you're going through puberty. What changes have you noticed? One other thing that will happen more with time is something called an erection. What have you heard about erections?"

Asking what a preteen knows lets you understand what level of education they have already received from peers, media, and so on.

Next, you can ask what feelings your preteen notices when they have an erection. They may notice a rush of energy, curiosity, confusion, fear, disgust, or embarrassment. Be sure to validate that erections are a normal bodily process, and every boy experiences them:

> "It's normal to have those. There is a good reason for them, too. Do you want to know what it is?"

Again, asking a question like this lets your preteen have some control over this part of their life. They can tell you if they are not wanting to know about this yet or if they are curious. If they say no, respect their boundary and circle back a few months later to see if they feel ready to talk. Whenever they decide they want to know, here is what you might say:

> "When blood rushes to the tip of your penis, it will stick up and out. It's called an erection. Have you seen that happen to you? If you don't touch it and let time pass, it will go back down. It's an automatic thing your body does, and it's nothing to worry about. If you ever notice it happening in public, you can simply adjust your seating or your pants so as not to draw attention to it. Any questions?"

As your preteen moves into the teen years (thirteen and up), you can also include an additional reflection on erections and their procreative purpose.

"Your penis has a very important purpose of being a sign of the capability we all have to be a gift to others. Your penis is the place that sperm leaves to help create a baby, with God's help, if you're called to that in the future. So, when you have an erection, you can be reminded that it's a sign of your capacity to, in your body, be a giver of life. Not every man (or woman) participates in giving new life through biological children. But all of us, in our bodies, can discover the "sign" of this calling, which is that we are meant to bear fruit in our lives."

## BODILY CHANGES OF BOTH SEXES

Just as it's important to talk with boys about what is happening in their bodies and those of their male peers, it is also helpful to tell them about what is happening in girls' bodies. One of the most common precursors to pornography is natural curiosity about bodies. Whether your son is attracted to people of the opposite sex or the same sex, talking with him about what is happening to girls' bodies as well as boys' bodies can reduce the likelihood that he will seek an education through porn. As you begin to talk with your son about his own body changes, you can also begin to explain the following:

"You know how we have talked some about how your body and other boys' bodies are changing at puberty? Girls' bodies are changing too. What have you heard about that?"

Your preteen might say something like, "I heard that boys grow taller and girls don't." At this point, you can highlight what is accurate about what they have heard and correct any misinformation gently:

"You are right that boys tend to grow taller at this time. In fact, girls also will get taller, but usually most girls don't get to be as tall as most boys will. But some girls will be taller than you when you are an adult, believe it or not. And some boys will be shorter than you. Remember, we are called to treat everyone with love and respect. This means we don't make fun of other people for how their bodies look, or about anything else, for that matter."

After hearing what a preteen already knows and correcting any mis-information, you can outline some of the common changes:

"When girls start to grow older, their bodies start to change because of the hormones that get released, which God made to help our bodies grow healthy and strong. Like you, girls will also get taller, grow body hair in their armpits and private areas, and start using deodorant. Their skin might also get those bumps called 'acne.' Some girls will grow a little facial hair as they become women, but they won't have beards or mustaches like some men do. Any questions about that?

"There are also things that happen to girls that don't happen to boys. This is because girls become women. One of the amazing things women's bodies can do is carry a baby and give that baby food to eat from their chest area, called their breasts. Their breasts are one of the private areas on a girl's body, just like you have private areas. As girls go through puberty, their chest will get larger, and they will have a monthly 'period,' which is when something called the uterus releases its lining if the woman isn't currently pregnant with a baby. This lining comes out and looks like blood. It might sound strange, but it's nothing to be afraid of.

"Women have such incredible bodies, and so do men! Our bodies have so many good purposes, and it's normal to be curious about bodies too. When questions come up about what's happening in women's bodies, or you hear things from friends or the internet about that, let's talk about it more. There is so much helpful information and sometimes unhelpful information out there, so we want to make sure you know as much as you want to know and that the information is accurate, okay? What questions do you have?"

An early teen may wonder if girls will have a penis or ejaculate. Calmly, you can tell them this:

"Girls' and boys' bodies are different, meaning that girls' bodies aren't made with a penis and boys' bodies aren't made with a uterus. So, boys ejaculate and have erections from a penis, and girls have a uterus and breasts. God made each of our bodies with special purposes, and our different parts tell us about those purposes. God is so smart and gives us a kind of map through our bodies to tell us what they can be for!"

Let's say you don't know an answer to a question your teen has about their body or other people's bodies. That's okay. You are not all-knowing, and you don't need to pretend you are. The key is, if you don't know something, delay the conversation and circle back.

Let's say your son asks, "What is a uterus for?" You may have never been taught about how to explain that. Here are a couple of options for how you might respond:

"Good question! Where did you hear about that? I am so glad we can talk about these things."

"Wow, that's a good question. I am learning new things, too, through your questions, so thanks for asking me. I am going to find the answer and let you know. What other questions do you have right now? That way, I can look into other things, too, while I am at it." (See chapter 3 for the answer!)

"Thanks for asking me! I think I know the answer, but let's find a time to talk about it in the next couple of days. It's not super complicated, but I want to make sure you have the right information. If you have other questions, let me know so we can talk about them too."

It's only chapter 2, and I know this can feel like a lot to take in. You can always go back to earlier prompts and review them, since none of these is a one-time deal. Now, let's turn to how you might have similar conversations with your teenage daughter.

# "WHAT IS HAPPENING TO MY DAUGHTER'S BODY?"

## EXPLAINING PUBERTY TO GIRLS

"Are you on your period?" This is a common question a teen girl might get when she is visibly upset, irritated, or tired. Said cynically, it can be incredibly hurtful and invalidating. Many adult women I meet with share that this comment was the most "education" they received about their bodily changes at puberty. Such comments do little to instill a reverence for and confidence in a young woman's emotions, the incredible gift of her developing body, and her feminine genius. Let's work together to offer something different, setting a better tone for how to talk about puberty with young girls.

### SETTING THE TONE

The way we talk about the female body, especially a young teen's body as it develops through puberty, matters. If we lead girls to believe that periods are dirty, a deficit, or something that makes us "dramatic," "emotional," and "overly sensitive" for a week at a time, we shouldn't be surprised when it is hard for women to experience body positivity or confidence about their sexuality due to shame. The way a young girl experiences her bodily changes is impacted by the initial conversations (or lack thereof) and tone when talking about menstruation.

Keeley still remembers her first period. An only child, she had no frame of reference for puberty, and no one ever shared with her about it. Her parents had gone for a hike, and she had decided to stay back in the family cabin because she had a stomachache. She woke up from a nap and found blood on her bed. She screamed for help and realized she was completely alone. "I am dying," she thought. She frantically called her parents, but because they were hiking, it took several hours for her to get in touch with them. When her parents returned, her dad said nothing and didn't look her in the eye. Her mom told her, "Congratulations, you are a woman!" and showed her where pads were kept. "I was not in the mood to celebrate," Keeley reflected. "I was terrified."

Because puberty is something each person moves through, proactive conversations can protect kids like Keeley from the shock and confusion of seeing blood and not knowing why. The science around why women have periods and the divine design behind it all are awe-inspiring. Of course, it's hard to feel celebratory if all you know about it is that you will bleed once a month and there are items to use to catch the blood. You can make a difference in your child's experience by explaining periods, making them less daunting, and treating them as something to be appreciated, even if they don't feel worthy of celebration!

## EXPLAINING PHYSICAL CHANGES

### CHANGES IN GIRLS[1]

- Breast growth
- Height changes
- Body hair growth
- Sweating and body odor increase
- Acne
- Menstruation
- Mood changes
- Sexual desire
- Hip growth and weight fluctuations

Let's look at a way of starting the conversation with your preteen girl about general bodily changes. It will follow a very similar model to chapter 2's conversation starter for preteen boys:

"Now that you are getting older, your body is going to start to prepare for adulthood more and more. This means you will get taller, for one, and your weight will fluctuate more as you are growing. Those things are normal changes that happen to every kid at different times. Have you noticed those changes in yourself or other people?

"Height and weight aren't the only changes that will happen. You will start to notice you might sweat more (and smell stinky more easily)! In the next couple of months, I can take you to pick out some deodorant that smells good to you, which you can use when you start to notice that you smell different. If you don't notice it, I'll also let you know if I notice. This happens to everyone around your age, so even if others aren't talking about it at school, it's very normal!

"It's good to know what's coming, so I want to talk about some of the other things you can expect as you get older. We've talked before about your genitals, such as your vagina. Those parts of your body will start to change as well. You may notice more hair growing in different places: around your pubic area—which is below your belly button and between your hips—and in your armpits. Your breast area will start to grow out, because breasts are what allow women to nourish a baby if we give birth one day. Breasts are a really beautiful part of your body that God made. When you start to notice changes in your chest or other parts of your body, know that it's normal, and it's exactly what God made your body to do!

"There are really good reasons why our bodies change, and we can talk about those more as time goes on, whenever you want to understand what is happening and why. It's also normal for this to feel uncomfortable and even weird for some people. We can talk about that too. What questions do you have so far?"

# EXPLAINING AND PREPARING FOR MENSTRUATION

## STEPS TO DISCUSSING BODILY CHANGES

7. Bring up the topic of bodily changes.
8. Ask what a child already knows about bodily changes.
9. Validate accurate information.
10. Correct inaccurate information.
11. List medical knowledge briefly.
12. Check for questions and invite follow-up.

The average age of a girl's first menstrual period is age twelve, with most girls having their first period between ten and fifteen years old. African American girls tend to begin puberty around age eight. This is, on average, sooner than Hispanic and Caucasian girls, who begin puberty around age nine. Keep that in mind for the timing of these conversations with your child.[2] For all preteen girls, breast-budding, growth spurts, and body-hair growth are good indicators of upcoming menstruation.

## TEACHING ACCURATE LANGUAGE FOR GENITALIA

Words for external genitalia should already be familiar to your child by this age, but if you're catching up, no worries! In this chapter, we'll address conversations you may have with your preteen daughter: speaking generally about the purpose of internal genitalia at ages nine and ten, and then introducing the concept of a menstrual cycle and periods between ages ten and twelve. Feel free to point to each body part on the diagram below as you walk through it:

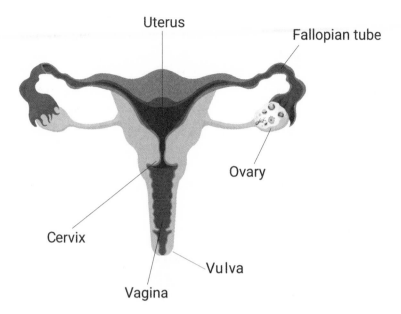

"One of the cool things about getting older is that you can learn more about your body and how it works. Just as you are learning about other aspects of creation in school, you can learn even more about your own body now. You may remember that I have explained before that you have genitalia, which are involved in creating children one day if God calls you to that. Right now, I want to show you what is happening inside your body, in areas you can't see.

"Your vagina is the place that connects the external and internal genitalia. It is an opening that is an entryway into and out of the body.

"Your uterus is a pear-shaped area where a baby can develop after fertilization. The wall of your uterus is created to contract (that is, get smaller) during labor, which is what helps move the baby out of the body through the cervix and vagina. If there's no baby inside your uterus, your uterine lining, which has thickened throughout the menstrual cycle, sheds once a month, which causes bleeding.

"Your cervix is the lower region of your uterus and becomes dilated (that is, expanded) during labor and delivery. It also is responsible for protecting against bacteria that could cause infection.

"Your fallopian tubes are the place where a baby is conceived. After the sperm enter your body through the vaginal opening, cervix, and uterus, one of the sperm can fertilize the egg in one of these tubes.

"Your ovaries are responsible for producing and releasing eggs each month and for giving your body hormones called estrogen and progesterone, as well as sex hormones that are also made by the male body. Each girl, at birth, has one million egg cells (oocytes). On average, about four hundred egg cells are released over the course of your life."

## EXPLAINING A WOMAN'S CYCLE

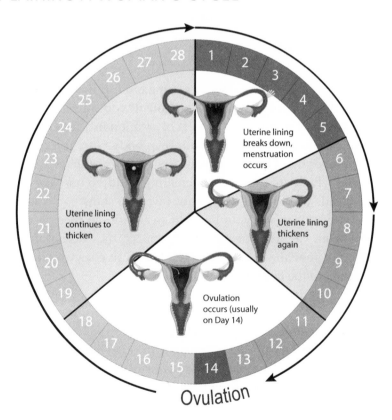

As you move into discussing a woman's cycle with your teen girl, you will want to use a diagram like this to be able to show her what is happening, and where in her body it is happening, as it relates to her menstrual cycle.[3] It is very common for teens to feel disconnected from the rhythms of their body, and this exercise can be helpful in reconnecting your daughter to her body and each of its parts in a meaningful way.

"Around this time of life, you will begin to have something called a menstrual cycle. It hasn't started yet, but it will in the next few years. It is something incredible God created that allows a woman's body to prepare for the possibility of having a baby if God calls us to that one day. For each of us, even if we never have a child, this cycle is a sign of God's intentional plan for our bodies. Our bodies, in having a cycle, show the intentional order in the way we are created by God. Our bodies also show that we are able to bring new life to the world, physically for some of us, and spiritually for all of us!

"Each woman's body, each month for many years, is on this cycle, where our uterus thickens in case it needs to hold a baby, and our body releases an egg from the ovaries. Since most of our eggs will not grow into a baby, eggs that aren't beginning to grow into a baby are released through something called menstruation, or a period. This is when the thickened lining around our uterus thins out, since we only need the lining to thicken if we are carrying a baby.

"You can understand where you are at in your cycle by the type of mucus that comes out of your vaginal opening. It's helpful eventually to learn about this mucus and other signs of fertility, but no need to worry about that now when you notice discharge. It's a sign from your body of where you are at in your cycle. What questions do you have about this?

"Pretty soon we will make sure you have everything you need to take care of yourself as your body changes. You can always bring your questions to me."

## PLANNING FOR PERIODS

In addition to explaining genitalia and their function and discussing the menstrual cycle, we want to help your preteen prepare for her period. Preparation matters more than many people realize. For girls, it is valuable to have a bag prepared with supplies for her first period. You can explain this ahead of time to your daughter and place a basket of supplies under the bathroom sink in multiple parts of your home, as well as creating a to-go bag to keep in her purse or backpack. This is a great step to continue the experience of your teen becoming an "expert" on her body. A basket that you provide your teen ahead of time could include things like a packet of ibuprofen, a couple of pads for heavy, moderate, or light days, a few tampons, an extra pair of underwear, a heating pad, a plastic bag for a to-go version of supplies for school, and maybe even some chocolate for good measure!

Here's one way you could introduce these supplies to your teen:

> "I wanted to pass along some supplies that will come in handy in the next few years. Your body is starting to change in some ways, as all girls start to around this age. One of the changes that will happen is the start of something called a period. What have you heard about it?
>
> "When your period first starts, you will notice blood on your underwear, which shows that your body is growing to become an adult body. Remember how we've talked about the uterus as a body part that exists to keep new life safe? Every month, your uterus has an outer part that gets thick in case you need it to keep a baby safe. When it gets the signal that there is no baby to keep safe, your uterus sheds that outer lining and it gets released from your body as blood. What do you think about that?"

Kids can have all sorts of reactions to menstruation. For many, it is odd. For some, it will feel scary. For others, it will seem exciting or cool. Normalize whatever your daughter shares with you.

A common question from a younger girl is, "Will it hurt?" You will want to share something like this:

> "It won't hurt like when you bleed from a cut, but sometimes you will have cramps in your stomach or a headache or aches in your body during or right before your period. There are things we can use to help with that kind of pain, such as medication, heating pads, a warm bath, and certain teas. So, when your period is happening, you can just let me or Dad know so we can help you get some relief, if possible. Okay?"

You will want to make it clear that periods last anywhere from four to seven days once they are more regular, but that at first, they may be irregular and less predictable. You will want to cue your teen into the fact that regular patterns of nourishment and refraining from excessive exercise are important for establishing and maintaining a regular cycle. You will also want to highlight how moods can fluctuate throughout a woman's cycle and (if your child has a phone) that various apps can help women track their period. Let's see what this could sound like:

> "At first, your period might be pretty unpredictable. I put together a little to-go bag of supplies for your first period. You can keep those items with you in case you notice blood in your underwear when you are at school or a friend's house. Your period will gradually become more regular and it's important to regularly nourish your body and refrain from overexercising to help your cycle regulate. You'll also notice that your emotions may change suddenly throughout your cycle. Some days during our cycle, we can feel really energized, while other days we may feel really tired and annoyed, or numb. On tired days, it's good to rest more and be extra gentle with yourself. There are ways to track your period so you can know what your hormones are doing on different days. Here's the app I use!"

## EXPLAINING HOW TO USE PADS, TAMPONS, OR MENSTRUAL CUPS

It is important not to assume that a young girl will know how to use a pad or tampon for the first time. Take time to sit down with your daughter, open a pad, and take apart a tampon or a menstrual cup to demonstrate different parts of it and indicate which parts remain in the body and which are to be removed (for example, removing a plastic applicator but leaving the cotton part inserted for a tampon). Let your daughter practice a few times, holding and taking apart the pieces of a pad or tampon or menstrual cup to understand how it works.[4] Doing this ahead of time will help a young girl have peace of mind and know what to do when the time comes.

In my work as a psychologist, I have heard horror stories about first periods. As parents, you are in the position to teach your daughters and equip them to step into this phase with more confidence and ease. They may not thank you when you have the conversation, but they will be protected from all kinds of situations that could arise when they are not prepared.

## BODILY CHANGES OF BOTH SEXES

Because boys' erections can happen around their siblings and peers, it's also valuable for girls to know what is happening in developing male bodies—especially if your daughter has brothers or male friends. Otherwise, seeing an erection and not understanding what's happening can cause fear or extreme discomfort for some kids.

Consider, for instance, the story of Tina, who came to see me for therapy. She recalled a highly uncomfortable situation that heightened her own sexual shame. She was about ten years old, and she was sitting in the car with her older brother, age twelve. She noticed that his penis was erect, and it scared her. She pointed and said, "What is wrong with you?" Her brother was terrified and didn't know what to say. To this day, Tina recalls her fear in that moment and remembers thinking that, when men have erections, it is a sign of a bad thing. When she came to me for therapy years later, as a married adult woman, she still struggled to see her husband's erect penis without having some level of anxiety.

Tina would have benefitted from someone explaining to her (and her brother) the medical reason for erections. Here is one way to do that:

> "Tina, just as your body is going to change as you get older, your brother's and male friends' bodies will change too. This means that, sometimes, you may notice a boy's penis sticking up. Have you ever seen that before? It is a sign that blood is rushing to that part of the body, which makes it stick out further. Sometimes a boy is trying to make this happen, but other times it just happens without their control—they might feel really embarrassed by it. This can happen to boys by accident from time to time, and it is nothing to be afraid of. But if there is ever a time when you see a boy in your class touching his penis because he wants to make it stick

out, you can let me know and we can talk about how to handle those moments. Remember, if someone ever asks you to touch his penis or make it stay up, that is not okay, and we can talk about those moments after. We don't touch other people's private areas and or let them touch our private areas."

Each and every conversation with your teen girl creates an opportunity for greater closeness and trust, an opportunity to be seen as a reliable guide and source of support as she matures. The more we become willing to step into these conversations, the more likely we are to raise confident, holy young women who know their bodies, experience gratitude for the beauty and mystery of their bodies, and steward them with ease in a world so ready to objectify. None of this is a foregone conclusion, of course. You could parent "perfectly" and still not have your child turn out the way you hope. This is a painful reality of surrender in parenting, to be sure, and an opportunity for our own sanctification and growth in trust in God.

# CHAPTER 4

# "HOW DO I PREPARE MY TEEN FOR PARTS OF PUBERTY THAT AREN'T SEX-SPECIFIC?"

## INTRODUCING ADDITIONAL TOPICS

In this chapter, we want to cover topics that aren't necessarily sex-specific. You will find conversation starters for setting boundaries around teens talking about pubertal changes, guiding your teen in how to respond to teasing and body comments, and helping your teen attend to hygiene and cleanliness as their body changes.

### SETTING BOUNDARIES AROUND THESE TOPICS

Many parents worry that talking with their teen, especially as early as age ten, so openly about bodily changes will lead a child to talk excessively about what they are learning with others. If you are concerned about your teen openly talking about this with peers and younger siblings, you could simply say something like this:

> "It's so great that we get to have these important conversations. These conversations are private, meaning we don't have them with everyone. We talk about these special things with trusted people, mainly our parents and, with

our parents present, our doctors who make sure our bodies work well. You don't need to bring up these conversations with friends or younger siblings, because they will get to learn those things from us, just as you did! It's not your job to teach others, since that's up to their parents. Does that make sense to you? Everyone will learn at their own pace."

## TEACHING HOW TO SPEAK UP AGAINST TEASING

When you are teaching your children about bodily changes, it is also a good time, if you have a few more minutes, to coach a child about how to respond when someone mocks them or other kids around them. A lot of kids will get teased as they start to develop physically, or if they are not developing as quickly as other peers. Girls often get teased if they develop breasts more quickly, and boys often get teased for not growing as tall. Acne is another common physical change for which kids will get made fun of. It is no small thing for a child to know how to stand up for themselves and others when these moments happen. Here's one way you can help prepare them for this:

"I am so proud of the person you are. One of the cool things about being human is that God made us with a voice to use to stand up for people when they are being made fun of. Sometimes people get teased in front of us, and sometimes friends will tease us. That's not okay. When you hear someone teasing a kid in your class about their height, what could you say back? What about if someone is teasing a girl in your class because her breasts are developing?"

Notice that the key, as always, is a dialogue, not a lecture! Your teen will feel honored and more open if you trust them to come up with an idea of how they could respond. If they give you a short answer like "I don't know," here's where you could go next:

"Do you remember the two greatest commandments? They are to love God with all your heart, soul, mind, and strength, and to love your neighbor as yourself. That means when you stand up to someone who is teasing someone else (even if the person they are teasing is you), you are following God's plan for us to love him and others. It's not easy in the

moment, and sometimes we stay quiet when we feel afraid.
When that happens, we can talk about it. What do you think
you would be afraid of if you heard someone teasing a kid
in your class? What would make it hard to speak up?"

Validate all the fears and challenges that could come up. When you
validate, you could say things like, "Oh, that makes sense," or, "You're
right, that's very difficult," or you could simply nod your head to show
you're listening.

Then, explore what could help your child face their fears:

"Now we know what can make it hard to speak up. If you
feel encouragement from God to say something anyway,
what would help you have the courage to speak up even
though it's hard?"

Once your child has a chance to respond, say something like this to
give them some tools to use to speak up:

"It's normal to feel scared to speak up, especially when it's
new. What can help is taking a few deep breaths—in through
your nose and out through your mouth—and a quick prayer
like 'Jesus, help me.' It helps to have a word to start with
that gets you speaking that is easier to get out. I use something like 'Hey' or 'Wait a second' to get me talking. Then
I can say something simple like, 'Why do you care? That's
weird that you would bring that up.' Then, I do something
called the 'broken record,' where I say something one time,
and if someone challenges me, I just say that again. Let me
show you what I mean: 'Hey, cut it out. Leave ____ alone.'
And if the person you're talking to challenges you or teases
you, you can say it over again: 'I said cut it out and leave
them alone. It's not cool or funny to be mean.' Then you can
simply walk away or change the topic, or go privately and
tell a teacher if they won't leave you or someone else alone.
And you can always tell me about those moments when
they come up.

"Speaking up is scary at first, and it's something to celebrate, because it's a way we can be like Jesus. When he saw

people being hurt, he stood up for them. He will help us be brave and do it too."

## RESPONDING TO BODY COMMENTS

In addition to talking about responding to teasing, we want to equip preteens to know how to respond to inappropriate body comments. This is especially important given how common eating disorders and unhealthy diet culture are today. You can make this teachable moment broad enough to account for insulting body comments more generally, or specific enough to help equip your teen to respond if someone makes objectifying comments about their genitalia:

> "Sometimes, people will think it's funny to make comments or jokes about someone's size or shape or weight. It is normal for weight to change over time as people grow. In our family we don't talk about body changes and comment on them. It's not helpful to focus on our body size and shape, or on other people's, because those things don't have anything to do with our value. That's why we focus on people as a whole. I can comment on your beautiful smile, or the way you light up a room when you laugh, but I won't comment on your weight or size, and I don't want you to comment on those things about other people either. If someone does say something like that about your body, you can ignore them, tell them to stop, or say something simple like, 'Please don't comment on my body,' and then walk away. As always, you can also talk with me about these things at home.
>
> "Sometimes people might try to make comments about parts of a person's body. Even if they are saying something that seems complimentary about that person's body part, it's not appropriate to reduce people to parts. You will hear guys and girls at times comment on a person's body parts, often when that person doesn't know they are being talked about. That can feel very violating and is not an appropriate way to talk about someone. We want to focus our comments about people on their personhood, which includes their body but isn't merely about their body parts. We want to be aware of how focusing on parts over the person objectifies someone.

If all I see are your body parts, I am not honoring you. When you hear comments about people's body parts, what could you do in response?"

Give your teen options here:

- Change the subject: "What are you up to later today? Did you see the game last night?"

- Redirect: "I don't want to talk about people's body parts. That's weird."

## OVERALL HYGIENE

Overall hygiene, including shaving, cleansing, and use of deodorant, are additional topics to discuss with your teen. You can have these conversations with your teen around age ten, or earlier if your preteen is starting to experience some of the changes that require these conversations.

### SHAVING

Parents approach conversations about shaving in all kinds of ways. Sometimes, a parent decides to make this conversation almost a rite of passage; you might plan a full day of hanging out one-on-one with your teen, which begins with (or includes) a facial hair and/or body hair shaving tutorial. Whether shaving becomes a full-day event or a shorter discussion on a random Sunday morning before church, here is one way you can introduce the conversation:

"Hey, I noticed your body hair is starting to come in. Do you notice that? What is that like for you?

"It's a really natural thing, but it can take some adjusting to. It means you are growing up to be an adult and maturing. One of the things that growing teens do to take care of themselves is learning to shave. I want to make sure you know how to do it, so when do you want to learn?"

This approach gives your teen an opportunity to share about what the pubertal change is like for them, and it also allows you to frame shaving as a way for your teen to take care of themselves. Allowing them to decide when they want to learn helps them retain some power and control in the midst of bodily changes that might feel scary and out of control.

Buy your teen a quality razor and some shaving cream, soap, or oil, and teach them the importance of applying the cream before shaving. This seemingly unnecessary direction is important since, left to their own devices, some teens may cut themselves significantly the first time they shave.

## ACNE

When it comes to discussing acne, be careful not to increase your teen's self-consciousness. Many parents will tease kids about acne, not knowing how much anxiety can emerge from these moments, especially if a teen is getting teased for the same thing in school. A well-intended, lighthearted comment can cause a teen to spiral to a place of insecurity. It's good to be careful about how we approach a conversation that probably feels easier for adults to talk about than it does for teens. Here's one sensitive way of beginning the conversation:

> "Have you noticed any bumps coming in on your face or those of friends? That's called acne. It happens around your age for lots of guys and girls. Keeping your face clean, drinking enough water, and trying not to touch your face with your hands can help a bit with it, but sometimes you will notice bumps no matter what you do. Again, that's normal. There are different facial cleansers we can use to help with it. Next time we are at the store, we can pick out a cleanser that you can start using to keep your face clean. How does that sound?
>
> "If people comment on these bumps, don't be surprised. Kids sometimes talk about others and try to make them feel bad when they already feel uncomfortable. If someone says something mean to you, we can talk about how to respond. For now, know that you can simply ignore someone when they do that, or you can say something like, 'Pimples are normal for a lot of people,' and leave it at that."

## BODY ODOR AND DEODORANT

The easiest way to introduce deodorant might be to wait until the next time you or your spouse is buying deodorant at the store. Take your preteen with you and show them the section. You can say something like this:

> "As you get older, your body starts to release hormones that make you sweat more and grow hair on your body. Adults wear deodorant to make sure we smell good even when we sweat. Now that your body is starting to turn into a more adult body, do you want to pick out your favorite scent to try?"

Whenever possible, we want to make these conversations natural, calm, and invitational. Bodily changes are no small thing, and addressing them proactively and frequently is going to set you up well to be a resource for all the conversations that are to come.

Let's turn now to "the sex talk" as we know it, building on everything we've already discussed. Hopefully, this conversation won't feel quite as overwhelming now!

# CHAPTER 5

# "HOW DO I ACTUALLY HAVE THE SEX TALK?"

## INTRODUCING SEXUAL INTERCOURSE

Maybe you skipped right to this chapter because you are desperate after a question from your teen that made you feel awkward. Or maybe you are trying to be proactive because you suspect the day is coming when you will get asked how babies are made. Or maybe you have already told your teen about sexual acts, but you want to know what you missed along the way in framing a Christian vision of sex. No matter your starting point, let's dive in.

### FRAMING SEXUAL INTERCOURSE

Framing is everything. We can frame sexual intercourse as forbidden fruit, a prize for good behavior, a chore to be endured, or so many other things. When I ask adults to reflect on the most helpful messaging they heard about sex when they were younger, they typically point to the value of knowing that sexual intercourse is a reality, a normal part of a marital relationship, and a gift from God. It's important for parents to be comfortable acknowledging to their kids that sex is something they do that allows them to participate in the divine life. This doesn't mean you should discuss your sex life in front of your kids at the dinner table, but acknowledging the reality of sex is not something to be ashamed of.

It is important to walk the line of not overwhelming a teen with sexual information, while also giving them a basic and medically accurate understanding of sexual intercourse. A lack of sexual education can actually pique a teen's curiosity about sex. When teens understand more about what sex is and how it works—especially when they are taught by people who underscore the sacredness and purpose of sex—everyone is better off.

## PROACTIVE CONVERSATIONS

Ideally, the first time your teen learns about sexual intercourse will be from you. Teens whose parents speak with them about sex are more likely to delay sex than teens who don't have these conversations.[1]

Some teens, especially preteens around ages nine to twelve, may not be willing to bring their questions about sex to you. One sex educator suggests the following prompt to begin this conversation proactively: "Have you ever wondered . . . what sex is?"[2]

### FOCUSING ON SCIENTIFIC INFORMATION

Part of the reason this book includes diagrams of sexual anatomy in chapters 2 and 3 is so you can reference these charts when you describe sex to a teen. Our bodies' sexual dimension makes sense in the context of men's and women's complementary roles in sexual intimacy. Showing side-by-side diagrams can allow you to help a teen see how men's and women's sexual anatomy each works together to create a baby. As you do this, I encourage you to use medical terminology and invite your teen to do the same. This alone will help your teen know that the topic of sex isn't off-limits or taboo. It will also help your teen see you as a resource for sexuality conversations. You want them to walk away from these conversations with you thinking, "My parent knows their stuff, but they don't expect me to know it all."

Whether your teen says yes or no to your asking if they wonder what sex is, you can offer this:

"It's important that we can talk about this, even if you haven't really thought about it before."

For a younger teen, keep things simple:

"Sexual intercourse is a gift created by God to help humans unite to one another and participate in his creation of new life. It draws together a man and a woman who are married to be as close as two people can be. In sex, a man's penis [point on diagram] enters a woman's vaginal opening. It's a beautiful thing God intended for marriage, because marriage involves a commitment where a couple can say with their bodies what they say with their whole heart and life: I give all of myself to you, and I receive all of you as a gift. Sexual intercourse is also the way that babies are created. A man's body releases sperm. A woman's body receives the sperm, and the sperm can unite with her egg, which is made from her ovaries [point on diagram]. This is how a baby can be created. What questions do you have? Remember, we can always talk more about this over time if you don't have questions now. It's such an important thing to be able to talk about with Mom/Dad."

Some teens may wonder if sex hurts. Here's how you might respond:

"Sex is actually created by God to be a pleasurable experience. It may not sound like it at your age, and that's okay, because sex is an act meant for adults who are married, not unmarried teens! It may be uncomfortable when a couple first begins having sex, but if there is pain in sex, there are ways to figure out how to relieve that over time."

For an older teen, you may build in more information about the reproductive aspect of sex:

"In sex, a man's penis is important because it's how God intended to release sperm inside a woman. What's amazing is that a particular sperm intended by God can join with a particular egg or eggs. If this happens, a baby begins to grow in the mother's uterus. Each baby, like you once were, is a gift from God. No matter the circumstance, any time a baby is conceived, the baby is a new life intended by God to bless this world.

And that's how sex can lead to a baby. What other questions do you have for now? Remember, we can always talk more about this over time if you don't have questions now. It's such an important thing to be able to talk about with Mom/Dad."

## OFFERING A CATHOLIC VISION

In addition to describing what sex is, we also want to infuse a Catholic understanding of sex. Here's how you might walk through each of these principles with your teen:

"Sex is freely chosen or consensual: Sex is intended to be an act between two married adults who can both say yes to the other. Sex is never meant to be forced. If anyone was to ever try to force sex on you, or any other type of behavior, you would never get in trouble for that. Your parents will help you know how to handle it. But know that it's not your fault if that happens. One of the ways God shows us what love is like is that he never forces us to love him. Anyone who really loves you would never force you to do anything against your will. Force is not love.

"Sex is purposeful: Sex has a purpose, like all of God's creation has a purpose. We look to the Creator to help us understand the purpose of all things, including our bodies. The purposes of sex are many: to unite us to our spouse, to allow us to be a concrete gift of ourselves to another, to participate in the potential of creating human life, and to reflect the unity between the persons of the Trinity in becoming a self-gift. Sex is meant for the security of marriage between a man and a woman who are committed to each other until death. Some people are called by God to stay unmarried, which also means they're not called to have sex. They're called to make a gift of themselves in many concrete and different ways, and singleness is another really good and purposeful way of living.

"Sex is beautiful: Sometimes people think of sex as dirty, or gross, or casual, or about using someone, or just about pleasure. Sex is not any of those things, even though it can sometimes be used that way. Sex is meant to be beautiful! In a secure marriage between two people who are working to invite the Lord to help them love their spouse and not use them, it is beautiful. Like any other part of a marriage, it takes work. But for people whom God calls into marriage, it is well worth it!

"Sex is meaningful: Sex has meaning. Sometimes people talk about sex or show it in porn as if it is meaningless, or as if it can be just as wonderful between strangers as it is in marriage. But that's not the point of sex. Sex without meaning becomes merely about using someone for pleasure. That teaches us selfishness, not love. And we are made for a beautiful love!

"Sex is fruitful: Sex between a man and a woman has the potential for bearing the fruit of new life. As Catholics, we believe that this design is intentional and we shouldn't disrupt it. The fruitfulness of sex reflects God, whose love did not stay within the Trinity but bore fruit in creating us. Love doesn't dwindle when shared; it multiplies! And sex that is open to this fruitful potential reflects the Trinity in a powerful way. Married couples are called to hold nothing back, to receive all that the other has to give, which includes our ability to create another person.

"Sex is realized most fully when it is faithful. This means sex is meant to be shared between two people, over the course of their lives, who have committed to choosing each other and no one else.

"Sex is unitive: Sex is meant to draw a husband and wife closer together. It allows each person to discover themselves more fully in the other.

"Sex is total: The total gift of a body (sex) should correspond with a total gift of the person (marriage)."[3]

## CATHOLIC FRAMEWORK AROUND SEXUAL INTERCOURSE

Sex is . . .

- Freely chosen
- Purposeful
- Beautiful
- Meaningful

- Fruitful
- Faithful
- Unitive
- Total

---

## WHEN THE "SEX TALK" WAS NOT PLANNED

Sometimes, kids will ask their parents about sex before parents can get around to sitting down and having the diagrams ready. Or kids and parents together might see or hear something about sex that starts the conversation sooner than they expected. If that's you, you are not alone.

Take the story of Karla. Karla was driving in the car with her daughter, Rosalee, and out of the blue Rosalee asked, "How do babies happen?" Rosalee was ten, and Karla was not at all ready for this question. Karla, playing it as cool as possible, did what we all can do when we are caught off guard; she delayed the conversation:

> "Good question! I'm glad you asked. Let's talk about it _____ when we have a little more time. What made you ask about how it happens? Were you feeling curious, or did you hear someone talk about it?"

This is a time-buying strategy to get your bearings if you got caught off guard. The key is to have the conversation, if possible, when you are calm.

Karla circled back to Rosalee the next day, which was a wise move. I know many parents who don't ever circle back, and unfortunately, this can send the message to your kid that you don't have anything to offer to the conversation. This is exactly the opposite of the message we want to send as parents.

Karla shared with Rosalee that babies are conceived when the sperm from a man and the egg from a woman join together in a woman's body.

"How do they join together?" Rosalee asked.

What Karla said is one approach you could take when your child asks the same question:

"Well, a man's body gives a sperm. That is kind of like a seed that sprouts new life from the ground. A woman's body receives the sperm, and the sperm unites with her egg. This happens in something called sexual intercourse. It's a beautiful thing God intended for marriage, because marriage allows a couple to say with their bodies what they say with their whole heart and life: I give all of myself to you, and I receive all of you, and this is a total gift of self. We hold nothing back, which means we engage in an act that lets a married couple give and receive totally, including their ability to create a baby."

Then, you could offer a bit more detail:

"In sex, a man's penis is important because it's how God intended to release sperm inside a woman. What's amazing is that a particular sperm intended by God can join with a particular egg or eggs. If this happens, a baby begins to grow in the mother's uterus. Each baby, like you once were, is a gift from God. No matter the circumstance, anytime a baby is conceived, the baby is a new life intended by God to bless this world. And that's how a baby is made. What other questions do you have for now? Remember, we can always talk more about this over time if you don't have questions now. It's such an important thing to be able to talk about with Mom/Dad."

## HOW DO BABIES COME OUT?

Another version of the sex question is a stand-alone question about pregnancy or childbirth. While you can certainly respond to this question when your child raises it, it's ideal to be proactive when possible. You could initiate this conversation when you see someone who has just had a baby.

Here's what you could say if your ten-year-old asks you, "How do babies come out of a mommy's belly?":

"I'm so glad you asked! Having a baby is one of the most incredible things. Like anything worthwhile in life, it can be hard in some ways. But it is one way God invites us into

creating new life. For people God calls to be parents, this
role is such a privilege.

"Babies grow in a mother's uterus for about nine
months. When they are healthy and ready to come out,
they will turn upside down so they can make their way out
of their mom. The opening to the uterus, called the cervix,
expands and allows the baby to come out through the vagina, the hole women have between their legs. Other times,
a doctor will help the baby come out through a surgery.
Maybe one day you will be a parent and get to witness it!

"What do you think of all that? Do you have any other
questions for now?"

This allows you to check on how your teen is processing this
information.

## ADDITIONAL TOPICS WITH OLDER TEENS

Other topics your teens (aged sixteen to eighteen) may wonder about
will include orgasms and ejaculation. Because nocturnal emissions can
precede puberty, you will hopefully have already had an initial conversation about ejaculation in that context. You may not explain every aspect
of this in one conversation, but here is a model for the moments when it
might be important to explain these concepts in detail:

## ORGASMS

"Orgasms can happen to men and women when they experience a climax in sexual pleasure. Orgasms, for men, happen alongside ejaculation, when semen is released from
the man's penis. The purpose of this semen is to enter the
body of the woman in intercourse. It's the semen that carries
sperm that, when fertilizing an egg, can create a baby."

For teen boys:

"You have probably already noticed erections and ejaculation. Those are normal things your body does that signal
the potential for fatherhood and for making a total gift of
yourself to another. What a gift!"

For teen girls:

> "You may have noticed times when you feel sexual excitement in your genital area. That isn't an orgasm, but it's a sign that your body has an ability for sexual pleasure. That ability is good, and it's meant to point us toward the goodness of our bodies and their capacity for total self-gift."

You can gauge if this last bit of information is helpful for your younger teen or something to hold until they are a bit older:

> "If you are called to marriage, you will experience sex. You will discover the beauty of sex together with your spouse. Orgasm isn't possible in every sexual act, and some people experience challenges with orgasm; if that ever were to happen, there are ways to help with that. That's adult stuff, so no need to worry about that now."

## SEX OUTSIDE OF MARRIAGE

Many parents hope that a prohibition approach to sex will work for teens. Too often, this means that teens who do have sex will keep it hidden, feel great shame, and likely compensate for that shame by isolation, irritability, withdrawal, and in some cases, more sexual activity. Further, if your teen is not sexually active, prohibition-only conversations can lead teens to harshly judge those who depart from this view, or to feel less than for their decision to abstain from sexual activity.

Media portrayals and experiences with friends or family may be the best way to discuss sex outside of marriage, since they are widely depicted in popular media and communities your teen is part of. Here's how you might introduce the conversation in response to a media portrayal:

> "Did you notice how that couple referenced having sex in that show? Some people haven't been formed to where they see the value of maintaining sexual activity for marriage. Even for those who have not refrained from sex, God is ready to help them come to know his plan more fully and can offer forgiveness and restoration to them."

When it comes to finding out the degree to which a teen's friends are discussing sex, here's another prompt:

"At this time, a lot of teens will talk about sex. Interestingly, because so many teens talk about sex, we can tend to think most teens are having sex. This actually isn't true! What have teens in your school been talking about when it comes to sex?

"It's good to know that, if you look at research, less and less teens are sexually active than years ago. In fact, most high school students are virgins, and the majority of those who have become sexually active admit that they wish they waited longer. This shows a growing awareness that high school isn't the time to focus on sexual relationships. It's the time to build rich friendships, grow as a person, date for some, and ultimately zero-in more on what God is calling you to do with your life. It's a time of great formation, and sex is not necessary for human formation. In fact, as beautiful as sex can be, sexual activity is not a requirement for a happy, whole, holy life."

Some parents want to discuss the reality of what could be done if a teen does become sexually active. Let's turn there next:

"Some people do engage in sex outside of marriage, as we've talked about before. What could you do if you found yourself in a situation where you had sex? I want you to know that, like anything else, you can talk to me about that, and I will not shame you or reject you. While we have shared about the value of sex being preserved in healthy marriages as God's best plan, sometimes we can struggle to live according to that. If that were to happen, God wants to be close to you in that and so do I."

## SEXUALLY TRANSMITTED INFECTIONS

Many Christian parents will forget to talk with their teens about sexually transmitted infections, yet another reality that is important in sex education. Of course, the ideal for most parents would be that this is not relevant. Even still, inviting conversation about it will help your teen immensely, whether they themselves are sexually active in adolescence or not. This conversation is not necessary in early adolescence (unless your teen has brought it up), but by the time a teen is around fifteen to eighteen, you could calmly introduce this concept.

> "What have you heard about sexually transmitted infections or diseases? Sometimes this will come up in health class, but I wanted to talk about it with you too. These are infections that can be passed from person to person through sexual activity. It's important for people who are sexually active to complete testing for these infections. For men and women, they don't always show symptoms right away, so regular testing is really valuable. For people who are not sexually active, there is no need to get tested, but it's a good thing to know about just the same."

## WHEN A TEEN DISCLOSES SEXUAL CURIOSITY OR SEXUAL ACTIVITY

In so many of these model conversations with a teen, we've concluded them by encouraging the teen to circle back and talk to you if they have more questions, or if they have an experience they need to process. You may be wondering, What happens when a teen does circle back? What happens if they express curiosity about or desire for sexual things, or if they disclose to you that they've been involved in sexual conversations or behaviors?

When this happens, the most important thing is to stay calm. I strongly recommend having a "first thing" you're prepared to say every time your teen discloses something that's hard for you to hear. Preparing for this conversation in advance can help you not to respond to your teen out of fear or anger in the shock of the moment. Your initial reaction is one way you can represent the attitude of Christ to your teen. Remembering how Christ receives and delights in every time we share ourselves with him—even when it involves sharing our pain, sin, and difficulties—can help you respond to your teen the same way.

No matter what your teen shares (including significant and traumatic events such as unwanted sexual touch or an abortion), it is better that you know than not know. Teens who carry the shame of these experiences without the love and support of family are likely to spiral further into hiding and challenges in this realm.

So, what can you say when a teen discloses sexual curiosity, activity, unwanted experiences (more on this in chapter 11), and similar things to you? Here are five messages I'd encourage you to communicate in a conversation like this:

## 1. Affirm

> "Thank you so much for trusting me with this. I am so proud, and God is so proud, of your courage in bringing this [question/experience/story] to me. It had to be hard to do that, and I admire you for it."

## 2. Clarify

> "What is it like for you to share this with me?"

(This question allows you to know what your teen is experiencing and tune into their needs.)

> "What more do you want to share to help me understand your question/the situation/what happened?"

If what they share is a situation:

> "Can you share more of what happened, either by writing it down or saying it out loud to me? That will help me know more of how to help you."

## 3. Normalize

> "You are not alone in having this [question/experience/difficulty.] That doesn't make it easy to deal with, but it does mean there is an [answer/way forward] for you. God will help us find the [answer/way forward]."

## 4. Provide Information

> "What specific questions do you have for me to answer? If it's one I am not sure about yet, I will find out for us, okay?"

5. Express Gratitude

> "I am so grateful that we have the type of relationship where you could come to me with this. How do you feel now that you have shared it?"

## CONCERNS AROUND DISRUPTING INNOCENCE

As we move through this chapter, some parents may be worried that talking about such topics prematurely will put thoughts in their child's mind that weren't already there. What I have found in my own counseling practice is that parents naming these topics to their kids does not usually instill ideas in kids' minds; rather, it signals to them that if and when such topics come up, trusted adults are not too fragile to talk about these topics. After all, many young people will encounter—or have already encountered—these ideas out in the world, and they may be curious about them or even consider experimenting with things they don't understand. Raising these topics in conversation opens the door sooner for your teen to bring their curiosities to you, rather than exploring them via pornography or in a relationship with a peer.

Of course, I do advise that parents use discernment with the level of detail they give their kids. Less is more with a younger teen. Use discernment, but do not let fear rob you of the opportunity to proactively invite conversation, difficult as it can be.

The framework we are building is meant to help you be a primary educator of your teen on all kinds of topics related to sexuality. One very common topic in this realm is self-stimulation, or masturbation, which we'll dive into next.

# CHAPTER 6

# "WHAT ABOUT MASTURBATION?"

## ADDRESSING SELF-STIMULATION

Vanessa remembers the first time she masturbated. She didn't know what it was at the time. She thought masturbation was a "guy sin," because at youth group retreats, the guys and girls were always split up. The girls talked about emotional chastity, and the guys about porn and masturbation. She had an image in her mind of what male masturbation was, and she had heard friends talk about things like "jerking off" and "cum," but she didn't have a clue that her efforts to self-soothe when she felt panicked and lonely at fourteen were also self-stimulation.

This started her journey of turning to masturbation for comfort. She felt ashamed and dirty while also feeling pleasure and relief, and she didn't have a clue that what she was doing was masturbation. It wasn't until long after this had become a habit of hers that she realized her behavior was masturbation. This crushed her; she believed she had been committing mortal sins for years. "How could I be so stupid?" she shared with me in a therapy session.

"Stupid?" I responded. "How were you supposed to know what you were doing? No one taught you. Masturbation was always paired with porn as a 'guy problem.' Many Catholic women can relate to this story, even if they don't care to admit it."

Stories like this show how important it is for us to have conversations about masturbation with young teens. They need to understand what this behavior is, how it can manifest, why people turn to it (not always out of lust!), and what they can do or who they can turn to if they find themselves engaging in it.

## WHAT IS MASTURBATION?

You may be wondering, "At what age do I start to explain masturbation to my teens?" It's important to keep in mind that, by the age of fifteen, nearly 100 percent of boys and 25 percent of girls will have masturbated to orgasm at least once. If you are hoping to shape your teen's views and behaviors related to masturbation, you will want to start explaining this concept before they begin to masturbate, if possible.[1] An older study that compared teen girls and teen boys found that by age fourteen, 62.6 percent of males and 43.3 percent of females had masturbated at least once.[2] Based on this statistic, I would recommend introducing the concept of masturbation, including a Catholic vision of sexuality and the purpose of stimulation in marriage, to teens between the ages of ten and twelve, depending on your child's maturity, level of exposure to media, and physical development. If your teen has unfiltered access to phones and social media, I would want to introduce the concept of masturbation around age ten, knowing that they will likely come across content related to masturbation by this time. Okay, let's dig into how we might introduce masturbation now.

### INTRODUCING MASTURBATION

Here's one way you could begin a conversation about masturbation with your teen:

> "There are lots of different ways teens try to get to know their bodies when they're around your age or a little older. One way that's common is something called masturbation. What have you heard about this?"

Asking this question allows you to get a sense for, as always, the messages a teen has already heard. This allows you to keep your description as discrete or detailed as necessary, given what your teen already may know. Here are some further clarifying things you could say:

"Masturbation is any type of stimulation (rubbing, touching) of your genitals with an object or your own hand with the intention of causing arousal. The genital area does feel pleasurable if it's touched in certain ways, and the feeling of pleasure isn't a bad thing. As Catholics, we also know that our genitals have a specific purpose, which is to be stimulated in the context of a relationship with your spouse, if God calls you to get married one day, in order to create new life. Some people will say you need to masturbate to be healthy. That's actually not the case. There are ways to be confident, healthy, and understanding of your body without that, which is good news.

"Our bodies are gifts from God. Your body is good, and the fact that your genitals can allow you to feel pleasure is part of God's beautiful plan for marriage. He made the sexual act not just as something that can unite two people and have the potential to create new life, but also as something that is meant to be really enjoyable! It is meant for the context of a total gift to another person, our spouse, which we can't engage in when there is no other person present. That's why God has helped us know that masturbation/self-stimulation is not part of his plan for our sexual lives, along with other sexual acts that are not in a marriage. These different acts are sin because they take the purpose of sex and move it out of the fullness of what we are made for."

Pause and ask your teen what thoughts or questions they have. Then turn the conversation toward how they'll interact with the idea of masturbation when they encounter it elsewhere:

"It's not uncommon for masturbation to come up as a topic with friends or even random people at some point or another. If someone was to ask you about whether you masturbate, what would you want to say?"

If your teen says they aren't sure, offer this:

"You could say something like, 'Why are you interested in that? And why do you care about whether I do or not? That's weird, don't you think?' Or you could say, 'No, I don't. I have found other ways to get to know my body and feel confident, so I don't need to do that.' Or you could just say, 'I'd rather not talk about that—let's change the subject,' especially if your teen has masturbated and doesn't want to lie about that. You could also say, 'I have. I am working on refraining from it since it's against my values.'"

These suggestions allow your teen to see that there is a way to own their decision about how they relate to their body, and it's a good way to respond to other questions they get from people about their sexual activity. These responses also reinforce the reality that teens never need to feel obligated to answer personal questions, especially when those questions are related to sex or their genitals.

## WHY DO PEOPLE MASTURBATE?

Your teen needs to know why people turn to masturbation, so that they can understand what it "does" for them and others, which is why I want you to have a degree of understanding of that. Too often, Catholic youth simply get the message that masturbation is wrong, full stop. This message never responds to young people's (understandable) curiosity about why masturbation draws people in, which ultimately makes it difficult for those who start the behavior to stop. For a teen like Vanessa, they may not realize until years later what masturbation actually *was*, which can lead to a whole other mound of shame and isolation. If we can't be curious about what a behavior is "doing" for us, we can't find replacement options. More than that, lack of curiosity leads to self-loathing, self-criticism, and self-rejection, none of which do anything but reinforce the very behaviors we may be trying to stop.

Most children begin to touch their genitals by the age of three or four. This is normal and not imbued with sexual meaning in most cases, even when it "feels good" to a young child. As kids get older, they may realize, even by accident, that touching their genitals creates a sense of pleasure or calm. Parents can often hastily react to this behavior negatively and harshly, without any conversation that helps a young person understand the behavior better. Even when parents don't react, without education, many of these kids develop habits of self-stimulation and shame about this long before they understand what they are doing and why.

Here's how you explain why people masturbate:

"I want to talk with you about why someone might masturbate. Sometimes people do it for comfort, or to help them sleep, or because it can feel good. While we want to understand why a person might *not* masturbate, it's important to know when you hear about it what draws people in and what might incline you to do it."

## FUNCTIONS OF MASTURBATION

- Self-soothing
- Calming panic
- Pleasure
- Release of sexual tension when feeling aroused
- Release in response to sexual fantasy/pornographic content
- Winding body down to sleep
- Exploration of body

Notice how neutral I am listing out these functions. That's intentional. Even if masturbation is not a necessary aspect of sexual development and can have moral implications (more on that later), understanding it requires calmly explaining what leads so many people to engage in it.

## MESSAGING ABOUT MASTURBATION

Too often, the message that masturbation (and porn, for that matter) is gravely sinful leaves people believing that there is nothing positive they should expect to experience from masturbation. This attitude can be extremely conflicting and "crazy-making" for teens, whose early experiences of masturbation are full of "good pleasure" and seem, for most, to have very few consequences. It's no wonder so few teens are compelled by a Catholic vision that paints masturbation as merely bad. As we will talk about more in the next chapter on pornography, behavioral change will be more lasting if we can help teens understand the bigger reason why God designed our sexuality to be pleasurable. As St. Thomas Aquinas reminds us, each of us is pursuing a good thing when we sin; however, there is a higher good available to us when we choose holiness, and sin inhibits our ability to encounter that higher good.

If you take away only one thing from this chapter, let it be this: Even while we set limits around self-stimulation, we want to be very careful not to send the message that pleasure is bad.

## CATHOLIC TEACHING ON MASTURBATION

A Catholic ethic on masturbation teaches that masturbation is a sinful and disordered behavior (that is, it goes against the natural order of our sexual organs and their purpose). It is morally problematic because it is pleasure—namely, orgasm—induced apart from a relational encounter of communion with an orientation toward self-gift. Of course, pleasure is not bad, and we certainly "induce" it in a range of ways that are not problematic. So those of us who want to help our teens understand Catholic teaching on masturbation need to first make sure that we understand that view and its complexities in our own minds.

Many of us have learned that masturbation is a sin, without hearing a compelling argument for why God would invite us to refrain from it. If you can hang with me, I want us to explore this topic for ourselves before we address how to talk about it with a teen.

The Catholic understanding of masturbation comes back to the very purpose of our genitals. In their essence, our genitals are a sign of the reality that humans are made by the Triune God who is perfect unity and relationship. God's love in the Trinity is also creative; that is, it is the avenue for new life. *Agape* love is sacrificial love. True love can't help but be shared. Thus, our genitals, incomplete on their own, are a sign of communion and our capacity to create, regardless of whether we realize that potential in a sexual union. The sign of our sexual nature, made for communion with God, signals what our bodies and souls are made for, even if we never engage in a sexual relationship. For those who do marry, stimulation of your genitals by yourself or your partner is intended to be oriented toward and within the context of sexual intercourse.

All of us have the capacity to receive and give pleasure in a range of ways. Some of these modes are always for our good, such as receiving or giving a smile. Some of these modes are sometimes for our good, depending on their context and moderation, such as consuming good food. Some of these, arguably, are never for our ultimate good, even if they feel pleasurable to us. As Catholics, we believe that this final category includes masturbation.

Catholic teaching, incorporating Scripture, tradition, and research from the natural sciences, upholds the following truths:

- Masturbation takes sexual activity outside of the procreative potential of our bodies and does not orient us toward that end.

- Masturbation divorces pleasure from self-gift.

- Masturbation removes the vulnerable element of sexual intimacy, which is its gift and invitation into an encounter with another who is invited to see, give, and receive.

- Masturbation can separate orgasm from its purpose in the context of intercourse, which is ultimately total gift of the self to the other.

From a psychological standpoint, there are additional meaningful reasons why God may caution us against masturbation as an end in itself:

- Masturbation, especially for men due to their sexual response cycle, can promote sexual dysfunction in sexual relationships.

- Masturbation can become habitual or compulsive, potentially taking away a person's ability to manage life apart from it.

- Masturbation can lead to foreclosure on moments of vulnerability with another person—moments when we have to communicate our needs and desires rather than taking matters into our own hands.

- Masturbation, when done apart from sexual intimacy between partners, is done in isolation, whereas sexual behaviors are meant for the context of communion with another person; so masturbation can exacerbate loneliness and poor social coping.

It is important to offer this teaching and hold it in tension with an acknowledgment of how many people have engaged in and/or currently engage in self-stimulation. This keeps us from shaming ourselves or our teens for engaging in masturbation. We can encourage faithfulness to God's design while refraining from self-flagellation or condemnation of those who engage in self-stimulation. God does not shame us or coerce us while he invites us deeper into the mystery of his plan for our lives.

## ADDRESSING ONE COUNTERARGUMENT

While it is outside of the scope of this book to address all arguments for masturbation being a good and necessary thing, I want to respond to one some readers (and some of your teens) will have.

A current narrative about masturbation I often hear is that men and women suffer in particular ways when they are told it is immoral to masturbate. Those who critique the Catholic view of masturbation frequently argue that young men and women need to be permitted to explore their bodies in order to effectively experience pleasure and reduce body shame. They might be especially concerned that young women are being taught to fear their body's capacity for pleasure, resulting in greater risk of future self-hatred.

One aspect of this perspective that I'm sympathetic to is the concern that young women, especially in religious contexts, are often framed as being uninterested (or at least less interested than men) in pleasure and sexuality. This narrative can lead to enormous shame about sexual desire for women who have a high sex drive. Meanwhile, women who have challenges related to experiencing sexual desire may feel that their challenges are "normal," assuming there is no way to build and increase pleasure and arousal in their marriages and sexual lives. This messaging often starts from a young age, when many teens are told that guys love sex and girls love emotional connection.

It's also the case that, if all we teach our young people about sexuality is what not to do, we leave a lot of young people who practice chastity unaware of their bodies and unable to "turn on" their sexuality in marriage or manage their sexual desires adaptively in singleness

Devin's story illustrates this well. Devin was told by her parents in a sex talk, "If you have sex before marriage, it'll ruin your life. Also, no touching yourself 'down there.'" This was enough to keep Devin from being sexually active before her marriage, and anytime she felt sexual arousal, she felt disgusted. As Devin approached marriage, she felt more and more afraid of sex and continued to feel disgust at the thought of being touched "down there." "How can I just turn this thing on that

I've seen as so bad and something to avoid at all costs for so long?" she wondered. Years into her marriage, Devin still struggled to experience pleasure in sex or to communicate about her desires in that realm with her husband. She still felt shame about sex, even though she tried to tell herself, "It's not bad now."

There are ways we can help Catholic children like Devin grow into adults who can step into marriage with greater confidence, freedom, and ease. And for those who don't marry, we can help teens grow into adults with integrated understanding of their body and sexual desire.

Recognizing the ways we've sometimes failed to encourage healthy body exploration and honor sexual pleasure can help us understand why some people are concerned about *how* we introduce Catholic teaching on masturbation to young people. Sexual relationships within marriage will always take work, intentionality, and growing as a couple, but teaching healthy exploration of one's body and understanding of the goodness within its sexual aspects is important.

Doing this *doesn't* require us to change or ignore Catholic teaching on masturbation. After all, there are ways to explore and understand our bodies and its capacity for pleasure without masturbation. Let's dive into that further now.[3]

## FOSTERING HEALTHY BODY EXPLORATION

If we aren't going to merely say no when it comes to masturbation, what is it that a teen gets to say yes to when they move away from masturbation or refrain from it?

As already mentioned, some will argue that masturbation is necessary for a person to gain self-awareness of their body. Requiring any one behavior to achieve healthy integration of your sexuality, like self-stimulation, seems to oversimplify the conversation. As Catholics, we know that being a fully alive human does not require any sexual activity (let alone masturbation). In fact, the perfect man, Jesus Christ, was never sexually active, and he was the pinnacle of human existence. Even when some believe masturbation is necessary for self-knowledge, we can offer a different vision for integrating our sexuality that allows us to discover the goodness of our bodies without, in the process, violating its very purpose as established by God and as the Church teaches.. If masturbation were necessary for our good and our salvation, it would be morally permissible, to be sure.

There are ways teen women (and men) can come to a healthy knowledge of their bodies without stimulating their genitals for pleasure alone. Further, the following tips will prepare a young person for the possibility of marriage and a sexual relationship in that context, without requiring self-stimulation to facilitate self-knowledge. Finally, to imply that masturbation is the only route to body awareness discounts the stories of many men and women who have never masturbated and are able to successfully enter into rich sexual relationships where they discover their body anew in relationship with their spouse.

## THE MIRROR

A common technique I recommend for parents of older teen girls is this: Offer your teenager the opportunity to use a mirror and privately look at her genital area and identify various parts using a nonexplicit diagram. (One is provided in the back of this book.) To be clear, teen boys should also be invited to look privately at their genitals—in fact, around age fifteen, they should begin checking for warning signs of testicular cancer—however, boys' self-examination won't require a mirror.[4] Giving a teen the opportunity to become familiar with their body can help honor their natural curiosity, reduce body shame, and orient them to the beautiful gift our body is. Too often, female bodies in particular are prone to objectification and framed around a sexualized purpose. Teens have a degree of innocence that may allow them to be able to receive the gift of their body through seeing and understanding its many incredible functions.

Here's how you could introduce this conversation with your teen:

> "We have talked before about how your body is changing at puberty. What kinds of changes have you been noticing?"

Allow your teen to share with you about any changes she or he is noticing. They may have questions about the changes they see, so make space for this:

> "What questions do you have about these changes?"

Notice that I am assuming the teen has questions. Instead of saying, "Do you have any questions?" I am anticipating and making room for the fact that there likely are some questions.

After addressing these questions, introduce the idea of the mirror to your teen daughter:

> "One thing that can help young women know their bodies is taking a mirror and a diagram and identifying different parts of your specific body. After a shower, you can take a hand mirror and look at your genitals and become familiar with how they look and what they are for. Once you know what's there, you can better understand how beautiful and good your body is. You can also understand what it points to, which is that all parts of our body, whether we use them or not, are there to tell us about God, ourselves, and our relationships with others."

## BUILDING SELF-CONFIDENCE AND KNOWLEDGE

We also want to talk about ways to help a teen build confidence and knowledge in their body, without relying on masturbation:

- Getting comfortable with your body using the mirror exercise
- Experimenting with different clothing styles
- Building physical strength through movement
- Tracking your menstrual cycle
- Learning a new skill
- Fostering talents
- Praying to see your body the way God sees it
- Making a gratitude list of all the things your body allows you to do
- Reducing social media usage or filtering out unhelpful content

One way for specifically teen girls to build body awareness and confidence—one that is growing in popularity today—is to track their menstrual cycle (we already discussed this in part in chapter 3). Get your teen an app or chart to map out her cycle and get to know the natural ebbs and flows of hormones. You could also look for opportunities to enroll your teen in a Natural Family Planning (NFP) class, so that she can understand how masterfully her body is made; even though she may not pursue marriage for many more years (or at all), NFP classes can help her think practically about what her body is doing throughout her cycle and why it matters.

### A NOTE FOR BOYS

There is a strong narrative that boys in particular need the release of masturbation for their health. However, a young man's body is designed by God to find release through nocturnal emissions or wet dreams. If a young man never masturbates, these emissions are the normative way to release semen. This is the incredible thing about the rhythms of our bodies. Women, if they do not conceive a child, will menstruate every month to release the unfertilized egg. They also experience a form of nocturnal emission that involves a spontaneous orgasm while they sleep. Men, if they do not engage in sexual behavior, will also ejaculate, releasing semen, while they sleep. Thus, we do not have to be worried about not being able to develop into a healthy adult sexual being without masturbation. Our bodies will engage in their own rhythms to ensure proper functioning. God has made ways for our bodies to naturally release and experience spontaneous orgasms. This is nothing to be ashamed of; it is a sign of the incredible purpose and masterful wisdom of God in creating our bodies the way he has.

## CONCERNS ABOUT AWAKENING SEXUAL DESIRE

As reflected on already in chapter 4, some parents will understandably worry that encouraging their teen to understand their body—explaining things like sexual organs, their function, and masturbation—will put ideas in a teen's head. This question, a valid one, presumes that we can stir up curiosity before its time. Do parents have the power to stir up thoughts in a teen's mind before they belong there?

This fear of awakening sexual desires or behaviors prematurely is common to so many parts of the sexuality conversation. In fact, we just talked about a very similar fear in the last chapter, and we'll address these dynamics in future chapters as well. Even apart from sexuality, concerns about planting ideas in teens' minds come up in relation to other topics for teens, including conversations about depression, suicide, and self-harm (especially cutting). We know from mental-health research that simply bringing up these topics does not make teens any more likely to engage in them. This same principle applies when it comes to talking with our teens in sensitive, age-appropriate ways about masturbation and their bodies.

Inviting a teen to explore their body in healthy and moral ways is effective and important because it goes beyond simply telling a teen "what not to do." It also offers a teen "what to do," opening up ways to integrate their sexuality positively and proactively.

Here's one final reason these conversations about masturbation and body awareness are so important: it is naive, in most family situations, to assume that your teen will not hear about what you are bringing up if you don't share it with them. Certainly, some teens have been in environments where parents are the first ones sharing with them about masturbation and sex—and this is ideal! However, many teens are being taught about these things from peers, social media, passing comments, or even class lectures before their parents address them. The internet is its own education, and it is full of misinformation and temptation.

If we don't shape the conversation around masturbation for our teens, someone else will. The same could be said for pornography. We will turn to that next.

# CHAPTER 7

# "WHAT ABOUT PORNOGRAPHY?"

## FORMING SELF-MASTERY

"I don't remember a lot of conversations with my dad growing up. But I do remember him lecturing me after he would discover me watching porn. After a while, it was like a routine. Watch porn, get caught, get a lecture, tell him I wouldn't do it again, and weeks later find myself back in the cycle. I knew my dad wanted me to stop, but he really didn't do much other than tell me what *not* to do. I don't honestly remember any conversations that helped me understand *why* I kept watching porn. I just felt like a monster."

This story is so common when it comes to the way pornography gets addressed in many Christian homes. The response of many well-meaning parents involves a conversation, a reminder that pornography is bad, and sometimes filters on phones or computers. This sends your teen the message that porn is harmful and sinful, but it only offers them what not to do. It doesn't effectively help them know how to stop doing what is deemed harmful. It doesn't help them understand where their desire to watch pornography comes from—a crucial step in changing behavior. It doesn't help a child understand the alternative strategies that they can develop, with the support of trusted adults, to manage urges to watch porn. And it doesn't often effectively keep kids from seeking out porn again.

So, what does effectively help your teen understand the harmful nature of pornography, without stopping there?

Let's consider the messages we want to send your teen about pornography, ideally both before and after your teen sees pornography (assuming that, unfortunately, most teens will be exposed to pornography at some point). In addition, let's identify some critical principles to use when having conversations about porn. These will help us avoid unintentionally shaming children, which ends up shutting down conversation, silencing and isolating teens, and typically leads to further porn use.

---

### MOVING BEYOND WHAT NOT TO DO

If all we teach kids is what not to do, they will struggle to effectively avoid porn or know what *to* do when they come across it.

---

## PROACTIVELY DISCUSSING PORNOGRAPHY

Proactive conversations about pornography will help a child more effectively know what to do when they see porn. These conversations can be casual, gradual, and intentional.

There are many settings where you can bring up pornography. Let's imagine you are picking up your eleven-year-old daughter from school. Her younger sibling is at a playdate, which means you have some concentrated time together. In passing, begin the conversation:

> "Emily, I've been thinking about how some kids start to come across something called porn around your age. Have you heard anything about that word?"

This gives you a chance to see what, if anything, your teen already knows about porn. Once you've done this, move into a brief synopsis of what pornography is and how it can pop up:

"Porn is any type of image, video, or writing that shows the human body or sexual behaviors in a way that's meant to make the person watching have a sexual response. It can pop up without our wanting it when we type something on the internet, friends can try to show us photos or videos, or there can be pop-ups on different websites or advertisements."

Give language for possible feelings your teen may have when they come across porn, and why those feelings are legitimate:

"When we happen to see pornography, even by accident, we can feel a lot of different things, such as excitement, curiosity, guilt, disgust, confusion, or embarrassment. Porn takes something incredible—the human person, our bodies, and our capacity for relationship with another person—and tries to create a false representation of the real thing. So, it can seem exciting and interesting, but also lead to shame and guilt and emotional pain."

Tell your teen what to do next if they see porn and what they can expect when they tell you about it:

"If you happen to see porn or find yourself going back to it, I want to invite you to tell Mom and/or Dad about it. Remember, as your parents we are here to help you with the things that come up that are difficult. I also want you to know that if you are honest about porn use, you will not get in trouble for it. We will work together to help you know what to do next. Anytime you tell me about things that have happened that are hard to figure out, I will be so proud of you for telling me the truth. I can't help you if I don't know what's going on."

Acknowledge the way pornography can pull us away from communion with God and others, and help your teen understand what we get to say yes to when we say no to porn:

"God wants for each of us to have a real freedom to know our bodies and their goodness, and to see and know the goodness of others. Pornography can make it harder to see ourselves and others in the way God intended. That's what

makes it something that God tells us to avoid. Sin is anything that damages our ability to see ourselves, others, and
God fully. It pulls us away from the fullness of life God has
for us, even when it feels good in the moment. Learning
how to say no to porn means saying yes to the freedom of
knowing God, ourselves, others, and the goodness of our
bodies more fully."

Set clear parameters that help a teen have more protection from easy
access to porn. You can even invite them into this conversation by helping you brainstorm what additional protections would be helpful, and
invite them to make sure those protections are working. Here's one way
you could say this:

"It is possible to do things that limit the likelihood of coming across porn. You'll notice that we have put monitors on
devices and blocks to protect you from seeing things that
aren't helpful for you. We also fast-forward scenes in movies
or shows that expose people's bodies in ways that make it
hard to see them as a whole person. The sexual act is something good, beautiful, and sacred. It's meant to be exclusive
to the people engaging in it, not something for us to view as
entertainment. So, we try to make it easier on you by putting
protections on devices. If you see things getting through the
blocks, let us know, okay? Can you think of other things we
could do to help you not see these kinds of images?"

## PROACTIVE CONVERSATION STEPS

1.  Summarize what porn is and how it can show up.
2.  Give language for what it can feel like to watch porn and why.
3.  Identify next steps after viewing porn and what to expect.
4.  Acknowledge the spiritual impacts of porn and the spiritual fruit
    of refraining from it.
5.  Set parameters for filtering exposure to porn and why.

## WHEN A CHILD HAS VIEWED PORNOGRAPHY

When we address porn use among teens, we should expect that many kids have seen pornography at some point, and that in many cases they didn't seek out their initial exposures.[1] The average child is exposed to pornography long before they have the ability to effectively discern how to respond. Many of my clients feel enormous self-blame for their pornography exposure, even though it was a friend, internet site, or mistaken Google search that led to their first exposure. Without any way to make sense of this experience, many teens cycle into a pattern of porn use that is hard to break on their own. That's where trusted adults come in.

## HOW DOES EXPOSURE HAPPEN?

Where are kids accessing pornography? Unsurprisingly, most kids will access porn through their phone, home computer, laptop, or tablet device. Fifty-one percent of eleven- to thirteen-year-olds have seen porn at some point, with that number increasing to 79 percent of sixteen- and seventeen-year-olds.[2] That means if you are a parent of an eleven- to thirteen-year-old, one in every two kids your child's age has already seen porn of some kind.

### WAYS CHILDREN ARE ACCIDENTALLY EXPOSED TO PORNOGRAPHY[3]

- Mistyping "sex" or "porn" in an unrelated Google search.
- Looking at a friend's phone and seeing pornographic videos as a result. (This is most likely to begin between ages eleven and twelve.)
- Receiving video or photo links from peers and clicking on links.
- Clicking on pop-ups and advertisements on gaming, sporting, or film websites or on social media platforms, many of which allow access to illegally shared content.

## WHAT IS PORNOGRAPHY EXPOSURE LIKE FOR TEENS?

Common emotional responses of your teen to initial exposure to pornography include the following:

- Disgust
- Confusion
- Pleasure
- Embarrassment
- Guilt
- Excitement
- Amusement/laughter
- Awkwardness
- Curiosity

Knowing these common responses will help you supply your teen with possible labels as they process their own emotional responses to pornography, allowing you to invite more detailed conversation with them. You will want to normalize the range of emotions a teen may feel when watching porn, to help them share more about what might be drawing them to it.

## WHAT DRAWS TEENS IN?

Parents often misunderstand the reasons why teens are drawn to pornography. Viewing porn can be a very mixed experience for many teens and is not always fueled by lust alone.

Common motives for watching pornography include the following:

- Coping with difficult emotions (boredom, sadness, loneliness, insecurity, inefficacy, futility, anger, disgust, shame, guilt)
- Distracting from pain
- Numbing pain
- Amplifying, extending, or controlling positive feeling state
- Replacing pain with pleasure

- Releasing emotions that are hard to release elsewhere (anger/aggression)
- Building awareness of one's body
- Feeling curiosity about bodies
- Wanting to punish oneself for bad behavior by doing something "bad"
- Seeking sexual release

When we frame porn use as merely a sign of lust, we forget that all behavior can have a range of motives. For instance, a person may steal from a place of greed, but they may also steal from a place of desperation or hopelessness. If we tell a person who steals out of desperation that they need to stop being greedy, they will probably not stop stealing, and they aren't likely to have a clear understanding of why they keep going back to the same unwanted behavior.

Why is understanding motives important? Not only does it help us think with nuance instead of framing porn as always a lust issue, but it can also help us foster curiosity with our teen about what might be prompting them to return to porn.

I try to cultivate a curious posture by asking one or all of these questions:

- What needs are being met by pornography use?
- What is pornography offering that a person is not accessing in other areas of life?
- What negative feelings is pornography relieving a person of?

## STRATEGIES TO ADDRESS PORNOGRAPHY

Once we understand more of what porn is doing for a teen, we can begin to consider what strategies might be helpful to address it.

### MANAGING YOUR OWN REACTIONS

One of the things I often hear from parents when they become aware that their teen has seen pornography is just how difficult it is to manage their own reactions. Just as your teen might have mixed reactions to viewing pornography, you might have mixed reactions to learning about it (or even imagining it).

I remember being on vacation with a mother named Sharon and her sweet boys. Her kids, both under five, were taking naps, and we sat and delighted in the boys' silly gestures, giggles, and play from earlier that day. Sharon said, "I hate to imagine that one day they will likely be exposed to pornography. I hate to think about that, but I know it's possible. It's so overwhelming even to imagine. I don't want that day to come."

So, how can we prepare for when that day does come? Suffering, sin, and temptation are inevitable in a fallen world. We are working in this book to help you protect against what can reasonably be protected against, prepare for what can be prepared for, and respond calmly, courageously, and charitably when days come that you hoped would never come (and to help your teen learn to do the same).

Many virtuous, holy men and women have been exposed to porn at one moment or another. I say this not to downplay the grief I feel about the prevalence and pervasiveness of porn, but to help us remember that God is sovereign and ready to help us where we are, in a world of radical exposure to sexual content. The Holy Spirit will help you navigate this world with your teen.

With that in mind, here's a map of how you can manage your own emotions as you respond to your teen's porn use initially:

- *Pause*: When possible, do not address the pornography immediately if you discover it by walking in on your teen or happen across it on their device. Discovery can lead us to be reactive, not responsive. If you are noticing a rush of emotion, pause and wait to have the conversation until you have clarity about what is happening to you.

- *Name and honor what you are feeling*: It makes sense if you are feeling sad, confused, guilty, angry, disgusted, horrified, defeated, scared, or grieved.

- *Seek out supports*: Talk confidentially about what you are feeling with at least one person who can honor what you are feeling before talking to your teen. This will help defuse the intensity of your emotions and let you show up as a parent to your kid.

- *Identify a low-stress time to talk*: Bring up what you saw calmly, while you are doing something with your teen (such as driving in the car, working on a task, or going for a walk). Doing something together can make the moment less intense, allow for moments of comedic relief, and create a dynamic where your teen isn't feeling as much under the microscope.

- *Describe what happened and how you felt about it*: "I noticed ___. I felt [concerned, hopeful we could talk about it, grateful I came across it] so that we can address it together." Keep in mind that your teen doesn't need to know everything you felt; focus on feelings that are constructive for them to hear.

- *Invite understanding*: "Can you tell me a little bit about when you first came across it and how long it's been happening?"

## HAVING INITIAL CONVERSATIONS AFTER DISCOVERY/DISCLOSURE

Let me show you an example of how to discuss porn use with your teen when you become aware of them viewing it.

Wanda, a single mom of three, is cleaning up the family room after a long day of work on a Wednesday night. She picks up a tablet belonging to her eleven-year-old son, Kyle, turns it on, and sees a pornographic video playing. Wanda is shocked. She didn't realize Kyle could be seeing this so young. She thought the day would come to address this, but certainly not so soon.

Even though Wanda feels scared, overwhelmed, angry, and disgusted with what she has seen, and heartbroken that Kyle has seen it, too, she decides to wait until the weekend to address it with her son. She knows that if she brings it up sooner, she will be reactive, and she needs some time to talk with a friend about her concerns and make a plan.

Wanda makes a plan to spend some quality time with Kyle on Saturday, after his football game. She knows that bringing this up before then could add stress to his day and make him distracted for his game. Wanda invites Kyle to go for a drive, so the conversation isn't as intense, and they are "doing something" together instead of just sitting together in a room.

One of the harder parts of the conversation is initiating it. This is how Wanda begins:

> "Kyle, I want you to know that I came across a porn video I saw on your tablet the other day. I am really grateful I found it, because I want to understand more about it and talk about how to help you with it."

If Wanda notices Kyle shutting down or getting defensive, she can say something to help:

> "I can tell this is a hard conversation to have. I am not angry at you, and I'm not going to punish you for this. Many teens come across porn at some point. It's normal to feel a lot of things when this conversation gets brought up: things like fear, embarrassment, guilt, shame, anger, confusion, and the desire to pretend like it didn't happen. It makes sense if you are feeling some of that."

Wanda can then ask Kyle more about his history with porn:

> "Can you tell me a bit about when you first came across porn? You aren't going to get in trouble. We will make a plan to help you with this, but I am not here to yell at you or shame you. I am proud of you for being willing to have this conversation."

Once she knows a bit about Kyle's history with porn, she can acknowledge that there are lots of reasons people come across porn:

> "There are lots of reasons we are drawn to porn. Sometimes, we are curious. Other times, something pops up that makes us feel a spark or excitement. What do you think drew you to porn first?"

Then, Wanda can start to understand more with her teen what porn is offering him. This may feel strange for her to say, but any behavior we engage in is "doing something" for us, or we wouldn't do it. Wanda can introduce this idea to Kyle and help him think through what it is about porn that feels like it is helping him:

"What do you notice about how the porn helps you?"

Kyle may not be sure, so giving some ideas based on what Wanda knows about common reasons for pornography use can be helpful:

> "It can feel comforting, exciting, interesting, pleasurable, intense, and other things. It can be an outlet when you are feeling lonely, bored, desire, sad, frustrated, or tired."

Then come up with a plan for how to cope:

> "When you are feeling like you want to watch porn, I want you to know that you can always reach out to me to talk about things if you want to, or just to have some company. We can have a code word to use, if you'd like, in case other people are around. If I can't hang with you, like if it's late at night or something, we can think about what else you could do to help. What do you think of that?"

## FOLLOW UP AND FOLLOW THROUGH

The key to addressing porn use (or any behavior in any child) is to follow up and follow through. Too many teens (and adults) who are regularly working to step away from pornography use recall that the most their parents did was have periodic conversations when they discovered pornography again. These conversations, even if had calmly, only left the teen feeling more isolated, ashamed, and alone in their use.

Here are several ways to follow up and follow through about porn use with your teen:

- Initiate monitoring of phones and/or internet use every few weeks, and be sure to tell your children ahead of time that you will be doing this. You could frame the conversation this way: "Phones and the internet are a privilege, and it's our job as parents to protect you from harm. There is a lot on phones and the internet that can harm us." Whenever possible, this ought to be a proactive step, not a reactive one.

- Use apps that are designed to monitor website usage, and set them up on your teen's devices. Do this, whenever possible, before your teen's first exposure to porn. Tell your teen that this is set up as you do it, to keep communication open.[4]

- Check in verbally every few weeks about how your teen is doing with viewing pornography. Do not rely on an app to check in for you.

- If you see your teen's mood changing, seek out intentional time together. Do something you enjoy together, and don't use every time you connect one-on-one as accountability time. That can feel to a teen as if they are reduced to their porn use, as if that is the only catalyst for your interest in them.

- Talk openly with your teen about how pornography is developed, including that many of the people filmed in pornography are coerced into certain sexual acts, drug use is heavily influential in that world, and experiences of abuse are common pathways for people to begin to step into pornography. Talk also about the inaccurate view of sexual intimacy that pornography offers.

- Come up with a list of solitary and family activities or coping skills that your teen could engage in when they are wanting to view porn.

- Pray together for grace from God to *want* to stop watching pornography if your teen does not feel a desire to stop it. And pray together for the grace from God to have the conviction and courage to reach for support to refrain from pornography when urges arise.

- Seek out a therapist to check in on your teen's mental health. Sometimes, pornography use is the "tip of the iceberg." It's a sign that, beneath the surface, there is emotional pain going unnoticed and unattended to. Respond by assuming there are needs, longings, emotions, and beliefs beneath the surface that your teen could benefit from getting support around. Normalize therapy as a way to check in on your mental well-being, not merely as a means to an end.

## WHAT IF OUR TEEN DENIES VIEWING PORN, BUT IS WATCHING IT?

Have you ever denied something you knew was true? We've all been there, unfortunately. Kids are known for this, but if we are honest, we don't turn eighteen and magically become, well, honest. This can help with empathy and understanding when your teen denies their use.

Denial is a powerful defense mechanism that allows us to maintain a level of protection from the pain of facing reality. While denial can be rooted in deception and manipulation, sometimes we deny because we are terrified, overwhelmed, powerless, or ashamed. Refrain from assuming your teen is merely trying to deceive you if they don't come clean right away about porn.

Remember, the part of your teen's brain that anticipates consequences, thinks about behavior, and plans for the future is not fully developed. This means we ought to expect teens to respond impulsively. This doesn't mean we enable their misbehavior or assume they can't grow in this area, but it does keep us from simply framing a teen who tells a lie under pressure as "a liar."

When your teen denies any misbehavior—especially something steeped in shame, like pornography—it's not always malicious. Be curious about what your teen might be afraid of if they told the truth. Consider possible fears like these:

- Loss of privileges (punishment)
- Loss of respect
- Disappointing you
- Angering you
- Disgusting you
- Confronting their own shame, disappointment, anger, disgust, or fear
- Loss of self-worth

Too often, when a teen denies behavior, we make the mistake of assuming malicious intent. However, more often than not, misrepresenting information or flatly denying something is a defense mechanism to protect ourselves, or simply a behavior motivated by a sense of panic.

Expect that, even when you have "concrete evidence" of your teen's porn use, they may deny it. When they do, it is better not to get into a "tug of war" about the truth. Instead, you can intervene by describing and observing the situation and your teen's response:

"I noticed there were some videos of pornography on your phone searches. I hear you saying you didn't search for porn. That may be the case, and it also may be hard to acknowledge what you did right now. Let's pause this conversation and take some time to sit with what I shared. Know that I am not bringing this up to punish you or make you feel worse. Honesty always is relieving, even when we are being honest about something we feel ashamed of. You can take the next twenty-four hours to come back to me and tell me if you did search for those videos. If you are honest, there will always be less consequences. You will never get in more trouble for telling the truth, even if it was hard to tell the truth right away. Then, we can work together on coming up with a way to help you with what is going on."

If the teen comes back and tells the truth, thank them for their honesty. Heap on praise of their clarity and courage.

"Thank you so much for coming back and telling me truth. I am so proud of you for doing that. I bet it wasn't easy to do! How does it feel to be honest even about things you don't want to face?"

Then, circle back to the original conversation.

"Now that we got clarity about what happened, we can work together to make a plan. What can I do to help you more with the pornography piece? I have some ideas, but I want to hear any that you have. You may not be quite ready to fully want to give it up, and that's not uncommon too. But maybe we can make a plan either way."

Collaborate and come up with things you are going to commit to as a parent, as well as things your teen can commit to, in working to change this behavior.

End your conversation with intercessory prayer. We often underappreciate the power of a parent praying for and with their child. Here's a sample prayer you could pray:

"Dear Jesus, we know you are here with us in each and every moment. You are always ready to hear what we are struggling with, and you rejoice in your child being honest with you. We want to be honest about how hard it can be in a world full of temptation to draw close to you, especially when we feel guilty and ashamed. Thank you for your mercy, your love, and your readiness to help us with what we have going on. We bring to you this struggle with pornography and ask that you guide and guard ____ and help them come to know how you see them and every other person we meet. Mary, wrap your sweet child in your arms and protect their heart. Root out anything that is not of you, and invite us in every moment to return to you with our whole heart. Amen."

## WHAT IF OUR TEEN DOESN'T WANT TO STOP YET?

If you are reading this section, perhaps it's because your teen has been honest with you about not feeling motivated to stop watching pornography. I want to start by complimenting you for having the type of open communication where they could be honest about this. Many adults I work with who experience difficulties with their pornography use talk about how much pressure they felt to "pretend" they would stop pornography even when they weren't ready to give it up. This only exacerbated shame, the very emotion that, among others, can trigger behaviors of sexually acting out.

So, let's back up. How do you make it more likely that your teen would be *honest* if they weren't ready yet to give up pornography?

### USING PARTS LANGUAGE

You'll notice in earlier scripts I made a point to name that a teen may not feel ready yet to fully stop. You want to emphasize this to make space for the possibility:

"Sometimes, if we are honest, a part of us *wants* to stop a behavior, and another part of us *doesn't* want to stop. For example, when I am feeling tired, a part of me may want to go to bed early, but another part of me wants to 'numb out' by watching my favorite TV series. That can happen with porn too. A part of me might want to stop, such as the part of me that believes it's not God's best plan for me or the part that wants to spend my time doing something else. A part of me might not want to stop, like the part of me that feels calmed by it or the part that feels energized when I'm bored. This is normal, and you don't have to pretend that those parts of you don't exist, okay?

"Are there parts of you that want to stop and parts that don't?"

This can get your teen talking about what might be motivating them to stop pornography use and what might lead them back to it.

The wonderful thing about our relationship with God is that he wants to help us when there are parts of us that want to turn to the thing that isn't his best for us. He is ready to offer the grace we need to *desire* what is for our ultimate good.

## PRAYING FOR THE DESIRE

You can encourage your teen to pray for the desire to change the relationship they have with porn, and you can even offer to pray with them.

"It helps me to bring God into situations where I have mixed desires. Scripture talks a lot about how we can have desires that conflict in the Christian life. God cares about all of our desires, even our desires to sin! When we bring our desires to him and don't filter, he will help us find a way.

"So, you can tell God about the things you like about porn. The parts of you that still want it can share that with him. Let yourself be honest with God, just as you are being honest with me about it all. He will not mock or blame you or be disgusted by you. He loves you as much now as ever.

"You can also pray for the *desire to want* a healthier relationship with porn. Ask him to open your eyes to what it's offering and where it may fall short."

## OFFERING RESOURCES OR EDUCATION

You can also offer your teen resources and education if they want to learn more about pornography, its effects, and the way it is intertwined with human trafficking in concerning ways. Sometimes this helps teens build understanding of why they might be inclined to move away from it.[5]

## SETTING LIMITS

Finally, you can set limits around use even in this context. It's not as if, because a teen says they aren't ready to stop porn, the porn is given free reign. Here's how you might talk about limit-setting in this situation:

> "It makes sense that you feel torn about stopping watching porn. As we've talked about, there are things it gives you that keep you going back. And even if, on some level, we know it ultimately won't satisfy, it does in the short term. I am so grateful you can be honest about the parts of you that want to (and likely will) go back to it. Knowing that, I want to help you with setting some limits around it still. I don't want this to be something we as parents are *forcing* you into, but I know it might feel that way. Let's talk now about limits to help reduce its place in your life, even while we know that it won't completely go away yet. Let's come up with some helpful limits together now.
>
> "Honesty is always best in this. We can check in on how you are feeling about it all, and we can continue to pray for God to increase your desire to replace porn with other things. And we don't ask for perfection in this (and neither does God), but simply the willingness to be open about where you are at with it."

I recognize, too, that some teens have younger siblings. It is valuable to acknowledge the following with them:

> "As you are working on understanding this and working through the conflicted feelings about stopping pornography use, we will use some filters on devices to buffer against exposing you and your siblings to it. Also, we want to acknowledge that siblings can see and come across porn when it's on common devices. We are going to keep computers in common spaces where there is more accountability, and we will keep devices out of rooms so that we can prevent those moments when you may leave something on a device and one of your siblings comes across it. Does that

make sense? What else might be helpful to limit exposing siblings as you are working on this?"

## TEACHING ADAPTIVE COPING

Regardless of whether your teen is ready to walk away from pornography use, you can introduce and teach your teen ways to cope with difficult urges. Internal coping skills are the things we find that help us manage distress that do not require resourcing support of others. Environment management strategies are the things we tweak in our environment to set ourselves up for success in behavioral change.

### INTERNAL COPING

- Identify cognitive distractions from porn that are not harmful in the same way porn use is. (For example, think of and imagine in vivid detail the future person you want to become. Think of and imagine in vivid detail your future vocation, plans, and hopes, and allow yourself to dream and imagine this future. Research a topic that is interesting to you. Think of something you are looking forward to in the next year, and imagine it in detail.)

- Identify, name, and reflect on emotions that may be triggering urges.

- Engage in physical exercise to release endorphins (pleasure hormones).

- Journal to contain or express emotions.

- Use expressive arts to contain or express emotions.

- Listen to music that channels the release of emotions.

- Engage in play. (Make a list of leisure activities to engage in that aren't isolating or solitary, especially when boredom is a trigger.)

- Challenge self-defeating thoughts when you fall back into a behavior with self-compassion. (Instead of saying, "I'll never stop. What's the point?" try saying, "I made a mistake. My past mistakes don't have to decide my future and don't define my value. I am still learning and growing, and God sees how hard I am trying and loves me unconditionally when I fall short. I can begin again. One day at a time.")

- Make a list of reasons why you want to live a life free of porn, and keep this in a place you can see it, or convey through art or a quote what it is that motivates you to refrain.

### ENVIRONMENT MANAGEMENT

- Change scenery. (Get up from the space you are in and go somewhere else.)
- Set up accessible activities that are within arm's length that aren't a device.
- Don't keep screens in bedrooms.
- Leave room doors open.
- Filter devices.
- Get out of bed right when you wake up and reserve your bed for sleeping.

## COPING PLAN

- Internal Coping (identifying things your teen can do on their own to manage urges)
- Environmental Management (identifying things in the environment that make porn use more or less likely and making adjustments there)
- Social Coping (identifying people and strategies for support when needed)
- Filtering Access (setting up filters on devices)
- Addressing Emotional Triggers (spending quality time together, seeking therapeutic support)

## PRIORITIZING ONGOING DIALOGUE

Remember, you do not need to address all your questions or concerns in one conversation. One step at a time, see if you can open up the dialogue.

Think about what it would have been like to have these conversations with your own parents. It can be overwhelming, to say the least.

If you notice your teen having a hard time with any conversation, let alone a conversation about something as vulnerable as pornography, you can acknowledge that difficulty and ask them to help you understand what it's like for them to talk about this with you. Then table the rest of the conversation for later, especially if it feels as if you're hitting a wall:

> "It seems as if you might be having a hard time talking about this. That makes sense; this is a tough conversation for anyone to have. There's a lot I might feel if I were you. What are you feeling?
>
> "Let's pause for now and come back to this conversation later. Thanks again for being willing to be honest with me about it, even though I know it's a hard conversation to have."

As always, follow up. Life is so full, and it's easy to let follow-up conversations fall to the back of the to-do list. But these conversations set your teen up to know that you will follow through. Be consistent in doing so, and trust that, even if your teen rolls their eyes at you for "always having to have talks," they will thank you one day for being an intentional parent who cares about doing what you said you would. It's no small thing.

As we bring this chapter to a close, I want to be clear that I am not offering a foolproof guide to avoiding pornography in your home or perfectly managing porn use. No foolproof guide exists; if it did, I'd offer it to you.

However, porn use is a reality to contend with, and one that many Christians must learn to navigate in an ongoing way. God works in the midst of our present world to lead us to holiness. For some of your kids, the path to holiness will involve exposure to porn. For others, the path to holiness will not include this component as heavily, or at all. Either way, take heart. There are things to be done to buffer against the harmful effects of porn on your teen. Most importantly, your accompaniment with them and ability to listen, receive, and speak into their experience in real time will help in more ways than you realize.

# CHAPTER 8

# "HOW DO WE RESPOND TO CRUSHES AND DATING?"

## FOSTERING HEALTHY RELATIONSHIPS WITH OTHERS

In this chapter, we want to cover attraction, crushes, and healthy ways you can interact around your teen's romantic interests. For thirteen- to fourteen-year-olds, only 20 percent have any past or current dating experience. For fifteen– to seventeen-year-olds that number rises to 44 percent.[1] So, for many parents, your teen actually may not officially date in adolescence. For other parents, your teen will be in at least one serious dating relationship before they head off to college. Because of this, we want to begin talking about what teens are noticing about attractions and crushes (in themselves and peers) between the ages of ten and thirteen. Some teens will not take any prompting to initiate these talks, and others would rather talk about *anything* other than crushes with you. Either way, setting up conversations to normalize attractions is a good next step in the direction of fostering healthy sexual development and integration of sexuality into personhood. Then, we will want to learn how to navigate all of the questions and experiences that reside in the realm of attraction. Let's dive into that now.

## TALKING ABOUT ATTRACTION AND CRUSHES

A common milestone that every person experiences in sexual development is their first awareness of attraction. Some people report feeling
initial crushes at a very young age, even as young as four or five. For
most kids, these crushes pass and they tend to go through a period of
time when crushes are less important. Some kids will even have a strong
adverse reaction to those they once had a crush on. Take Chloe, who, after
having "a boyfriend" in kindergarten, came home from school in second
grade announcing, "I hate boys. They are gross!" Just a few years later,
in fourth grade, Chloe might start to notice feelings of attraction again.

When your preteen first begins to experience attraction and crushes, he
or she might not be sure what to do with it. Proactively talking about this,
like everything else we have covered already, is important. Some parents
avoid talking about attractions because they worry about making too much
of it or bringing too much attention to what is already a significant focus
of peoples' minds. In fact, opening the door to the conversation will be the
very thing that helps normalize it and springboards future conversations.

Let's think about how to initiate this conversation with a preteen
(eight- to twelve-year-olds):

> "In the next couple of years, you might be more aware of
> crushes. You can always talk about crushes at home if you'd
> like. Whether you get married one day, are single, or become
> a priest or religious, you will experience attraction to people.
> Crushes are normal and helpful in pointing to the type of
> people you are drawn to, and there is nothing to be ashamed
> of in being drawn to someone.
>
> "Attractions are a normal part of development. Some
> people might notice being drawn to the same sex and others
> to the opposite sex. As you become aware of these, know
> you can talk to us about them. Attractions can feel confusing
> for sure, and we are here to help you make sense of them."

Next, you want to help your preteen reduce any feelings of guilt for
their attractions (and for spontaneous responses, such as an erection) in
response to sexual stimuli.

"You will notice your feelings toward people, both people you know and people on TV or in movies or in public. You are not doing anything wrong if you notice a beautiful or attractive person.

"It's not a sin to feel attraction to someone. When we are drawn to someone, we are being drawn into the beauty and goodness within them in some way.

"If you see an attractive person in the store or at school, that is a wonderful thing. You can thank God for the gift of that person and for your ability to feel a response to their goodness!"

## HELPING TEENS LEARN TO RESPOND TO ATTRACTIONS AND DESIRE

We can discuss more fully the concepts of stewarding our attraction and lust as well with our teens. There is no specific age for this, but you can lay a foundation for highlighting our ability to respond to attractions, rather than being ruled by them. This framework can be offered gradually and frequently once your preteen is noticing their attractions:

"We can certainly choose to respond to our attractions in healthy and unhealthy ways. If I am responding in a healthier way, I am able to see and hold that the other person is a whole person. I am not going to reduce them to body parts or the way they look. And if I start by noticing parts of them that I find attractive, I can acknowledge that and shift my attention to their face, their eyes, and allow myself to thank God for their beauty without reducing them to that."

In this case you are helping your teen expect the moments when they focus on "parts" of another person and lose sight of the "whole" person, and you are also gently offering a way to respond in those moments.

"We can also find ourselves responding to our attraction in unhealthy ways. We call this lust. When we forget that a person is another person and view them as an object for us to use, we can be responding in a way that is unhealthy.

"The wonderful thing about being a human is we can grow in mastery of ourselves, with God's help. He is ready to help us see each person, not as an object to use, but as a person to love and respect. It is a process, for sure, and God is merciful when we find ourselves lusting. When I find myself caught up in looking at a person in a less healthy way, it can be helpful first to acknowledge what I am feeling, then shift my focus. I can also pray for them and ask God for the grace to see them more fully.

"Sometimes we can even have thoughts that pop up where we imagine kissing someone or being close to them or them liking us or other thoughts like that. Those are normal too. We can choose how to respond, even though we can't choose our thoughts. One way to respond is we can follow those thoughts and build a fantasy out. Another way to respond, which is what allows us to honor that person as a gift, is this: Just like with our attractions to beautiful parts of people, we can also simply notice the thoughts and then shift our attention back to what's happening right in front of us. We can't stop our thoughts simply by telling ourselves to 'stop it.' We can learn to shift our attention to something else, though, as long as we can acknowledge the thought and practice staying present where we are."

## RESPONDING TO ATTRACTIONS IN THE SHORT-TERM

Now that we have covered how to talk proactively and respond initially to attraction and crushes with your preteens and teens, we want to look together at how you can continue this conversation throughout the teen years.

I want to highlight one important piece about attractions for now: You might be inclined to downplay the attractions and crushes of your teen. In doing so, teens will often feel as if you "don't get" the significance of their attraction or crush on someone. It might also make them less likely to come to you, if they feel as if you will not take the experience seriously or will diminish it as a phase. Remember, teens feel deeply and fully a lot of times. Even if it doesn't seem significant to you, it likely feels significant to them. The more you ask questions and honor the significance, the more they will invite you in as the years unfold.

## EXPECTING QUESTIONS ABOUT CRUSHES AND ORIENTATION

Attraction and crushes as well as orientation questions often become a focus for many teens. It will be helpful to assist your teen in preparing for pressure in this realm.

Let's talk first about helping your teen anticipate pressure about crushes and dating:

> "When you have a crush, you don't have to *do* anything about it. You don't even have to tell people if they ask. Of course, you *can* tell someone if they are a close and trusted friend, but it's important to know that they might try to tell you what to do about it. Sometimes people might share that information with others or pressure you to ask someone out or tell them you like them. Crushes are fun to simply enjoy and delight in. If you don't want to date someone, you don't have to. If you ignore people who try to pressure you to open up more about your attractions, they will eventually stop bugging you."

Many of your teens will also be asked, "Are you straight? Gay? Queer? Bi?" To prepare your teens for these questions, by ten to twelve you will want to acknowledge that these questions will come. Here's how you might address that:

> "You know how we have talked some about attractions and how you will start to notice those more? Because of this, attractions can become a bigger focus of conversation with friends. Have you noticed this?
>
> "There might be moments when people will ask you who you have a crush on, and whether you are attracted to people of the same sex or the opposite sex. They might use words like 'straight,' 'heterosexual,' 'gay,' 'lesbian,' 'bi,' or 'queer.' There are lots of words people might suggest to you too.
>
> "Our attractions are something precious and important and sacred. We can have many kinds of attractions. Some of these are good and holy. Some are less so. God's grace is needed by all of us to steward our attractions and purify them. Whether they are directed toward people of the opposite or same sex, they can urge us to act in ways that

are not God's best for us or others. They aren't something that everyone has a right to know about, especially people we aren't close to. Also, because of your age, attractions are simply that. Understanding our orientation and labeling our attractions publicly usually happens later, and it's not necessary to do that now, even when you hear others doing so. Our orientation is when our attractions last over time. So, what could you say when people you don't know well ask you who you are attracted to? Or when people try to suggest labels?"

Here are some suggestions for how a teen might respond to peers who start to insert language and categories when they are young. With strangers or acquaintances, they might say:

"I don't tend to talk about things like that with people I'm not close with."

With friends they are closer to they might say:

"I am not focused on figuring out labels right now. I have my whole life to figure that out."

## DATING

Think for a moment of your family values that are important to pass on regarding dating. Jot down a few in the margins. Having a framework for dating is so helpful, because it offers teens something concrete to step into.

So, how would you discuss dating with your teen? You might want to start at around age eleven or twelve, even if your child is not thinking much about dating yet. Remember, being proactive is always best. Ironically, at this age, some children will not want to talk with you. They may show discomfort or annoyance. That's okay. Validate those feelings and highlight the importance of having this conversation even still.

"Honey, I want to talk a bit with you about dating. Have you heard of friends starting to date?

"One way people respond to attraction at your age is pursuing dating. In our family, we [list out family dating expectations]. If you date, keep in mind everything we've already talked about regarding sex and sexual behaviors, and we can talk about that more practically when you date. Figuring out how to manage sexual desire and talk about it with trusted people becomes more important when you date.

"If you find someone you want to date at school or in your friend group, we would love to know. Sometimes I know it can feel odd for some people to talk about crushes with parents. You may hear about friends who keep their crushes and the person they are dating a secret from their parents. You don't have to do that, since we have open communication about these things in our family.

"We do ask that, if you are dating someone, you let us know so we can get to know the person you like. We'd love to meet them and have them over to the house sometimes so we can get to know them better."

## SINGLENESS

The reality is that the majority of a teen's years leading into adulthood are spent single, and for some singleness will be a lifelong path. Singleness is such a gift even while it has its own challenges. Singleness can be a rich time of formation and growth as a young adult, and your guidance can help foster that!

There can be a lot of social pressure toward dating, both for guys and for girls. This can lead to shame and insecurity when teens aren't dating. How many of us dated someone because we thought we "should" at some point in adolescence? We can equip our teens to normalize singleness and recognize its value, too!

"There are lots of good reasons to stay single, even when you're attracted to someone. Attraction doesn't have to dictate whether or not we're in a romantic relationship.

"Can you think of some of the reasons people might actually like being single and what the good parts of it are?

"Singleness allows us to prioritize getting to know ourselves, investing in friendships, and growing in confidence that doesn't hinge on having a romantic interest. Sometimes people who are dating someone may seem confident, but a lot of times dating can actually be a filler for insecurities.

You can grow to be confident with a boyfriend/girlfriend and without them.

"Being single doesn't say anything about how desirable or strong or capable we are. Some people might give you a hard time for being single. How could you respond if someone did give you a hard time for that?"

---

## RESPONSES TO TEASING ABOUT SINGLENESS

- "I am focused on other things right now."
- "I don't need a boyfriend/girlfriend to be okay."
- "I'm not worried about it. I don't know why it matters so much to you."

---

### FRIENDSHIP

Regardless of whether your teen ends up dating in adolescence or not, we always want to bring them back to what can be such a rich part about this time of their lives: friendships. Here are some conversation starters about friendship and how it can intersect with other aspects of a teen's life:

"Sometimes people start dating and they can get lost in that and lose sight of friends. Have you noticed that at school?"

"Who would you say are your closest friends? What are the things you are learning from your friends? What are the things you get to offer in your friendships?"

"What might help you if you start dating to remember not to let your crushes become a higher priority than friends, at this time in your life?"

"What would be helpful from Mom and/or Dad if we start to notice that you are focused more on dating than friendships? You can also ask your friends what would help when they notice that. It would be hard to hear that, but good friends will tell us the truth."

Remind your teens, "Friends will be there if relationships end or don't work out the way we hoped. A lot of times we can get lost in a romantic relationship if we aren't prioritizing time with friends."

## STEWARDING ATTRACTION IN THE LONG-TERM

### DISCUSSING VOCATION

Now, we want to turn to vocations and the way you could introduce and talk about marriage, priesthood, religious life, and singleness to teens, especially older teens.

### DISCERNING VOCATION

Discerning one's vocation can be an enormous burden to so many Catholic young people. Many young adults spend years waiting for their vocation to become clear, fearful of desires along the way, and viewing God as a trickster who may spring a vocation onto them without their permission and without their freedom. You have the opportunity to ease fears and offer opportunities for your teen to witness vocations, ask questions about vocations, and trust you as a reliable guide.

When introducing the concept of vocation, here's one way you might start the conversation:

"Did you know that, through the Sacraments of Baptism and Confirmation, you receive your 'common vocation'? This means you receive the pathway by which you are called to be a saint and evangelize, or lead others to Christ.[2] By the time of your Confirmation, you have the graces to live out the particular ways God is calling you to love in daily life. Whether you are at school, at home, with friends, or alone, the Holy Spirit is always ready to help you become more like Jesus every day. Pay attention to the spaces and places you feel most alive, and that may help you discover the path God has for your life."

We want to make space for teens to discover God's call by inviting them to notice the particular ways God is calling them to love him today, in their common vocation. It is more likely that their particular vocation will emerge most fully in this context, rather than by trying to will themselves into an abstract knowledge of their particular vocation.

---

## HONORING A RANGE OF VOCATIONS

Too often, parents talk about "when you get married . . ." as if marriage is a given. This does not help those young people who experience attraction to the same sex, those who are single, those who wonder about a religious vocation, and so on. It also can unintentionally reinforce a distinctly secular idea that people are expected to marry as a type of societal goal for each person.

In order to broaden the pathways for teens, who are told so often that romantic love is the pinnacle of human experience, we want to talk about vocations that flow out of our common vocations as well. We want to avoid pitting marriage and celibacy in competition with each other or viewing those who pursue celibacy or marriage as more or less sacrificial in their love for God.[3] Let's turn now to discussing particular vocations:

> "As you respond to the ways God is inviting you to love him and others today, you will discover what can be called your particular Vocation, or 'capital V' vocation (as I like to say). This might include singleness, marriage, priesthood, or religious life. Wherever God takes you, I will feel so proud to witness how he reveals his plan for your life. He has so much goodness and beauty in store for you, whether you are single for a time or permanently, get married, or become a priest or nun."

### HOW TO "SHOW" VOCATION

- Host a book club at your home (co-ed or same-sex), and invite people from diverse vocations. Invite your teen to sit in, be present, and interact with different people.
- Have priests and religious over for dinner or a game night, and let your teen encounter them "off duty," as fellow Christians seeking to follow God.

- Bring your teen to weddings, priestly ordinations, and professions of the vows of religious sisters. Let them encounter the presence of God in the beauty of vows made out of love for God and others in a radical self-gift.
- Allow your teens to witness you resolve conflict if you are married. Show them apologies, warm greetings, and pauses for intentional goodbyes with your spouse, as well as healthy conflict (avoid blaming, name-calling, and villainizing the other).
- Invite single people of various ages (widows/widowers, friends, family members) into your family traditions. Christmas-cookie decorating, birthday celebrations, graduations of children, or whatever it is will enrich your family life and show that people can belong no matter their call.

With an older teen, who has the ability for more abstract thought, we can help them to *imagine* a range of paths, through any of the following conversations:

"Marriage is a beautiful way to reflect God's love for each of us, even in all of the challenges of two imperfect people building a life of love together. Like God's love, it's free, total, fruitful, and faithful. What do you think it would be like to be married?"[4]

"It's so incredible to have priests dedicated to the service of the Church. They have a unique part in bringing Christ to us through the sacraments, their prayers, their sacrifices, and their fatherly love when they are reflecting God's love well. No priest is perfect, and yet God shows us what he can do with any one of us—shape us into servants capable of bringing his love to the world. What do you think about what it would be like to be a priest? What appeals to you? What doesn't?"

"I am so grateful for our family friend _____. As a single person, they have freedom to serve God in their relationship with him, their job, and in relationships with many people. They can come over for dinner and be part of our lives, and that's because they are free to go where God calls them, without having their own family to care for. What could it be like if you were single for your life? What would be the blessings? What could be some challenges?"

"Did you see the religious sisters at Mass? It amazes me that there are so many options for committing your life to God. Sisters are active in the world for the good of the Church, whereas nuns take vows of poverty, chastity, and obedience in a monastery where they serve God through prayer and concrete acts of service in a life of quiet. They show us that we are all called to live a life of dedication to God in our own particular way. Can you imagine being a religious sister or nun? What are you drawn to about that? What doesn't appeal to you?"

Notice that I am not recommending you tell a young person what they "should" do. This can put undue pressure on teens and add a layer of fear to some about disappointing parents, especially in cases where it's clear that there is a preference one way or another. You want to open up a conversation and share a bit about the particular vocations, without foreclosing on one option. Even if you have a sense that your teen may be called in some particular direction, refrain from too easily projecting your sense on your teen. This leaves room for the Holy Spirit to work. Finally, remind your teen that God works with our desires, not against them. Our vocation is not necessarily the task that is hardest for us or the one that demands the most sacrifice.

### CHASTITY IN ANY VOCATION

Chastity, the successful integration of our embodiment into our person-hood, is a virtue that is cultivated in freedom, not a power play. Chastity is a virtue, which means a disposition toward the good that can be culti-vated over time. This implies that chastity is not something we gain from intellectual knowledge alone, any more than I can fully realize the virtue of prudence by reading a book about financial stewardship.

A comprehensive picture of chastity is beyond the scope of this book. But I want to name that many people have been hurt by unhelpful frames of chastity. Some popular messaging about chastity can make abstinence, and even cultivating chastity, out to be an end in itself. It can frame a satisfying marriage as the "prize" for chastity.

For Christians, the goal of our lives is not behavioral compliance; it is more perfect communion with God and others. Thus, we want to help young people recognize that, while there is enormous value in abstinence in adolescence, the culmination or realization of virtue around sexual appetites is not to be discovered merely in what we say no to.

Chastity, like all virtues, is the pathway for growing in Christlikeness. Some teens will discover and live out chastity in a range of ways from a young age. Others may struggle immensely with chastity, and it can be a point of real difficulty in ongoing ways. The goal, ultimately, is to help each person discover the call of Christ in their life and relationships and to turn to Christ when they fall short. If we are honest, all of us fail to perfectly live out virtue in our sexual lives. This is why we want to present chastity as an integral part of any vocation and help point our teens to Christ as any challenges arise when they are pursuing virtue.

## CHASTITY CONSIDERATIONS

I have asked many people what drew them into a Catholic ethic of chastity and what pushed them away. This quote illustrates one common theme I hear: "The same thing that turned me on eventually turned me off. What turned me on was the fantasy that there is a soulmate for you, fear of not having a successful relationship or marriage, fear of having family look down on me. What turned me off was how it gave me shame and fear around having sex. . . . If there was less shame and taboo around sex, I would have been able to learn first the importance of respecting yourself and your body and that sex is a sacred thing that should be treated with intention and care."

When introducing the concept of chastity to your teen, you could offer this:

> "I know we have talked about chastity before in our family. We want to talk about it continually as you get older.

It might make even more sense why chastity is hard and important, now that you know what attraction feels like!

"You are capable of living chastely, which will allow you to more fully glorify God with your body. You will fall short in that throughout your life, and you are not alone. Christ, who was fully human, knows intimately the reality of our desires and our struggles. He wants to walk with you and help you respect yourself and others through respecting boundaries for physical touch and finding ways to show you care that honor someone's worth.

"No matter what path you take in life, whether you are married or single, the call is chastity. There will be joys and sorrows no matter which vocation it is, and chastity is difficult for each of us. Whether you are married, single, a priest, or a religious, there will be grace to help you. In the context of community, a life of prayer, and faith, we can step into our callings, not knowing all that they entail, bringing our imperfections to Christ who loves to draw close to us, especially when we are finding it difficult to manage our desires in a healthy way."

## SEXUAL BOUNDARIES

Let's talk a bit about sexual boundaries. These conversations are essential by around age thirteen, whether or not your teen is dating actively. As a teen gets older, the conversation will likely need to be more specific, but the early teen years are a time when a teen is vulnerable to someone crossing sexual boundaries if they don't have some understanding of *how* to say no and *what* to say no to.

Unfortunately, some teens will have unwanted sexual experiences that demand a response from trusted adults. These are incredibly difficult to navigate. Chapter 10 will focus more explicitly on how to respond in these situations. For now, we want to lay out a framework for initial and proactive conversations that pave the way for more open dialogue as a teen gets older.

Some important boundary areas to discuss with your teen are holding hands, kissing, caressing, making out, oral sex, and sexual intercourse. Too often, we forget that these behaviors tend to build on one another, and failing to discuss them leaves teens to their own devices. Especially in an age of frequent "hookups," it's important to remember that your teen needs to understand bodily boundaries even if they aren't in a romantic relationship.

I want to acknowledge one caveat here. Different families may encourage their kids differently in this space. I am simply going to describe what I consider to be healthy recommendations.

When it comes to holding hands, this can be a really lovely way for young people to express affection. Here's how you might introduce that concept to your preteen:

> "You know how you give hugs to people you care about? Another thing that people sometimes do when they have romantic feelings is hold hands. In some cultures, people hold hands as friends, without meaning something romantic by it. Have you ever held someone's hand? If so, what was it like? If not, why might you decide to ask to hold someone's hand? Where we live, holding hands is a way to signify a level of exclusivity—you don't just hold hands with anyone. People hold hands for a purpose, and it's something to ask someone about before you do. If someone else asks to hold your hand, it's up to you to decide whether or not you want to do that. And if you ask to hold someone else's hand and they seem unsure about it, you can tell them that you will wait until a time they are sure they want to. Even if someone says they'll hold your hand, if they show with their body or their words that they aren't totally sure about it, you should respect that by not moving forward with holding their hand. That's true for all touch, actually."

Notice how the emphasis on asking someone about hand-holding lays a foundation for continued conversations about the importance of consent.

Regarding kissing, here is a way to introduce the topic to a preteen. Whenever possible, build off things they have already encountered, whether it be couples' relationships around them or things they see on media. These are teachable moments to draw from:

> "Have you noticed how Mom and Dad kiss when we say hello or goodbye? We also kiss other times as a way to show

each other affection. We don't kiss just anyone, because kissing is a pretty important way of showing a particular person you are romantically committed to them in some way— such as in dating or marriage. In some cultures, kissing is also something you do with family members—especially a kiss on the cheek or forehead. That kind of kissing means something different than when you kiss someone you're romantically interested in. Have you ever kissed someone?"

A younger teen might remember kissing a baby or a crush, or being kissed by a parent. You can point out how trust is formed with people we kiss. We don't kiss just anyone. Then you can help your teen prepare for how they might interact with kissing in the future:

"As you get older, there will be times when you may want to kiss someone or someone may want to kiss you. If you want to kiss someone, it is essential to ask them before doing it. Just because you want to kiss someone doesn't mean they want to kiss you! So it's good to ask before you do it. It'll save you the awkward moment of their not wanting to and your assuming they do.

"Sometimes, a person may try to kiss you without you wanting it. What could you do if they did that?

"You can move your face away. You can tell them you don't want to do that. If you are confused about whether you want it, you can say, 'Not now.'

"I know this might not be something you have to face anytime soon, but if you do have a moment when someone tries to kiss you or does kiss you without you wanting it (or does anything else you don't want physically), remember this: It is not your fault. And your parents are always here to help protect you and help you figure out what to do when those things happen. We will not punish you for something that is not your fault, even if you worry that you did something wrong. Even if it's hard to say and hard to hear, we would always rather know than not know."

Saying this allows you to prepare for a common experience among youth and young adults, while encouraging your teen to look to you as a resource and guide.

## INTRODUCING OTHER CONCEPTS

In addition to more innocent activities like hand-holding and kissing, young people—especially young girls—also need to be educated about sexual or sex-adjacent behaviors outside of sexual intercourse. This is especially crucial because we know that many young people will be asked to do one or more of these behaviors at some point in their teenage years. Without being too descriptive, you can talk with them about the following:

> "When it comes to romantic feelings, sometimes someone may ask us to do something or be touched in a way that we are not comfortable with. What could you do if someone asked something of you physically or did something physically you didn't feel comfortable with? For example, if someone came up and hugged you from behind, what could you say and do?
>
> "You could move your body away from them. You could say clearly, 'Stop.' It's not rude to say no to someone. Whether someone is touching us in a way we aren't comfortable with or speaking to us in an uncomfortable way, we can focus first on getting out of the situation, and we can always talk about it with adults we trust."

## GETTING MORE SPECIFIC

Coaching through this is really helpful with preteens, and with teens fifteen and up we can get more specific about these behaviors.[5]

You could name one or two of the following words (there is no need to talk about every one of them at once) to a teen in any given conversation, ask them if they know what they mean, and remind them to bring such topics to you if they are curious, rather than looking to peers or online only.

Rather than trying to address all these behaviors at once, you will want to establish open lines of communication for your teen to bring questions about these behaviors to you. If your teen is not bringing up anything related to these terms and you have a sense they are aware of them, you might bring up a phrase like "nudes" and ask if your teen knows what it means. If they don't, you can describe it medically and tell them to talk to you if anyone asks them to engage in it. In these conversations, you want to strike a balance, accounting for your teen's development and exposure while also expecting that many kids will be exposed to these ideas by friends, the internet, or media.

We will cover the technology-related topics in chapter 12, but here's how a conversation could look talking about oral sex or anal sex with an older teen: "Have you heard the phrase 'oral sex' or 'anal sex'?" If your teen says yes, you can follow up by asking, "What have you heard?" If they say they haven't heard of those terms, you can say something like this to introduce the topic without getting more detailed than necessary:

> "These are words for adults and not topics for people your age to talk about. Some young people will try to ask you for those things or talk about them. Just as if someone is talking about drugs or alcohol, you can choose not to engage if the conversation shifts to that. You can also say something like, 'I am not comfortable with this. I'd like to change the topic.' Or you can simply change the subject."

Here's how you might bring up an even more serious topic such as unwanted sexual behavior. Start simply, giving just enough information to invite conversation and not so much that it overexposes your teen. I would aim to bring this up around the same time you explain sexual intimacy to a young person:

> "We've talked about sex, what it is and who it's for, and how to respond if someone tries to push you to engage in a sexual behavior. Remember, we can always talk about these things together. There is nothing that's too much for Mom/Dad.
>
> "Believe it or not, sometimes people will even try to put pressure on another person to do sexual things, even if that person is too young to know what those things are. This is why it's important for us to talk about this, even though it's difficult, in case anyone ever tries to put that kind of pressure on you. It feels good when people say nice things and compliment you, but some people will do that as a way of convincing you to do sexual things with them. If that happens, or if you find yourself in a situation where something is happening or is being talked about that you don't understand, or don't want to do or have done, let us know and we will help you."

## ZOOMING OUT FROM ATTRACTIONS AND DATING

So often I am reminding teens that, in a world where attractions are seen as the most important thing, there is so much to attend to and focus on beyond romance and dating. "You will be growing and maturing and experiencing this world of attraction throughout your life. There is no rush in figuring it all out now."

I want to invite you to echo this with your teens in subtle ways as you talk with them about the world of dating. Help your teen invest in interests, hobbies, friendships, service, and a range of other pathways for connection and meaning.

## WHEN TEENS FEEL INSECURE ABOUT NOT DATING

Many teens who aren't dating can experience a hit to their self-worth when so many others are dating. This can happen when a teen doesn't get asked to a dance or doesn't have anyone who says yes to them, has a sudden breakup, or opens up about simply feeling "weird" or "ugly," as their body starts to change with puberty.

### VALIDATION FIRST

Most parents and well-meaning trusted adults move quickly to minimizing fear, offering attempts to comfort by saying, "You aren't weird or ugly." It's not that you can't say that, but as always, begin first with validating the experience.

- "It makes sense that you feel this way."
- "You're right, it is difficult when other people seem to have it easier when it comes to dating."
- "It's easy to question your worth when this isn't happening for you."
- "A breakup is hard. Take your time to feel it. I'm right here."

### NORMALIZING THE EXPERIENCE

After validation, the next step is normalizing the experience, so they know they aren't alone. Say something like, "It's understandable that you have those thoughts and feelings. Many people feel that way when they don't feel chosen or wanted. I've felt that way for sure."

After normalizing where you can, the truth you want to speak over your teen is going to be more easily received. Like any of us, teens don't want mere reassurance, advice, or a quick fix. They want and need to be heard, seen, accepted where they are, and encouraged in the midst of it as well.

### OFFERING ENCOURAGEMENT AND AFFIRMATION

As for speaking truth over your teen, keep it simple. "You are incredible. You are loved. You are a treasure. You are beautiful. You are so good." Continue to hold space for both affirmation and acceptance of where things are. Say something like, "I know this is really hard right now, and I also have hope that you will see more each day how incredible you are, no matter what your dating status is."

## WHEN TEENS GET OVERLY FOCUSED ON CRUSHES AND ATTRACTION

If you notice your teen is caught up in crushes and attraction, whether they are dating someone or not, normalize their draw to this. At the same time, challenge them to invest just as much, if not more, energy in friendship. Here's how you might say it:

> "I noticed you and your friends talk a lot about who is dating who, who likes who, and all that. It's really normal to be interested in that. Remember that you have lots of time to invest in dating for years to come, and now is the time to prioritize friendships where you can—yes, talk about crushes, but also be kids, do silly, spontaneous things, build memories, and do not get too caught in drama. Crushes will come and go, but the memories and passions and interests you build in this time of life will be there for years to come! And when there is drama with friends, remember, I am here to be a listening ear for you."

## WHEN TEENS' FRIENDS GET OVERLY FOCUSED ON DATING OR SEXUAL ACTIVITY

Some teens will not be very interested in dating, while they may be surrounded by people who do. You will want to normalize that not every teen cares about dating the same way. Just as it's normal to have crushes, it's normal for many teens not to date or want to in high school. You'll want to frame this as a strength, even if it might isolate them from others sometimes.

> "Are a lot of your friends talking about and focusing on dating? I noticed you mentioned ____ has a boyfriend now. What's it like for you when your friends are dating?
> "Is dating on your mind?"

Assuming your teen says no, be sure to highlight that as a positive thing:

> "I really admire that about you. There are so many important things to pay attention to and grow in at this point in life. If you end up dating, it'll be a wonderful thing, but you've got so much time for that, and sometimes dating in high school can make things more complicated. Have you noticed that at all with your friends?"

Let your teen talk about what they notice about the impact of dating on their friend group. Be sure to ask them about the benefits of dating and the drawbacks. Then, they can start to recognize the degree to which they want that in their life:

> "What are the benefits of your friends' dating? What has been difficult for you about it?"

As always, validate, validate, validate. Don't be afraid to draw from your own wisdom as a parent about when dating started in your friend group, but whenever possible keep the focus on reflecting the wisdom your teen is showing by their thoughtful reflections. That will help grow their sense of self-worth and confidence in ways that are hard to fully appreciate.

One final piece of this discussion is bringing up sexual activity in friend groups. The average age of first intercourse is around the age of sixteen or seventeen.[6] Forty-two percent of teenage girls and 44 percent of teenage boys between the ages of fifteen and nineteen have had sex.[7] So, depending on your teen's peer group, it is likely good to have these conversations by age fourteen or fifteen, if we are being proactive:

> "You might start to hear more about your friends having sex at this time. A lot of times people who have sex will

talk openly about it, which can make it feel as if everyone is having sex. The truth is, less than half of teens have sex, so not having sex makes you a part of the majority! When you hear things from friends about sex, please know that you can bring those conversations up at home. Curiosity about it is normal, and you can also shift the conversation if you aren't interested in that topic with friends.

"How would you like to respond if your friends are talking about sex?"

This question can empower your teen to think through how they might respond. Sometimes, they need permission to draw from the wisdom they have, instead of a how-to. You might even be impressed by the thoughtful responses they come up with!

As we bring this chapter to a close, we want to shift to a realm of same-sex sexual attraction, orientation, and labeling, as well as the questions that your teen might have about those aspects of experience.

# CHAPTER 9

# "HOW DO I TALK WITH MY CHILD ABOUT GAY PEOPLE?"

## ENGAGING WITH SEXUAL ORIENTATION QUESTIONS

In this chapter, let's turn our focus to having conversations with your teen around same-sex attraction and desire and those who identify as LGB.[1]

This chapter aims to be helpful for all of us, whether you are parents who want to prepare for the possibility of your teen disclosing about same-sex desires or a same-sex or bisexual orientation or whether you are a parent trying to better understand how to talk with your teen about sexual orientation and how to relate to LGB-identified friends and family members. It will equip you to be thoughtful in how you talk about people who identify as LGB, in order to prevent you or your teen from regrets about those conversations later, in the event they did disclose a non-heterosexual orientation at some point.

This chapter won't comprehensively cover how we make sense of the shifts and trends in LGB identification, although that is no less important to understand. We will focus, instead, on how we want to talk with the next generation of Christian youth to engage with this changing landscape and to respond to their own experiences of attraction and/or that of their peers.

## THE CURRENT LANDSCAPE

I want to start with acknowledging and describing the current landscape that youth are experiencing when it comes to sexual attraction, orientation, and identity labels.

The majority of adults experience exclusive attraction to the opposite sex (92.1 percent of adult men and 81 percent of adult women).[2] At the same time, 1.3 percent of adult women and 1.9 percent of adult men identify as homosexual, gay, or lesbian, and 5.5 percent of adult women and 2.0 percent of adult men identify as bisexual. We could say that there is a 6.9 percent chance that your daughter will identify as LGB in adulthood and a 3.9 percent chance that your son will identify as LGB in adulthood, but the likelihood is probably higher than that, given the trends we are seeing among Generation Z. Among Generation Z adults, 18.7 percent identify as LGB.[3] This means that, while your child may not identify as LGB, nearly one in five of their friends will.

Increasingly, we are also seeing more teens report shifts in the ways they identify in adolescence. One study found that 19 percent of teens surveyed shifted in identification over the course of three years from heterosexual to sexual minority identity labels, with 26 percent of girls and 11 percent of boys reporting this.[4] In that same study, a slightly larger percentage, 21 percent, reported shifts in their experience of attraction over the course of high school, with 31 percent of girls and 5 percent of boys endorsing these shifts in attraction. This indicates that a larger percentage of teens than previously seen are using labels to describe an experience of non-heterosexual attractions, and it is likely that the percentage will be even higher by the time you read this book. For our families, it is more likely than ever before that your teen, even if they do not identify as a sexual minority, will know people in their life who do.[5]

The data I offer above highlights why it's going to be so important for you to initiate conversations with your teens about same-sex desire, labels, and those who identify as LGB, even if you don't, to your knowledge, have a child who experiences same-sex desire.

First things first: let's begin with language to make sure we have a solid foundation to dig deeper into this conversation.

## KEY TERMS

Language is one of the major points of focus and disagreement among Christians when it comes to conversations about same-sex sexuality. Should Christians who are attracted to the same sex call themselves gay? Does being gay mean you will only be satisfied in a same-sex sexual relationship? Is that kind of relationship inevitable or more likely if you use the common vernacular term "gay"? Or, as a Christian, should you say "same-sex attracted"?

Those better qualified than me have wrestled deeply with this.[6] But I want to define terms to see if we can't forge a way forward together.

---

### KEY TERMS

- Sexual minority(ies): An umbrella term for individuals who experience sexual attraction/orientation/identity in distinct ways from the numerical majority's experience of sexual desire.

- Same-sex or bisexual attraction/desire: The experience of romantic/sexual affinity for people of the same sex and/or people of both the same and the opposite sex. For teens, this experience most often emerges as crushes, which can be on celebrities or friends. Whereas a person with heterosexual attraction notices they have crushes on people of the opposite sex, a person with same-sex sexual attraction notices they have crushes on people of the same sex or both sexes.

- Orientation: The experience of persistent and enduring romantic attraction in a particular direction over time. A person exclusively attracted to people of the opposite sex may use the word "straight" or "heterosexual" to describe their pattern of attraction. A person exclusively attracted to people of the same sex over time may use words like "same-sex attracted," "gay," "lesbian," or "queer" to describe their pattern of attraction. A person who has experienced attraction to people of both sexes may use the term "bisexual," or they may use a descriptive label like "attracted to both sexes," or they may simply be known as "straight" or "heterosexual" because they are in an opposite-sex relationship despite persistently experiencing same-sex desires.

- Homosexuality: A term used in historic medical writings and Catholic doctrinal documents that applies, when used in the *Catechism*, either to patterns of same-sex sexual attraction over time or to engaging in same-sex sexual behaviors. This term is not widely used in common vernacular and is unlikely to be used by teenagers today.

- Sexual identity: The way in which a person may communicate their sexual attractions and sexual orientation as an aspect of identity to others through various labels. This can include terms such as "heterosexual," "straight," "bisexual," "same-sex attracted," "gay," or "lesbian." Some will use these words to indicate that their sexual orientation is integral to their identity, and others will use one of these words as an adjective to describe an aspect of their experience. The *Catechism of the Catholic Church* and various encyclicals define "sexual identity" as one's identity as man or woman, rather than defining it in terms of patterns of sexual desire and the ways people may identify as a result of these patterns. I offer you the above definition of sexual identity as well in order to account for the common way people may use the term "sexual identity" in informal conversation, since so often parents may be confused with a different use of this term than what they have read in Church documents.

- Sexual fluidity: The experience of some level of shift in sexual desire over the course of one's life. Such shifts are more common among women than among men, but this doesn't mean that *all* women experience these shifts or that *no* men experience these shifts. Some uses of this label emerge from gender paradigms and imply that all forms of sexual expressions that spring from desires are morally neutral or positive, which would depart from a Catholic understanding of sexual expression.

- Queer: An umbrella term to describe people who experience sexual desires that depart from the majority. Queer has increasingly become a word that teens are drawn to in order to reclaim what used to be used as a derogatory term directed at sexual minorities.

## ADDRESSING COMMON QUESTIONS

Now that we have laid a foundation of language that you will want to know to have these conversations, we want to turn to common questions your teen might have about sexual orientation, including questions about causation, change, and the use of labels, either for themselves or for their friends.

## CAUSATION

What causes same-sex sexuality, or any one of our patterns of sexual desire? This question has been the focus of significant amounts of research, therapeutic investigation, and personal self-reflection. I fear I will disappoint you with the simple truth: We don't know.

What we do know is that, for any one of us, there are many factors that contribute to something as complex as our sexual orientation. According to our best current understanding, both biology and environment can play some role in experiences of sexual orientation, and explanations that deny either one are often overly simplistic. The *Catechism of the Catholic Church*, long before this debate was settled (and perhaps it will never fully be settled), made it clear that the causes of homosexuality are "largely unexplained."[7] Thus, I would caution you and your loved ones from fixating on this question. If God needed us to know the cause of same-sex desires to effectively care for one another, I believe we would know the answer to this question.

There are certainly a range of theories about same-sex sexuality that have been circulated. Whole books could be—and have been—written on these theories or on debunking them.[8] This has such an impact on the questions of so many Christian parents, whether your teen identifies as a sexual minority or not.

"I don't want a therapist who tells my daughter she was born this way," a concerned mother once told me. She believed that bullying had confused her daughter to think she was gay. "Her friends kept telling her she was gay. Everything changed after that." When I asked how old her daughter was when she experienced this, she said, "Seventh grade." As she shared with me all the reasons she didn't think her daughter was "really gay," I thought to myself that seventh grade is the same age sexual attractions emerge for many teens.

This mom was right that "born this way" is probably an overly simplistic explanation for her daughter's sexuality. But the belief that bullying must have confused her daughter into thinking she was gay was also overly simplistic. Certainly, her explanation can't describe the experiences of many people who are attracted to the same sex. Some people report feeling differently compared to their same-sex peers for as long as they can remember, and they experience same-sex attractions in tandem with bullying around sexual orientation, rather than as a consequence of it.

When Christians push back on the idea that there might be any biological pathways that lead to same-sex sexuality, this can too often send the message to teens that we believe attractions to the same sex are chosen or subject to change if they try hard enough to address environmental factors. In fact, many gay teens I meet with spend years—yes, years—wracking their brain to figure out how to change their orientation or undo whatever environmental factor they have been told causes same-sex desires.

While we want to push back on the notion that people are simply born gay, it's also important to push back on the notion that there are no biological indicators of same-sex desire.

Ultimately, it seems likely that, for any person who is attracted to the same sex, there are a range of possible pathways that could have contributed to their experience. Just as there are many ways to get from the East Coast to the West Coast of the United States, and I can't tell you how someone got to the West Coast simply by virtue of the fact that they are there; it is too simplistic and reflects faulty research to assert one causal theory for most or all people who experience same-sex sexual desire.[9]

As Christians, it is good to be reminded that the question of causation has little bearing on the call of the Christian sexual minority. Whether a person is born with some level of disposition toward same-sex desire or there are some environmental processes at play, or both, the call of the Christian sexual minority is the same.

When talking with your teen about causal theories, here's how you might start:

> "There has been talk over the years about what causes a person to be attracted to the same sex. Do you ever wonder about that?"

If your teen hasn't wondered, you don't need to instill too much interest around this. Rather, you could simply acknowledge that, though people have many theories, the best science suggests that we don't know. Remember, we are trying to position you as a reliable source of knowledge.

> "We actually don't know what causes same-sex desire. There's not strong evidence for any one theory. Some people will say people are born gay, and others will say that same-sex desire comes from environmental factors. But the Church and the best of science are clear that the causes of same-sex desire are largely unknown. Christ, in redeeming us, can help us live virtuously with the desires we have, even if we don't know how they came to be."

For a teen who is trying to understand their own personal sexuality, here's what you might add:

> "It's normal to ask questions about how your sexual desires came to be. You may even hear theories from other people about it. I just want to remind you that those are simply theories. People might assume you were born gay or that something environmentally led to your attractions. When people suggest these theories, that's the kind of thing you can talk about with me more. If people start to suggest theories when you aren't asking for that, you can simply tell them that you are not interested in talking about how your attractions came to be with them.[10]

"Knowing how something we experience came to be can only take us so far. What's most important to me as your parent is helping you learn to talk about your experiences with God and invite him into them. He is a good Father and is ready to guide you in a path of thriving in him. He wants to hear about your desires and longing and to help guide you to discern how to follow him in the midst of them."

## CHANGE

Another common question your teen may ask is this: "Can sexual orientation change?"

It depends on what we mean by "change," I suppose. Entire books have also been dedicated to this question.[11] If you are interested in reading more about the Christian history of promoting sexual orientation change, Greg Johnson's book *Still Time to Care* is the most robust look you will find.[12]

As background, I want to name that sexual orientation change is not as simple as an on-off switch. It is not as if psychological treatment can simply manipulate attraction. As already mentioned, we also know that sexual fluidity exists, meaning that the strength, persistence, and direction of some people's attractions can shift on a continuum over time. This is more often the case for women than men. For instance, as already introduced in this chapter, about 19 percent of adult women report some experience of sexual attraction to women at some point in their life, while only 6.9 percent of adult women adopt labels that are non-heterosexual.[13] However, this certainly doesn't mean that all women experience sexual fluidity or that we could simply change a person's orientation if we wanted to. Even among people who do experience fluidity, the foundational studies on sexual fluidity suggest that these shifts occur outside of the person's control, not as a result of efforts to change sexual orientation.

### ANSWERING "CHANGE" QUESTIONS

When a teen wonders if attractions can change, it is helpful to frame this question around fluidity rather than change (which implies a more black-and-white shift). Here's how I might do so with a teen who is needing formation about the experience of attraction when they do not experience same-sex desire.

"Sometimes we can think of attraction in categories that are black and white. Either I am attracted to men or I am attracted to women. It can be a little more complicated than that, especially when you are a teen. Most people are exclusively attracted to the opposite sex. There are people you will meet who are exclusively attracted to the same sex. And some people experience attraction to people of the same sex and the opposite sex. Sometimes, attraction can shift over time. We don't know concrete ways to change and manipulate attractions, though, and some people have been harmed by efforts to make their attractions to the same sex go away. We aren't required to have attraction to the opposite sex to be holy. Heterosexual people don't have the market on holiness.

"If you don't experience attraction in a particular direction—for example, if you aren't attracted to people of the same-sex—even if people encourage you to consider that, you don't have to. Sometimes people can worry that attractions could 'pop up' later when they hear about that happening to others. For now, let's not focus on attraction too much or worry about new attractions unfolding. I want you to know that no matter what, we can talk about your attractions in our home.

"You may hear people talk about 'fluidity' with attraction. Sometimes, when people do this, they will be communicating that all forms of sexual expression are morally neutral or good. As Catholics, we understand that our desires and longing are not sinful in themselves, but for all of us, our desires can be ordered and expressed in keeping with God's commands. Our desires can also be disordered, misleading, and conflicted with other desires, which is why we need discernment to understand how to respond to them."

## TALKING ABOUT FLUIDITY WITH A TEEN WHO IS ATTRACTED TO THE SAME SEX

Many parents I talk to are worried about their teen foreclosing on labels too early in development. Certainly, this is an understandable fear with the increasing pressure on teens to identify with labels early. We want to balance this fear with the reality that some teens who experience same-sex attraction at puberty will continue to experience this over time, with no fluidity to be had.

When we talk about the possibility of sexual fluidity with our teens who are attracted to the same sex, we want to be careful not to undermine a teen's disclosure of same-sex attraction or promise that fluidity in attractions is likely or probable in their case. For teens, when parents respond to disclosure of LGB identity labels with the assumption that this is a "phase," most teens think, "Challenge accepted. I will prove just how much this is *not* a phase." This can create an adversarial relationship between parents and a teen, where the teen feels as if they are not believed and sets out to assert an identity more strongly.

Thus, rather than focusing on whether your teen's attractions could or will be fluid over time, I would encourage you to focus on receiving your teen where they are. To account for fluidity, you could respond in this way if your teen is talking with you about their attractions:

> "I appreciate your being willing to talk about this with me. It sounds like you have been attracted to [girls/guys/both sexes] since about puberty. Puberty is when humans start to notice attraction, so it makes sense that you would notice it around the same time. Some people experience fluidity in attraction over time, meaning that their attraction to one sex or the other can increase or diminish. Other people experience attraction to just the same sex, just the opposite sex, or both sexes, and it persists over their entire life. Either way, as your family, we want to help you understand your desires and discern God's plan for your life, no matter whom you're attracted to. God has good things in store for you—most importantly, for you to be a saint! I love you so much, no matter how your attractions evolve over time."

## A WORD ON CHANGE

While I will do (and have done) therapy with an individual who has had an experience of trauma and is a sexual minority, and I am happy to work with them on treating trauma-related symptoms, I do not believe therapy around those symptoms will eradicate a person's same-sex desires. After years of working with clients, I have not seen attractions go away as a result of trauma work, family-of-origin processing, and so on. While attraction patterns may show some fluidity for some people, meaning a person may experience greater attraction to a different sex or less attraction over time, I have not seen strong clinical or research evidence of changes in attraction, per se, as a result of clinical intervention. People most often will report change in behavior or use of identity labels, but not attractions themselves.[14] I do not recommend that people pursue attraction-change as a clinical goal and would caution you from bringing your teen to someone for care who is attempting to change your child's orientation.[15]

## MOVING PAST DEBATES AROUND LANGUAGE AND LABELS

One topic that is likely to come up with your teens is how to understand the use of sexual orientation and identity language. This is a controversial conversation in Christian circles, and there are a range of resources that weigh labels conversations differently.[16]

All the time, I use terms to describe my experience and aspects of my identity that have the potential to be misconstrued or box me in. For example, I call myself a psychologist, and using this language is not more likely to make me an atheist, despite the fact that most psychologists do not believe in God. Additionally, when I call myself a psychologist, even while I acknowledge that much of psychology is rooted in anti-Christian ideals, I am not asserting that my profession is the most important aspect of my identity or is above my identity as a Christian or a daughter of God.

Another tricky word I sometimes use to describe aspects of myself is the term "feminist." In some contexts, this word helps me talk about my passion for honoring the dignity and role of women. Because there is so much divergence in views of feminists, both historically and currently, some people may misunderstand what I mean when I use this word. However, rather than throwing away the term as something inherently at odds with Catholicism, I choose to take what is good about the word and leave what is not; I use qualifications to add nuance to what it means to be feminist.[17]

As a therapist, I have found that when people I work with use language like "gay," that language can actually take power away from the word, diminishing that person's fear around sexual desire, rather than giving the word more power. I have also found some people who use other words, like "experiencing same-sex desire" or "same-sex attracted," can integrate their desires in sustainable ways. Additionally, I have witnessed people who refused to call themselves "gay," fearing that word would lead them to act out sexually, but then who shared later about the patterns of shame, secrecy, and sexual acting out they faced as they avoided the word, which functioned as a way to disavow their desires from a place of shame. If our goal is holiness and chastity, it's not clear that the use of one word over another magically renders a person more or less capable of virtue.

There is no official stance in Catholic magisterium documents about appropriate language to use to talk about one's sexual orientation.[18] Different ministry groups have advocated for one term over another, but this advocacy is sometimes rooted in sociocultural debates rather than in a historic ethic. What the Church is clear about is that we ought not to *merely* see one another as defined by our sexual desires.[19] Whatever terms you and your teen use to talk about sexual orientation, it is important that you refrain from reducing your teen or their friends to their sexual desires, as if their experience of sexuality ultimately defines their personhood.

## TALKING WITH YOUR TEEN ABOUT OTHERS' LABELS

I want to turn now to two sample conversations, one with a teen who is asking about labels related to friends who are starting to use terms like "gay," "lesbian," and "bisexual" and one with a teen who is asking about the use of labels in their own life.

### FOR PRETEENS

"A lot of people are drawn to using labels at this point, and it's probably wise to not get too caught up in labels now, since you are still learning about your attractions at this point. When using labels, it's good to remember that we are describing persons who can't be merely reduced to any one label. You are not defined by your attractions, even when you use language to communicate your attractions and desires."

### FOR OLDER TEENS

"More people might use labels now since attractions tend to stabilize as we get older. If you experience exclusive attraction in one direction, it's not likely to suddenly change, which is why people might start to use labels more often. What questions do you have about labels (for yourself or your friends)?"

### FOR ALL TEENS

"Let's think together about some of the benefits of labels when it comes to sexual orientation for Christians:

"Labels can help you communicate about your experience of attraction succinctly.

"Labels can signal to others who have that shared experience a sense of community and belonging.

"Labels can invite others to learn more about what you mean by the labels you use.

"What are some of the drawbacks?

"Labels can lead to misunderstanding.

"Different generations might hear and react to terms differently.

"Labels can feel reductive of your unique way of living out that experience, especially when your experience departs from the mainstream understanding of sexual orientation."

## HELPING YOUR TEEN RESPOND TO QUESTIONS ABOUT THEIR OWN LABELS

It is highly likely that your teen will be asked by others about their own labels. Here's how you might discuss this:

"Your sexual desire is a personal reality that is a sacred aspect of your experience. This means people don't have a right to weigh in on it simply because they want to. There is a tendency today for people to feel that they can speak into your labels simply by knowing about your attraction patterns. Setting boundaries when you don't feel ready to talk about it with someone is a good idea and something we want to support in our family. If someone asks about your labels, you could simply say, 'I am not really interested in talking about my orientation with others.' Or you could tell them that you aren't focused on that right now. Or you could offer the label you use, clarifying that it doesn't capture all that you are."

## ENGAGING WITH LGB-IDENTIFIED FRIENDS

Wyatt came home from his eighth-grade retreat and opened up about it with you. He spoke about many aspects of the weekend, and then brought up a piece he wanted to talk more about: "My friend Keith came out as gay."

Here's how you might open this conversation:

"How is it for you to hear this about your friend? It seems like a sign of trust in you that Keith shared that with you.

"What questions came to mind for you when your friend shared this?"

This question allows you to respond initially to what your teen is thinking through. Your teen may have questions about any number of things, including the following:

- Labeling

- Questions about how to be a friend to Keith

- Moral considerations regarding same-sex sexual behavior and/or relationships

You can also prompt your teen to think through moral concerns, recognizing that Keith may or may not be in a position to have this conversation with Wyatt right now:

"Many times when someone comes out as gay, we might wonder about what God says about same-sex sexual expression. What questions come to mind for you about that? I am sure it's a lot to think through for Keith and for you. I hope we can talk more about how you might think that through and even share your perspective with your friend in a respectful, kind, and loving way.

"We don't want to assume what Keith believes about the morality of same-sex sexual expression simply because he identifies as gay. There is a growing number of Christians who use those labels and subscribe to a Catholic understanding of sexuality. If you were to ask Keith right away what he thinks about the moral questions, he might feel reduced to his attractions by you. With time, God may provide opportunities for you to talk about morality together. Since Keith is also a baptized Catholic, he has the capacity to come to understand his sexuality through God's eyes, through the graces of the sacraments, his friendships, and prayer. In the meantime, you can be grateful to know this aspect of Keith's experience.

"If you were to find out that Keith disagrees with a Catholic ethic, you can pray for the wisdom and timing to talk with him about that. Fraternal correction, the idea of challenging a fellow Christian's beliefs or behaviors to call them on to greater virtue and prevent further harm to them, is best when it springs out of a trusting relationship and is done privately. Jesus called his followers on to virtue in areas where they fell short in the midst of real encounters and relationships, where he saw them deeply and they knew of his love for them. The same invitation is for us. Talking with one another about morality is most effective when it springs from authentic relationships, where we are known and loved deeply."

We often forget that what we want to help cultivate in our teens is a love for their friends that allows them to pray for their good. After all, to love *is* to will the good of the other.[20] Even more than telling someone what we think (and God thinks) they ought to do in life, we want to be steadfast in willing the good of another. Borrowing guidance that will show up later in this chapter, here are a few final things to point out to your teen, if they share about a friend who comes out:

> "In addition to being a loving presence in your friend's life and praying for wisdom to discern if, when, and how to talk together about sexual ethics, we are called to pray for our friends. Remember, there is no greater love than to lay down one's life for one's friends.[21] It is a sacrifice to pray for those we love sometimes, and it's no small thing. We can pray for Keith to experience healthy and God-honoring relationships, cultivate his gifts, and be free from toxic shame now that we know more of what he is navigating.[22] I am grateful that you have Keith as a friend and he has you!"

## MORAL CONSIDERATIONS FOR CATHOLICS[23]

With the caveat that we will not move immediately into offering Catholic teaching on sexual ethics, I want to discuss how parents can communicate a Catholic ethic on marriage and sexual expression to your teens who will have questions about sex as it relates to LGBQ-identified friends.

### EXPLAINING CHURCH TEACHING

Increasingly, teens will have friends and family members who enter into gay partnerships and will wonder about Catholic teaching on these relationships.

> "What does the Church teach about gay sexual relationships/marriages? People who are attracted to the same sex are capable of a life of virtue just like people attracted to the opposite sex. Part of living a virtuous life is stewarding our sexuality, and so the call for a Christian gay person is to discern how to steward their sexuality, whether it be through singleness, heterosexual marriage, or a religious vocation.
>
> "A Catholic understanding of sexual expression is that it is blessed by God when it is between a man and a woman in the context of a sacramental union that is free, total, lifelong, and involves sexual acts with the capacity for procreation, even if that procreative element isn't realized because of infertility.

> "For any of us who are not in a sacramental marriage, sexual acts would be morally impermissible. That would mean that same-sex sexual behaviors, among other sexual behaviors outside of the context of sacramental marriage, are not blessed by God.
>
> "It's understandable if you have questions about these beliefs, for you and/or for your friends. It's also understandable if you have doubts around these beliefs. What questions or doubts do you have?
>
> "There are a lot of competing messages about sexual ethics today, and some are really compelling! When questions come up, I hope you bring them to me. I may not always have the perfect answer, but it's important to me that we wrestle with our faith honestly."

If you aren't sure about how to answer certain questions, if your teen makes a point you haven't thought of, or if you simply want to honor your teen's thoughtful question even while feeling as if you have a solid response, reflect something like this:

> "That is a really valid question. I appreciate how reflectively you are thinking about this. I wonder if we can look into this more together and bring in some other perspectives to help us think this through. Would you be open to looking into that more together?"

Notice here that, even if you have the right answer, you are inviting your teen to follow their curiosity, doubt, and questions and bring them to reliable guides, including you. You are also venturing with them on a journey to come to know the truth of human sexuality, rather than signaling to them, "This is the truth; take it or leave it." This alone will help your teen learn more than just *what* to think, but also *how* to think about deep and important questions like sexual ethics.

## ENGAGING WITH PEOPLE WITH DIFFERING BELIEFS

Your teen will likely encounter many people who do not live according to a Catholic ethic. It is also important to help your teen to know how to engage with others who have different beliefs.

"Sadly, many people have not been formed in a Catholic understanding of sexuality, which is informed by scripture and Church tradition. Even when they have, some people do not express their sexual desires in keeping with that ethic. A same-sex sexual relationship is one way that people might express sexual desires apart from a Catholic ethic. It's certainly not the only way that can happen, as many people you meet in your life will engage in sexual acts outside of God's plan.

"What are important principles to keep in mind when you relate to friends, family, and acquaintances who do not live according to this ethic?"

Allow your teen to explore what feels important to keep in mind as they engage people they love.

I also want to offer a few principles for engaging with people of different beliefs:

1. Listen with the intention to understand.

   - Build a relationship of trust where we learn about a person more globally, their quirks, personality, passions, wants, longings.

   - Learn about another person's perspective, to the point where you could articulate their beliefs as well as they could.

2. Honor areas of agreement and critiques that are valid.

   - Point out superordinate values and goals that you can agree on.

   - For example, acknowledge what you can agree on in this way: "We need more Christians who see the minority and value the marginalized like you do."

   - For example, acknowledge the harm done by Christians in the realm of expressing sexual ethics at times (i.e., purity culture, shaming people for their attractions, etc.).

3. Hold a person's humanity as you engage their ideas.

   - Reflect the strengths and global experience you have of a person, their virtues, their hopes, your belief in them, and their capacity for virtue, even while acknowledging ideas that you see differently.

   - Pray for courage to speak honestly about where you disagree, and do so with humility.

- Reflect areas of unknowns and questions you have without answers, while honoring answers that you find in the Church for your questions.

- If a person is causing you to think twice about your perspective, humbly share that: "Your point about ____ is something I want to sit with and pray with more. It's a good point I haven't thought about before."

4.  Point a person to Christ in every encounter.

- Remind a person of God's love for them and his invitation and desire to wrestle with this with them in prayer and relationship with God.

- Point a person to the ways you have experienced life-giving aspects of Catholic teaching.

- Relate in a Christlike way when you engage with someone, and demonstrate how his grace equips you for this.

- Repent when you fall short of reflecting the Father's love. (For example, "I was unkind and demeaning in how I talked with you when we were arguing. I am sorry. That's unacceptable.")

Before we move on from this section, I want to offer a couple more questions to open up conversation with your teen about engaging with peers and adults they disagree with on sexual ethics:

> "What fears come up for you as you interact with people you love who understand sexual ethics differently?"

You might name that people can fear saying the wrong thing, being hateful, shaming others, being shamed or ridiculed, and so on.

> "What opportunities arise and gifts can flow from engaging with people who think differently?"

## RESPONDING TO PUSHBACK FOR CHRISTIAN ETHICS

Some parents wonder what to say if your teen is called a "bigot" for their beliefs on marriage, assuming the teen agrees with a traditional Christian ethic.

Increasingly, Christian teens could be framed as bigots or hateful for their understanding of morality and ethics when it comes to sexuality. In my own life, I have certainly heard people assert that anyone who does not have an affirming view of gay sex is bigoted.

At the same time, we can acknowledge that there are certainly times when the association between Christian sexual ethics and bigotry fits. Christians have in concrete ways communicated hostile, demeaning, and dehumanizing responses to people who experience same-sex attraction and may or may not identify as LGB. Sometimes, those who are fellow Christians who communicate our sexual ethics do so with a degree of vitriol and harshness that leaves behind all manner of charity.

I have sat across from many clients who had to leave Christian schools because of the level of harsh and dehumanizing bullying they were experiencing, simply for being perceived as "gay" by peers. I have heard countless stories of responses by Christians to LGB-identified people that have asserted, "We love you," but communicated anything but.

We want to hold all of this in great tension and with gravity when talking with young people about how Christian ethics may be perceived and why.

Cody, a fifteen-year-old boy, came home from school and was pretty irritable and short with you. Because you are learning that, for teens, irritability can be a sign that something deeper is going on, you reflect what you notice:

> "Cody, I notice you are a bit short right now. Sometimes that happens when you've had a hard day. Can we talk about how you are doing?"

Cody starts to tear up. He shares that he had been asked by a friend at his Catholic high school what he thought about gay marriage. Cody recounted how he shared with his friend what he had come to believe about a Catholic vision for marriage, and how many things are not blessed as sacramental marriage within that context, including gay sexual relationships. This is where Cody really began to cry. "My friend said she doesn't want to talk to me anymore because I am the bad type of Christian. I am afraid she will spread negative things about me. I tried to tell her I don't hate gay people but she wouldn't take it."

How could you respond to this or other moments when your teen is feeling alienated for their beliefs?

1. *Offer comfort* through physical affection or verbal validation.

2. *Clarify and validate a range of feelings* about the circumstance and how it transpired.

3. *Express your pride* in the courage of Cody in sharing honestly about his faith. "It must have taken a lot of courage to speak up in that way."

4. *Invite reflection on what was said and how it was said.* Your teen may, at times, use a tone when disagreeing that is harsh and lacking in tact. If this is the case, help Cody explore if there are ways he might have communicated his beliefs more calmly and kindly. Invite him to apologize to his friend for ways he may have done so, if that applies. If not, help him understand the value of self-reflecting in those moments, even if he feels he did nothing wrong.

5. *Acknowledge the reality* that some people have mistreated and dehumanized gay people while communicating Catholic beliefs. Acknowledge also that some will misunderstand Christian ethics, and validate how painful that can feel. Acknowledge that many have not had good formation in the faith through no fault of their own, and we are called to pray for and be kind to people, even people who attack us.

6. *Connect to spiritual realities* including how Jesus, too, was misunderstood for his teachings. Highlight the power of reflecting care, charity, compassion, and conviction while doing so with the humility of Christ. Remind your teen that perhaps their friend will grow in understanding over time, and even if not, it is valuable to be able to share calmly with others.

7. *Make space for questions* that your teen may have coming up from the conversation. Perhaps the teen felt stumped by other aspects of the friend's response. Or perhaps the teen does have their own questions about why Catholics believe what we do. Invite these questions and others to shift the focus toward learning and growing in maturity from a difficult encounter.

## WHEN YOUR TEEN EXPERIENCES SAME-SEX DESIRE

Now that we have talked through how a parent might talk about same-sex sexuality and LGB-identified people with your teens regardless of their orientation, we want to turn to gleaning some wisdom for parents who have a teen who is a sexual minority.

## RESPONDING TO DISCLOSURE

There should be no surprises here in how you respond to a disclosure of same-sex sexual attraction or identity. This response will follow the same general principles as responses outlined in previous chapters addressing other disclosures:

1. *Express gratitude and unconditional love through words and actions*: Highlight the courage it takes for them to share vulnerable parts of their heart. Give your teen a hug or some alternative form of affection. "Thank you for sharing this with me. I love you so much and am so grateful you trust me with this."

2. *Be curious about your teen's experience*: Ask, "What is it like to share this with me?" It could be everything from terrifying to relieving to hopeful to uncomfortable to weird. Do not make the moment about you.

3. *Invite more conversation, now or later*: Ask the teen if they would like to share more about their journey of becoming aware of this experience, or if they want to wait for that conversation another time. Some teens will want to open up more, and others will have fatigue simply from the disclosure and want to come back to it. "I'd love to hear more about what it's been like for you, and also I can understand if you want to have that conversation later."

4. *Commit to initiating future conversation, and follow through*: Ask the teen if they would like you to initiate future conversation or if they would like to. "You always have the option to come to me and bring it up, and I also know that sometimes it is easier for parents to bring it up so the pressure isn't all on you. Which would you prefer?"

5. *Offer to pray together*: Refrain from using prayer time to jump ahead to future-oriented thinking, or from making the prayer about asking God for a shift in attraction patterns. I would recommend keeping the focus on gratitude for what was shared and for grace to know of God's unconditional love and wisdom in all that life brings. "Would you like to pray together and thank God for this moment of honesty?"

6. *Anchor your teen in the life of the Church*: Remind your teen that God loves them, they are wanted in the Body of Christ, and God has answers to their every longing for identity, community, intimacy, and purpose. "I am so proud of the person you are becoming, who can share so courageously about intimate parts of your heart. I realize it can be difficult to know if there is a place for you in the Church, and I want you to know that there is a place for you and you are loved deeply by God. He is not scrambling for a plan B for your life, and he is ready to offer you a path to thrive in him. We can talk more in the future about what that path can look like."

## A HELPFUL PARENTAL RESPONSE TO DISCLOSURE

"When he told us, we were quick to listen and affirm our love for him. We also asked questions, seeking to understand his journey and help him feel loved and accepted. We let him know that he didn't need to answer our questions unless he wanted to (which he did). I told him that I would be praying three things for him: to always (1) have healthy belonging with godly intimacy, (2) use his gifts without hindrance, and (3) not experience unhealthy shame."[24]

## OTHER CONVERSATIONS BEYOND DISCLOSURE

### DISCUSSING SPIRITUALITY

One thing I hear too often from teens I meet with is that their same-sex sexual desire precludes them from a relationship with God, especially if they aren't yet submitting to a Catholic sexual ethic. One teen shared, "Anytime I had a crush on someone of the same sex, and especially if I dated someone, I would stop praying. I stopped because I felt like God didn't want to talk to me when I was doing something wrong. I thought he didn't care about me if I was going to walk my own path."

This illustrates one of the most important needs of sexual minority youth—finding ways to grow in their relationship with Christ. Teens will receive significant messaging from the mainstream LGBT community that being gay requires them to walk away from God, or else be shrouded in shame and loneliness. No wonder so many leave the Church. Thankfully, resources continue to emerge that can help sexual minority teens foster spiritual maturity and holiness and live as Christians who are faithful to a Catholic ethic and discovering community and freedom from shame.[25]

As a parent, you can do the following to help cultivate your teen's spiritual life and relationship with God. If we want teens to invite Christ into their understanding of sexual morality, it will most easily happen if they already have lines of communication open with him. You can help with that:

- Invite your teen to share about their faith journey and how their relationship with God has been more broadly.

- Ask questions about how they see their faith and sexuality intersecting and what questions they may have about that.

- If your teen is questioning their faith (as many teens do), normalize their questions and honor their courage in asking hard questions. Invite them to remember the many holy men and women in scripture who wrestled with God. Encourage them to bring their doubts to Christ, instead of feeling as if they have to have the answers right to approach him.

- If your teen has rejected their faith, be curious about what led them to that. Keep in mind that this is not uncommon, and it may for some teens be driven by shame ("I am bad so God doesn't want me") and/ or fear ("I am afraid of what God would ask of me").

- In subtle and not-so-subtle ways, look to answer the questions most teens are asking beneath the surface of what you see and hear from them: "Who am I? Am I wanted here? Do I belong? Does God love me? Does God like me? How will my needs for intimacy be met? What is my purpose? Can I experience the fullness of life as a Christian?"[26]

- Point your teens to models of Christian faith who share their experience.[27]

## DISCUSSING SEXUAL MORALITY

As parents, you will want to normalize the fears and doubts that your teen might have in considering Catholic teaching on sexual ethics. After all, how many of us were convinced by every aspect of a Catholic sexual ethic in high school? While the law is not gradual, there is gradualness in when and how we discuss sexual ethics. Too often, I see parents use initial disclosure of same-sex attraction as a time for these conversations. Well-meaning parents feel a sense of urgency here.

Just as we would not immediately tell heterosexual teens, "You know you can't have sex with them," when they talk about a crush, we ought not be fear-based in our response to sexual minority youth who share about their attractions.

As you noticed, in giving you a model for disclosure, I refrain from jumping to moral and ethical questions on day one. That is not because those questions are unimportant. Rather, it is simply not necessary to reactively respond and list out moral expectations around sexual behaviors right away. After all, merely telling teens what not to do more often compels them to walk right up to the line. Remember, we are setting up these conversations with the expectation that, as we build trust and communication, there will be many more opportunities to talk about sexual values.

As I mentioned, the moral and ethical questions are of great importance. Timing is key. Here's how you might open various threads of dialogue about Catholic morality:

> "Have you thought much about how a Catholic ethic on sexuality impacts your understanding of sexuality? What have you thought about that? What questions do you have about Catholic teaching on sexual ethics?"

Validate the understandable questions your teen has. Do this *before* offering answers to their questions.

When offering answers, share how you process Church teaching, almost as if you are inviting them into your thought process, not lecturing them.

Explain sexual stewardship to your teen:

> "While none of our attractions and orientation are chosen, a person can discern how to steward what they experience. The invitation to sexual stewardship exists equally for all people, though it will have particular complexities for LGB people."

Your teen may speak to how it feels as if their call to chastity is more demanding. Validate this for them as well:

> "There are unique demands placed on you, for sure. It is costly obedience. God rewards us for the surrenders and acts of obedience to him, and if we are honest, many times surrender is painful and difficult. With prayer, the grace of the sacraments, friendship, and strong community, you can live a virtuous life. God will provide and has particular gifts to offer the world through your witness."

Commit to walking the journey with your teen as they discern a Catholic ethic. Be available to listen to their tensions as they bring their questions, hopes, and longings before the Lord.

## FROM THE CATECHISM

"By the virtues of self-mastery that teach them inner freedom, at times by the support of disinterested friendship, by prayer and sacramental grace, they can and should gradually and resolutely approach Christian perfection."[28]

## SEEKING YOUR OWN SUPPORT

Many parents need support in processing their own reaction to their teen's experience of attraction. If you are a parent struggling to accept the reality of your teen's attractions, there are increasing resources for you on your own journey.[29]

## VALIDATING YOUR RESPONSE

It has been said that "when a child of Christian parents comes out of the closet, the parents go into the closet."[30] This is important for fellow Christians to know. I meet with countless parents every year who have a child who is gay, and when I ask them, "Who in your faith community knows?" the common answer is no one. This is often out of fear or due to unhelpful reactions from fellow Christians. We all are responsible for one another and for accompanying one another through the challenges of this life. We as the Body of Christ can do better for parents of youth who disclose same-sex sexuality.

---

### PARENTAL RESPONSES

The variety of emotions and thoughts a parent may feel when a teen comes out may include the following:[31]

- Shock: "Is this real?"
- Confusion: "What is happening? Are you sure?"
- Anger: "Why is this happening?"
- Fear: "What will happen to my child? What will others think? What does this mean for my child's relationship with God?"
- Grief or loss: "The life I envisioned for my child or for me may not happen."
- Guilt: "I must have done something wrong."
- Shame: "I am a bad parent. Why didn't I know sooner? Did I cause this?"
- Support: "I am here for you. I am not going anywhere."

---

## WHAT YOU MAY NEED FROM YOUR FAITH COMMUNITY

I often ask Christian parents I meet with what they need from fellow Christians in their church or local community when it comes to processing their own reactions to a teen sharing about same-sex sexuality. They have offered the following:

- A listening ear: "I am listening. I hear you. I want to receive more of what this is like for you."

- An understanding of the parent's ability to hold both the love they have for their child and the fears and concerns they hold for their child: "I can see both how much you love your child and the concerns and fears you hold."

- A commitment to prayer for wisdom, clarity, and peace: "Can I pray with you and invite the Holy Spirit to offer you wisdom, clarity, and peace in this time?"

- A reminder that they are not alone: "There are many beautiful Christian parents and families like yours who are wrestling with this."

- Encouragement to maintain open communication with their teen: "There are ways Christian families find to navigate a future together. It's important to keep lines of communication open whenever possible, even though it's way harder at times."

- Practical help: "Can I bring over dinner or some groceries tomorrow night?"

- Hope that their teen can have a beautiful life as a Christian: "I believe that God can shower many gifts on your child, and they can experience spiritual maturity and virtue."

- Withholding a tendency to offer answers right away or to try to answer questions of causation or change: "A part of me wants to try to give answers or ask my own questions, and I'm not going to do that because I want to give you space to voice your own."

For each and every teen raised in Catholic homes, my hope is that they can be witnesses to the world by radically embracing, loving, cherishing, and accompanying those who identify as LGB along a path of approaching Christian perfection. In concrete reflections of unconditional love in a community of Christians, I have seen more and more sexual-minority teens be drawn into a life of virtue. We need more saints who have responded to God's grace and accepted his call to glorify him in this way. Your teen could be one of the saints who reminds the world that, yes, regardless of a person's sexual orientation, they can live in full communion with God and others.

As we bring this chapter to a close, we will turn now to a related but distinct conversation with your teen about gender and transgender-identifying people.

# CHAPTER 10

# "HOW DO I TALK WITH MY CHILD ABOUT TRANSGENDER PEOPLE?"

## ASSISTING A TEEN IN NAVIGATING GENDER-RELATED QUESTIONS

The gender conversation is one of rising importance, and we can't avoid it if we want to be good parents who show our kids the essential role of our faith in understanding everything and everyone we meet. Increasing numbers of young people are sharing about experiences of gender distress, adopting a range of labels that depart from the binary, and / or subscribing to theories about gender that depart from a Catholic worldview. Even if your teen does not experience personal questions about gender, they will be invited into encounters with those who do. This is yet another area where you can equip your teen to thoughtfully, courageously, and compassionately engage in conversation with others regardless of whether they themselves experience gender distress.

### DEFINING TERMS

As we begin, we want to define terms that will be important. These terms will shift and change, to be sure, but there are some elements that you can draw from, even if certain terms fall in and out of favor. I am being descriptive, not prescriptive, when I lay out these terms. I am not telling you that all of these terms are in keeping with a Catholic understanding, but that these are terms you and your teens will hear and will want to have context for.

## KEY TERMS

- Biological sex (natal sex, birth sex): The combination of chromosomes, gonads, and anatomy that typically reflect whether a person is born male or female.
- Sex assigned at birth: This term was originally used to describe times when, because of a disorder of sex development, a child was unable to be clearly identified as male or female, or their sex characteristics were such that medical intervention occurred to align them with one sex. This term has increasingly been used by proponents of certain gender paradigms to replace "biological sex." These proponents assert that sex differences do not describe essential differences and are only social constructs. Thus, they say, sex is merely assigned at birth and is able to be divorced from gender.
- Gender: The psychological, social, and emotional aspects of what it means to be a man or woman, masculine or feminine.
- Gender identity: A person's psychological, emotional, and physical experience of themselves as male or female or masculine or feminine or an alternative gender identity.
- Disorders of sex development/Intersex: A diverse set of "medical conditions that involve the reproductive systems and refer to atypical development of anatomic, gonadal, or chromosomal sex."[1]
- Gender role: The range of roles that are typically delineated in generalized ways between men and women. These are defined by culture or family expectations and societal standards; they can vary across context, time, and place.
- Gender-related distress: The distress caused by questioning gender, feeling outside of gender norms in meaningful ways,

and/or struggling with one's experience of the sexed nature of one's body.

- Gender dysphoria: The experience of debilitating psychological, physical, and/or emotional distress around the disconnection a person feels with their sex at birth. This often coincides with the belief that a person is or wishes to be of a different sex and to be perceived as such, even while they recognize and accept the reality of their biological sex. This is a current diagnostic term used by clinicians and medical professionals. Not every person with gender distress has gender dysphoria, and not every person who uses a transgender/nonbinary label experiences gender dysphoria.

- Transgender: An umbrella term to describe the many ways a person may experience their gender identity as different from the majority of the population.

- Nonbinary: An umbrella term for an experience of gender that does not reside within the binary of male and female.

- Emerging gender identities: The range of terms that have emerged to describe gender identities that depart from the binary understanding of sex and indicate a fluid understanding of gender and sexual orientation. These include genderqueer, pangender, gender fluid, gender nonbinary, queer, gender-creative, and others.

- Cisgender: This term is used by some people to describe a person whose experience of gender is consistent with their biological sex—that is, someone who is not transgender or nonbinary.

## STARTING THE CONVERSATION

We are called to *engage* conversation about gender when forming young people, and if we are honest, it can be *really* difficult. We want to pray for courage as we enter in, because we will need it!

### RAPIDLY CHANGING LANGUAGE

The conversation around gender identity has evolved rapidly and for a variety of reasons that cannot be easily described. I remember publishing a book with Mark Yarhouse called *Emerging Gender Identities: Understanding the Diverse Experiences of Today's Youth*, released in August 2020. Less than six months after its release, one book review was written about it that struck me. The person wrote something to the effect of "This book is overall helpful, but a little outdated." A book that was written in 2019 and released in 2020 was already deemed insufficient by virtue of how quickly the conversation, agreed-upon terminology, and trends have continued to shift. All that to say, if you feel at all overwhelmed, intimidated, frustrated, and confused by this changing landscape, you are not alone.

Holding all of the feelings you're bringing into this space, let's agree that the time for engaging this conversation is now. Insofar as you see the value in starting a conversation (regardless of whether your teen is themselves wrestling with gender), here are some starters for doing so:

- Reference pop culture or your teen's local community: "I saw / heard that _____ recently shared they identify as [transgender / nonbinary]. What have you heard about that?"

- If you don't have a recent reference, you can raise the subject more generally: "One of the things that is a big focus of conversation right now in our culture is gender. How often does that conversation come up with friends, in school, or online?"

- Ask about their understanding first: "What have you heard about gender? What do you think about what you've heard?"

- Ask about their connection to peers who have adopted a different gender identity than their birth sex: "Many people know someone who identifies as a different gender than their biological sex. How about for you?"

- Ask about their questions before projecting your own: "Sometimes we hear about something and, even when some of it makes sense to us or we agree with it, some parts can feel confusing, or we can have questions about certain aspects or things we don't agree with. When you think about the ways people talk about gender today, what things do you resonate with? What things don't make sense to you, or what do you disagree with?"

## CHALLENGING THE GENDER PARADIGM[2]

Sometimes it can feel like, to uphold our parental responsibility, we need to aggressively challenge and offer the "right answer" immediately. In my work and relationships with teens, I find that this common strategy Catholic parents take when challenging the gender paradigm is arguing against the child's theory. I have not seen this be effective, even if what you are saying is absolutely true. If you jump too quickly to digging into arguing against a theory, as with any conversation, you will turn what is meant to be a conversation into a monologue. Many of us don't like monologues, but I can tell you that teens simply tune them out. Perhaps this is why so often efforts to challenge the gender paradigm result in little other than anger, miscommunication, and division in families I meet.

## MODELING HUMILITY IN THE CONVERSATION

Humility doesn't mean passivity, permissiveness, or silence on important topics. But even our Lord showed moments of withholding true information about himself and his mission from a place of humility and wisdom. Let's consider how you might model this as well.

A helpful image for ongoing gender conversations, specifically around engaging with the gender paradigm, is that of doing a puzzle together. There is a good bit of collaboration, and you as the adult have something unique to offer in likely having more experience working with puzzles. But your teen also has something important to contribute. Further, sometimes it's the younger of the two puzzle-makers who finds the key piece. The goal I would hold out for you as you talk with your teen is helping them build their critical thinking about gender, rather than giving them the answer you want them to end with.

# PROPOSING A CATHOLIC ETHIC

But what about when it is time to propose a Catholic ethic? What do you say when your teen asks you what God has to say about the binary, for instance? Let's look at that now.

### TEACH THROUGH MODELING

When sharing your own thought process, think of it as a form of modeling:

> "When I hear that a person's sex and gender is only a construction, and there is nothing core about people that is biologically determined when it comes to sex, there are things I agree with for sure. I agree that there are certain things about our gender that are constructed: like girls typically keep longer hair in our culture, but in other cultures its guys who keep long hair. So, the idea that girls ought to have longer hair is socially determined. What other things do you think of that are socially impacted?"

### CALMLY IDENTIFY POINTS OF AGREEMENT AND DISAGREEMENT

Validate and agree with what you can of your teen's thoughts. When you disagree, try *calmly* saying something like this:

> "What I can totally agree with is _____, whereas I see _____ differently.
>
> "When I hear that sex and gender are a construction, there are also things I question about that. It feels a bit black and white to say it's all only constructed by society. What things about biological sex do you think are determined by objective things, things that don't change based on your society?"

Let your teen parse out these things further. If your teen says, "Nothing!" don't panic.

### REFLECT CRITICAL THINKING

Simply offer a way of thinking of the objective realities:

"When I think about the argument of social constructivists, I can't help but look to a Catholic understanding of sexes. I think about how our chromosomes (XX/XY), with some exceptions for some people, are determined by God prior to our being born. These don't ever change, no matter what. It reminds me of other fixed things, such as our eye color and our natural hair. I also think about how the body is programmed at puberty to help us develop in one of two ways: into a female adult body that will have periods and have the possibility of pregnancy and nursing, or into an adult male body that will produce semen, have erections, and ejaculate. These don't seem to be just things society constructs; they also reflect a bodily reality we approach and have to contend with.

"Even though people can do things with medicine and surgery to change how their body develops, we can't make a biologically male body do all the things a biologically female body does, or the other way around. And as Catholics, we believe the way God made our bodies is part of our essence, and stewarding those bodies is important. This doesn't mean there is no place in the Church for people who identify as transgender, or that people who have transitioned are to be rejected by us. In fact, we ought to be the most vocal advocates for the dignity and worth of people experiencing gender distress. As a Catholic teen, you can stand up for those who are mocked for their gender experience. Church teaching offers a vision for helping people thrive, and that requires nuance and understanding as well as clarity about essential realities."

## WHEN YOU HAVEN'T NAVIGATED THIS CONVERSATION WELL BEFORE

Perhaps you have already tried to have this conversation with your teen, and it has gone poorly. Maybe it has blown up, and your teen has discounted your perspective or said they don't want to talk with you about gender because of your beliefs.

Steve came up to me after a talk a few weeks ago. "I am here as a testament that your advice works," he said smiling and with tears in his eyes. I asked him what he meant, and he went on. "I followed your recommendation of apologizing to my teen children for the ways I have discussed gender in the past. I apologized specifically for my harsh and demeaning tone, my pride and arrogance in implying my children have nothing to contribute when I would talk over them in these conversations historically, and the ways I claimed Catholic teaching as justification for my mocking and ridiculing of people who disagreed with me. That one apology has changed my relationship with my daughter in a powerful way. She has never been so willing to talk with me and listen to me as she is now."

Steve's story is not the only one. Countless times, repairs of relationship are needed for improved communication and trust. The gender conversation is no exception to this.

## A BRIEF EXAMINATION OF CONSCIENCE

As Catholics, we see great value in an examination of conscience. In my own life I have needed to reflect on and repent of the ways I engaged with gender minorities in a way that failed to reflect Christ. If I can't repent in my own heart to the Lord, how can I honestly move toward reconciliation with those around me who have been hurt by my approach? Can I accept responsibility for the ways my own sinfulness has inhibited opportunities to share a Catholic understanding of gender, rather than scapegoating others as the ones to blame?

Perhaps we can enter into a brief examination of conscience now related to how we have engaged with transgender-identified people, people who advocate for the gender paradigm, and our own children who may be drawn to this theory:

- Have I mocked, demeaned, or ridiculed people who identify as transgender or people advocating for them?

- Have I justified harsh treatment or cruel comments in the name of "truth" and poorly reflected Christ in the process?

- Have I remained silent when others mocked or ridiculed gender minorities out of fear of being thought poorly of in my community?

- Have I been silent about concerns I have with the gender paradigm out of fear of not being liked by others?

- Have I misrepresented information to prove my point?

- Have I asserted as Church teaching things that the Church doesn't actually teach about gender?

Now that we have reflected on ways we may have fallen short in our approach, I pray that you will invite our merciful Lord into this space with you. He is ever ready to forgive and help us begin again.

## WORKING TO REPAIR

After examining your conscience in prayer, you are in a better position to circle back to your teen and enter in conversation again, as you invite the Lord's grace into such difficult spaces.

- *Set the stage*: Try reapproaching this conversation when you feel calm and your teen seems calm. Name any fears you have about starting the conversation out loud to your teen. You are modeling healthy vulnerability when you do so, and it often makes the other person less defensive to know that you bring your own concerns into it. You could say, "I am a bit nervous to bring this up because it hasn't gone well, and it's important to me to get better at listening as your parent because you deserve that."

- *Alter tone*: A calm tone can be the most impactful aspect of many conversations. Content (what you say) often matters much less than tone (how you say it).

- *Summarize*: Say back what your teen has told you before about not wanting to have this conversation: "You have shared before that you don't want to have a conversation with me about gender because of [my faith/beliefs/how you feel disrespected]."

- *Clarify for accuracy or a fuller picture*: "Is that right? Is there anything else I have done or not done that made you not want to talk with me?"

- *Validate and take responsibility*: "It makes sense that you don't want to talk with me right now, since these conversations haven't gone well in the past. I have been [avoidant/passive/rejecting/aggressive/had a hard time listening]. I have, at times, misrepresented Christ and Church teaching. I take responsibility for that because if I were you,

I wouldn't want to talk to me either! And the story gets told (and is sometimes true) that religious people are cruel when it comes to this topic."

- *Apologize*: I am sorry for the ways I have hurt you in trying to have this conversation. That's not okay."

- *Commit to action*: "I know it will take time to rebuild trust, and it's okay if you aren't ready to forgive me yet. I want you to know that I am taking steps to learn more and grow in how I talk about this. It will take practice, and I won't be perfect at it, but would you be willing to be patient with me as I learn?"

## WHEN YOUR TEEN EXPERIENCES GENDER DISTRESS OR QUESTIONING

When your teen is struggling with gender-related questions, you also need guidance on how to respond. Other books, including some I have coauthored, have been written about this, but I will weigh in now on how you might initially respond to disclosure.[3]

## RESPONDING TO DISCLOSURE

We want to briefly acknowledge common ineffective or harmful strategies:

- *Avoidance*: "I don't know what to say or how to say it, and so I skirt around the topic whenever possible. If my teen shares about gender questioning, I deny that by silence."

- *Passivity*: "When gender comes up, I stay silent or say vague comments about creation or God's intent without asking questions or digging deeper. I fear that the more I say, the more I will be expected to talk about something that I am not equipped for."

- *Absolute Approval*: "I will support whatever you decide even if I have questions or concerns about your pathway. I fear harming you if I do or say anything else."

- *Absolute Rejection*: "I will not tolerate any questioning about gender or pushing back on norms. You are delusional and confused, and you need to get over this or we will not be in relationship."

- *Accusing*: "You don't listen to me. I explain everything we always taught you about our faith and about sexuality, and you just don't care."

- *Aggression*: "I am disgusted by you. There is no place for you in my home." This also can include harm through physical, spiritual, sexual, and psychological abuse and neglect in order to punish a teen for their disclosure.

When it comes to helpful responses to disclosure, we will unpack a very similar response to the one we laid out in the last chapter. Here is a framework for how to respond to a disclosure around gender distress:

1. *Express gratitude and unconditional love through words and actions*: Highlight the courage it takes for your teen to share vulnerable parts of their heart. Give your teen a hug or some alternative form of affection. "Thank you for sharing this with me. I love you so much and am so grateful you trust me with this."

2. *Be curious about your teen's experience*: Ask, "What is it like to share this with me?" It could be everything from terrifying to relieving to hopeful to uncomfortable to weird. Do not make the moment about you.

3. *Invite more conversation, now or later*: Ask the teen if they would like to share more about their journey of becoming aware of this, or if they want to wait for that conversation another time. Some teens will want to open up more, and others will have fatigue simply from the disclosure and want to come back to it. "I'd love to hear more about what it's been like for you, and I also can understand if you want to have that conversation later."

4. *Commit to initiating future conversation, and follow through*: Ask the teen if they would like you to initiate future conversation or if they would like to. "You always have the option to come to me and bring it up, and I also know that sometimes it is easier for parents to bring it up so the pressure isn't all on you. Which would you prefer?"

5. *Offer to pray together*: Refrain from using prayer time to jump ahead to future-oriented thinking. I would recommend keeping the focus on gratitude for what was shared and for grace to know of God's unconditional love and wisdom in all that life brings. "Would you like to pray together and thank God for this moment of honesty and invite his wisdom in for how we navigate this as a family?"

6. *Anchor your teen in the life of the Church*: Remind your teen that God loves them, they are wanted in the Body of Christ, and God has answers to their every longing for identity, community, intimacy, and purpose. "I am so proud of the person you are becoming, who can share so courageously about intimate parts of your heart. I know it can be difficult to know if there is a place for you in the Church, and I want you to know that there is a place for you, and you are loved deeply by God. He is not scrambling for a plan B for your life, and he is ready to offer you a path to thrive in him. We can talk more in the future about what that path can look like."

## NAVIGATING POST-DISCLOSURE FAMILY LIFE

Many parents who want to strike the balance between love, support, and critical reflection have likely heard several options from a range of Catholics they trusted about what to do following a disclosure:

1. *Cut off and course-correct*: Some parents are encouraged to cut off a teen's phone completely, shut off social media use, and limit interaction with any of the friends who were also questioning their gender. This is a fear-based strategy, where the parents use their power to shut down contacts that they fear will influence their child. Some teens may end up complying in the short term, others may secretly maintain contacts, and almost all teens will build resentment and a strong attachment to the "black-listed" people and information in the long-term.

2. *Give blind approval*: Parents are also often told by others that, if they challenge their teen at all or question the conclusions about gender, they could cause harm and make their teen depressed and suicidal. This resonates with the parts of parents that are afraid of losing connection with their teen and overtly harming them. Many parents share about how they have had a good relationship and don't want to change it. One parent said, "I never want our child to think our love is conditional, and I've heard that people who identify as transgender can be suicidal more often. I'm afraid if we question her, we will lose her." This is another fear-based approach if withholding any questioning or curiosity about their teen's shift is only done out of fear that the relationship will be ruined by anything other than approval of the young person's current discernment.

3. *Commit to principles and critical reflection*: I encourage parents to choose a different path from the paths of coercion/course-correct and blind approval. I invite parents to come up with principles they will live by and communicate to their teen. These principles might include a desire for unconditional love, open communication, authenticity with one another about their perspective, and commitment to move forward as a family. Even though they recognized that they would not necessarily agree with each and every aspect of the best way forward, that didn't have to mean the end of relationship. This also means each of them committing to learn separately and together about what the teen is experiencing and refraining from simplifying all of the experience to any one factor, without discounting a range of possible factors contributing.

When it comes to ways to respond to your teen, here are some suggestions in line with the third approach, committing to principles and critical reflection.

1. *Prioritize intentional family time (centered around common interests or hobbies)*: This is not at all a way to eradicate distress about gender. By suggesting it, I am not implying that families with these experiences are somehow to blame for their child's gender distress because of a lack of quality time. The purpose of this recommendation is to help zoom out from the focus on the child's gender and toward connection about things the family can find common ground within, especially since there is a tendency for everyone to hyperfocus on gender.

2. *Put away devices at meals to increase connection (for all family members, including parents)*: This is a way to increase connection, rather than a way to merely cut off contacts and alienate a teen from their friends.

3. *Seek out a competent therapist for overall psychological health for your teen and your family*: Be willing to join therapy sessions for your teen and/ or attend family therapy or your own personal individual therapy. This will allow you to acknowledge the ways your emotional challenges and/or aspects of your parenting style may not be helping your relationship with your child. This is a practice in humility and can go very far in improving communication and the quality of your relationship with your teen.

4. *Focus on individual or family goals*: This strategy of zooming out from gender allows for a young person to broaden their understanding of

their goals and hopes for the future and plan concrete steps to achieve their goals. Your child may have a desire to become more effective or skilled in some area of their life, or your family may have goals you want to accomplish together. Help cultivate these goals.

5.  *Make space for spiritual questions*: Every teen needs people to bounce off spiritual questions with. Many Christian teens believe that God wants our right answers and good behavior and that we can't bring unfinished questions to him. They can struggle to be honest in prayer. Invite your teen to journal and reflect on and bring their spiritual questions to God and you without a filter. As parents, you can model this as well (i.e., sharing about doubts, questions, or honest prayers you bring to God about many things instead of seeming to have all the answers figured out). Invite them to reflect through ethical questions about coping with gender, and be willing to be a sounding board and guide for this.

6.  *Fill life with opportunities to be stretched*: Find ways to help your teen get out of their comfort zone, open them up to new experiences, and allow them to grow in knowledge of strengths and interests.

7.  *Invite reflection*: Encourage your teen to reflect on their journey, with the help of therapeutic support, pastors, mentors, and peers. Invite reflection on morality and ethical considerations around what is often offered as the "answer" to young people for addressing and navigating gender questions.

8.  *Seek education*: Be willing to educate yourself along the way. Seek out trusted voices, and allow yourself to grow in knowledge of the experience of gender distress, language, categories, factors, and helpful approaches. Seek out voices of people who have lived experience of gender distress and people who have practical knowledge from accompanying gender minorities. Avoid perspectives or media sources that focus more on debating ideology than engaging people. There is a place for that, but many Christian parents find that the rhetoric within those circles does not equip them to calmly engage their loved one.

## A RANGE OF PATHWAYS

So many parents I meet with hope I can predict the outcome of their teen's gender questioning. I cannot.

For some teens, especially those whose gender dysphoria starts at a young age, the distress can get worse through puberty and continue into adulthood. Gender dysphoria will be part of some people's experience long-term. Supportive approaches, therapy, and time off social media are not guaranteed "cures" for gender distress and shouldn't be treated that way. What these approaches do is allow space for a young person to discern adaptive coping that corresponds with their faith and increase practices such as distress tolerance, acceptance, emotional regulation, and resiliency that will serve them for their entire lives.

## WHEN DISTRESS CONTINUES

As I already mentioned, sometimes gender distress will persist into adulthood. Take, for example, the case of Sammy. Sammy experienced gender distress from about the age of four. Sammy had been homeschooled throughout his life and was one of two kids. As long as his parents could remember, Sammy did not think about or experience himself as a boy. He often made comments about how he would like to get rid of his penis, or he would ask, "When am I going to have breasts like you, Mom?" When he spoke about himself in the third person as he got older, he would say things like, "Me and the other girls." One time he attended a healing service at his Catholic parish and afterward was crying the entire way home. "I prayed for God to make me a girl and it didn't happen," he said as he wept. Sammy's parents got him into therapy as he entered junior high, because he was experiencing significant depression and suicidality. Through therapy, Sammy began to manage his depression and also grew in his ability to manage gender distress in a variety of ways. He used a nickname, Sammy, and he shared that he didn't mind male pronouns, as long as his parents knew and believed him that this was a struggle for him and called him Sam or Sammy, rather than Samuel. Sammy had a hard time going to youth group at his Catholic church, due to feeling excluded at times and bullied for being "girly," and his parents worked to find him mentors to grow in his faith and avenues for connections with peers in other ways. He also grew to love Eucharistic adoration, because it allowed him to be alone with the Lord and feel safe and supported and received, without social pressures.

Before the family moved out of state halfway through high school, Sammy had tweaked the way he dressed to allow for wearing styles, colors, and textures that he enjoyed, and he kept a bit of a longer hairstyle. Sammy's parents worked with Sammy's high school to allow Sammy to use a teacher's bathroom in school because he used to simply avoid going to the bathroom in school, a common strategy of teens with significant gender distress. His parents found ways to help Sammy cultivate his strengths and abilities to where he developed greater self-worth, self-confidence, and hope for his life, even though his dysphoria still ebbed and flowed in intensity over time. The family wasn't sure how Sammy would discern managing gender distress long-term, but they were hopeful that they could move forward as a family.

## WHEN DISTRESS SUBSIDES

Many Catholic parents I talk to worry about peer and social media influence when it comes to gender. The story of Kylie illustrates the valid place for this concern, but I do not share it to imply that Kylie's experience is everyone's experience. In fact, some people wrestling with gender seek out people they can talk to about shared experience, as we all do when we are struggling with a particular challenge. Seeking out support from peers does not always mean the peers are the cause of gender distress. With that important distinction in mind, here is Kylie's story.

Kylie showed no signs of gender questioning from early childhood. That is, until about the age of sixteen. After being on TikTok and Instagram very regularly, Kylie told her parents, "I am not a girl anymore." Kylie began to dress differently, she cut her hair short, and she asked her parents to call her Kyle.

Kylie's parents didn't immediately cut off her friendships or media usage. I find that doing so is a fear-based strategy that leads many teens to secretly seek out friendships or use of media. They did prioritize the above recommendations for steps after disclosure, took more of an active role in Kylie's life, and in certain cases limited media usage over time so Kylie could focus on schoolwork, friendships, and activities.

How did things shake out for Kylie? Upon returning from her summer camps, after a year of therapy around her overall mental health, and after incorporating the above strategies with her parents by her side, Kylie shared this with her parents: "I think I am more settled with being a girl now. I did have questions, and I realized that they weren't stupid questions, but they also didn't have to be my questions forever. I heard so much about how it's cool to be trans/gay/nonbinary that I didn't realize it can also be cool to be me. No one forced anything, but I'm thankful you let me figure this out, and you didn't tell me, 'I told you so.'"

## NAME AND PRONOUNS

One of the most common questions I get asked in my work in gender is around adoption of a teen's chosen name and pronouns, if these differ from the legal name and pronouns that correspond with their biological sex. This is a valid and complex question, and it comes with a range of possibilities that vary greatly from case to case.

We make a mistake when we try to offer a one-size-fits-all approach to this question. An "always yes" mentality fails to account for the teens who may not benefit from adopting a different name and/or pronouns due to the level of upheaval they can experience as they explore gender and the way this can become a distraction from their daily life. An "always no" mentality fails to honor cases where it can be helpful for a teen's parents to make certain accommodations to account for the teen's gender-related distress.

### DISCERNING DIFFERENT APPROACHES

We need to remember that teens can have many different motivations for exploring their gender or requesting a different name or pronouns. Some are experiencing very painful gender dysphoria and are asking others to use language for them that doesn't increase this pain. However, this isn't everyone's story; especially today, some people who explore transgender identity for themselves don't experience any dysphoria. How you interact with your teen's request to use a different name and pronouns might be very different depending on the reason they are making that request. I do, however, trust the Holy Spirit to guide families in this space.

If a teen makes an initial request about their name and pronouns, because there are various experiences that might be motivating them, I'd encourage you to learn more before responding. Ask them if they are willing to have a conversation about what they're thinking and feeling so you can better understand their reason for making this request. Hearing what your teen is experiencing can also give you a chance to think through the various impacts your responses to your teen might have and help you discern how best to proceed.

Here's a story that illustrates how an exploratory conversation like this can be helpful for the parent/child relationship and for finding a way forward.

I met with Deb and their dad, a single parent, for a consultation.[4] Deb, a recent high-school graduate, goes by Deb (instead of their legal name Debbie) and uses 'they/them' pronouns at work, with friends, and with one of their adult siblings. Deb uses the label "nonbinary" to describe their experience. When I asked about what drew Deb to this label (a helpful question to ask your teen!), Deb shared a belief that, as a Christian, they ought not use a label that directly counters their birth sex. "I know I'm not a man," Deb shared, "but it is hard for me to hear people say 'she' about me. Identifying as nonbinary and using 'they/them' pronouns helps me avoid the word 'she' without using 'he' or identifying as male."

Throughout our consultation, Deb's dad made it a point to call Deb, Debbie, seemingly in hopes of teaching Deb something or correcting Deb somewhere along the way. In those moments, Deb subtly winced. In talking one-on-one with Deb, Deb shared that they felt invisible and misunderstood, and Deb was pretty emotionally closed off as a result.

Deb tentatively brought up the name/pronouns discussion with her dad in our consultation. As Dad responded, his biggest fear was a fear common among Christian parents: "I don't want to tell you a lie. I just don't see you that way, and 'they' is hard to switch to and wrap my mind around. It feels awkward."

Deb nodded passively. I could tell that this conversation typically went this way. Deb would share a request, Dad would react out of fear and concern, and Deb would shut down, feeling alienated, misunderstood, and self-critical for even trying. The cycle of estrangement would continue.

I tried to help disrupt this cycle by modeling being curious about Deb's experience of name/pronouns. "Before we move on, Deb," I said, "can I ask a couple of questions to understand your request better?"

Deb was surprised but said, "Sure."

I asked, "What would it mean to you if your dad did use your nickname and 'they/them' pronouns?"

Deb answered, "Even though I would know he still doesn't agree with me in how he thinks about gender, it would mean he sees me where I am right now and recognizes this as where I am today in my understanding. It would feel kind of like he is holding up a mirror to me: it would reflect back to me where I am at, even if he doesn't see the same things in me that I see when I look in the mirror."

"What does it mean to you when Dad doesn't use your nickname and 'they/them' pronouns?" I asked.

"I feel really dismissed and discounted," said Deb. "It feels as if he is denying that this is where I am at right now, like he just doesn't want to look at me at all while I'm in this place."

Questions like these can bring clarity to how a child experiences their parents' decisions. This helps parents gain perspective on their own choices, regardless of whether they change their minds.

In this case, Deb's dad decided that he would be willing to use the adjusted name and consider using "they/them" pronouns, because he knew what this choice was communicating to Deb and what it wasn't communicating. In the meantime, he decided to avoid pronouns when possible.

Many Catholic parents worry that, in using an adjusted name and pronouns, they are telling a lie or communicating agreement with a belief that they don't agree with. Deb's story reminds us that language can be messy, and sometimes the same words will be understood very differently by different people. For that reason, it's important to carefully communicate what we mean and don't mean by different words. Deb's dad found a way to maintain his convictions and be honest about his disagreement with certain beliefs about gender, while also acknowledging where his adult child was at that time and reflecting his child's experience in his speech. If Deb had said, "Your using my chosen name and pronouns would mean you finally agree with the way I'm understanding and expressing my gender now," we could imagine Deb's dad making a different discernment about name and pronouns.

## MAINTAINING RELATIONSHIPS THROUGH DIFFERENCE OF PERSPECTIVE

One of the most common challenges I see in families is maintaining relationships when there are different perspectives on gender. While this is certainly true no matter what the differences are around, when there are differences in understanding around gender, there are unique challenges facing families today. Because I shared above a story about a family where accommodations for name/pronouns were made, I want to offer an example of a family where these adjustments were not made, and how the family navigated that together.

Jacob came to see me for therapy, describing symptoms of depression and gender-related questions. Jacob's identification had shifted several times in the past six months: he had identified first as trans, then as nonbinary, then as genderqueer, then as female.[5] His sexual orientation labels had also shifted from pansexual to asexual to lesbian. He was spending a lot of time exploring content on social media about sexuality and gender. His parents, a Catholic couple, were worried because he had never showed any signs of distress about gender until he shared this information with them two months ago.

About three months into therapy, where we were initially addressing and treating his depressive symptoms, Jacob asked to meet with me and his parents. We did so, and Jacob shared with Mom and Dad, "You need to call me Jane and use 'she/her/hers' pronouns. If you don't, it'll tell me that you don't really care, even though you say you do." This opened up an important conversation for the family, and one I want to walk you through, especially if you relate to Jacob's family's story.

In our therapy session, I first validated Jacob's experience: "It is understandable that this is difficult for you. I often hear that the only people who truly care about a transgender person will support every aspect of their gender process. I am guessing you have also heard that." I also normalized the challenge he felt with his parents: "It is really hard when people don't agree with us, especially our parents."

Next, I shared some perspective: "I know from working with lots of families like yours that every family member has their perspective, and it's really valuable to figure out how to move forward together even when we don't all agree on the best approach. This usually means in adult relationships that everyone is willing to understand one another, even and especially when there is disagreement. If your mom and dad said, 'Our child doesn't love us because he thinks differently about gender,' I would challenge them on that. Can I challenge you a little bit too?"

With Jacob's permission, I offered this observation: "I have found that there is a way to stay connected to parents when you think differently about this gender journey."

What's most important about this story is how Jacob's parents demonstrated this reality for Jacob: even though they weren't on the same page, they were committed to respecting Jacob in the midst of their differences.

Jacob's dad spoke first. He started by validating Jacob, something he had been learning about in the reading he was doing outside of our sessions. He said, "I am proud that you had the courage to speak up to us about your question. It makes sense you would want us to use the name and pronouns you use with your friends. So, thanks for taking a risk and making that ask."

Then, he checked in on how Jacob was feeling about the conversation: "How was it to bring this up?"

Jacob responded, "I was so nervous to do it, but I feel relieved to get it out."

"Good!" Jacob's dad said. He continued, his tone calm and tender: "I want to be honest with you like you are being with us. If I was to simply call you Jane and 'she,' I wouldn't be honoring where I am at with all of this right now. As much as I care about you, and I want to do the things that lead you to feel cared for, I also want to be honest that I am just not there yet. It took you time to get to where you are, and I think it will take us time on our own journey. I know that's not what you want to hear, and I can understand if it's frustrating."

Jacob acknowledged his frustration but didn't shut down.

Jacob's mom chimed in next: "An image comes to mind for me of a five-lane highway. The story that gets told about families like ours is that we all need to be in the same lane on the highway, or else we can't be close and can't love each other. My hope is that we can be in different lanes on the same highway, but always going in the same direction, and going together. You are exploring your gender and asking important questions, and we want to support you in doing that. This means that, as has already happened, in some weeks or months you have been in the second lane from the left, while in others you are in the far right lane or the far left lane. Our goal is to stay in the middle lane, so that we can go with you where you are going without changing lanes with you. I know that's not what you want to hear today, and I also hope you can know that we are open to journeying with you where you go, even if we aren't always in the same lane."

Then, Jacob's mom offered an alternative solution, a sign of willingness to negotiate: "What we can commit to right now is avoiding using any pronouns, when possible, and not saying your name unless it's necessary, if that would help at all. Or maybe we could find a nickname that feels comfortable for all of us."

In this story, Jacob's parents are highlighting (and normalizing rather than shaming) his developmental process of exploration. As much as they have their own thoughts, feelings, and reactions to him, they are treating him like the young person he is, respecting his feelings and thoughts and honesty, and asking for mutual respect for their feelings and thoughts and being honest in return. They go beyond simply saying no. They commit to journeying with their child, even if they don't see eye to eye on every aspect of his path at the time.

Here are some helpful guidelines for parents to respond to a teen's request with respect by honoring it, even when they are not in a position to do what the teen has asked:

1.  *Honor the question and the courage it takes to ask it*: Emphasize your teen's bravery in speaking up even when you don't know (and may have enormous fear about) the answer.

2.  *Validate the desire behind the request*: Acknowledge the very normal desire to have parents on board with the path a teen is on. (Some teens "go underground" with their experience, hiding it from their parents, and this is harmful in the long run. I always remind parents that a teen's inviting them in is actually a sign of respect and trust, even when they are telling you things that are difficult to hear.)

3.  *Check in with your teen*: Ask your teen how they are feeling about simply bringing this topic up. This question lets you slow down the

conversation, keep from moving into a lecture or hasty answer, and really tune in to your child's experience.

4. *Check in with your tone*: Is your voice raised? How do you access the tone of voice a diplomat would use, coming across as calm, strong, and reflective rather than fearful (which can manifest as fragility / passivity or dominance / aggression)?

5. *Be honest in response to the specific request*: Share gently about where you are in your understanding and ability to honor the request (or not), and validate the feelings that could arise from your teen in response. This helps deescalate tension and can help your teen to still feel seen in their experience.

6. *Offer the image of a five-lane highway*: Offer this image and your commitment to your child to "go with them, even when we aren't always in the same lane." Many teens fear being cut off, which can make it hard for them to fathom the words of unconditional love that you may say.

7. *Distinguish your family culture from the cultural narrative, and show a willingness to be flexible*: Distinguish your family's values from the narrative that sometimes gets told about Christian families to teens: "If you loved me, you would agree with everything I say or believe today." Instead, replace this false story with a truer story: "We can *imperfectly* love one another and *not* see eye to eye on everything and be very respectful of one another in it." Commit to finding one thing you can do to help lessen the pain your teen may be feeling related to gender.

8. *Check in again and invite further dialogue*: Your teen may not be ready to talk more, but make sure they know you're willing to continue the conversation. If they are angry and hurt, don't focus all your attention on battling against their anger by proving you care. It is sometimes best just to honor a teen's feelings by saying, "It's understandable to be angry. I get angry or hurt, too, when people I love don't agree with me on important things, and I don't feel seen in my perspective. We may need time to cool off, and that's okay. Know we are here and willing to pick up the conversation when you are ready."

Notice how the conversation modeled above is not one-sided. This is a big difference between parenting a teen and parenting a younger child. Many teens (and most adults) are pretty masterful at showing they are listening enough to not get in trouble while totally checking out. I call it the "glazed nod." As soon as you go into lecture mode, take note of the glazed eyes, lack of expression, and automatic nods. If you see this, you have lost your teen's attention.

Instead of reacting in anger when discussing an already difficult topic, notice your teen has tuned out and remember that their attention span is developmentally less than an adult's at this point. Remember you, too, may also check out when not feeling heard or seen as a real person. When you notice a teen is checked out, pause and name out loud, "I am losing you, aren't I? I went into lecture mode." Acknowledging this can lead to a good laugh and brings you back to the goal: authentic dialogue and modeling of mature engagement about such important matters. Of course, as we've seen already through this book, this dynamic is true for all kinds of conversations we have with our kids as they become teens.

Specifically when it comes to gender, parents can be often framed as the enemy or threat to a teen. It can be powerful for a teen to know that you, as their parent, are able to model effective, calm, and constructive conversation about intimate questions they may have, about their own gender or that of their friends. The more you can receive your teen in their questions about this topic, the more they will turn to you as a reliable guide in difficult spaces to navigate.

Mistakes will happen all along the way, especially insofar as there are points of disagreement about gender with your teen. When things get heated, pause the conversation and commit to coming back to it another time. Seek outside help when it would be beneficial to have someone mediate conversations. And apologize when you say things that are harsh, mocking, or cruel. Modeling each of these principles as signs of healthy communication will benefit your teen as they learn these skills for their adult life. Remember, the goal is ultimately fostering holiness in your teen. This is possible in tandem with a teen wrestling with gender or asking questions about their friends' experiences. It's not just possible—it's essential, and you are an important part of the process.

# CHAPTER 11

# "WHAT IF THEY TELL ME SOMETHING BAD HAPPENED TO THEM?"

## RESPONDING TO UNWANTED SEXUAL EXPERIENCES

The innocence of a child, no matter their age, is worthy of protecting. Tragically, we know that horrific experiences can occur, even when you establish appropriate rules, boundaries, and oversight. While the principles of this chapter can be helpful for a range of traumatic experiences, our focus will be on the aftermath of unwanted sexual experiences.

For those of you who have survived experiences of trauma, please know that this chapter could be particularly difficult for you. Take the time you need to process what comes up for you related to your own trauma. Be gentle with yourself. If this information is not relevant to you right now and you are experiencing other overwhelming circumstances, give yourself permission to come back to this content when life has settled down. You could also find a trusted person to walk through the content with you. Be aware that if your child does disclose an unwanted sexual experience to you, that disclosure could evoke your own fear reactions; you'll need additional support in place to help you respond effectively.

# WHAT IS AN UNWANTED SEXUAL EXPERIENCE?

An unwanted sexual experience is physical contact and/or a verbal exchange in which a person is unable to or compromised in their ability to freely say yes or no. This situation can involve caressing, kissing, the showing of genitals or masturbating in front of you without your permission (exhibitionism), watching you as you undress without your permission (voyeurism), fondling, oral sex, or vaginal or anal penetration, as well as comments that are sexual in nature.

It is important to help your teen understand the reality that unwanted sexual experiences sometimes occur. Ideally, this conversation would occur prior to your teen having this kind of experience—or, better still, even if they never have this kind of experience. Girls are more likely to endure unwanted sexual experiences; 82 percent of all sexual assault victims under eighteen are female.[1]

> ## COMMON REASONS YOUNG PEOPLE DON'T DISCLOSE UNWANTED SEXUAL EXPERIENCES[2]
>
> - Shame, guilt, embarrassment
> - Confidentiality concerns
> - Fear of not being believed
> - Fear of retaliation

Here's how you might introduce this concept to a younger teen:

> "As we get older, we get to learn new ways of protecting ourselves and others. Just as there is good in the world, there is also evil and sin. I don't say this to scare you, but to help you be equipped to know what to do if a person is trying to do something wrong. You already know that some kids and adults do things that are appropriate, and others sometimes do things that are inappropriate. It would be inappropriate for someone to hit you, for instance, no matter what. It would also be inappropriate for someone to cruelly mock you. If those things happen, I always want to know so I can help you manage it, even if it feels hard to say out

loud. What are some other things that are not okay to do to someone?"

Allow your teen to share. Validate what they are saying by responding, "That's right."

Next, turn the conversation toward inappropriate behaviors that are sexual in nature. You could tweak the phrasing depending on the sex of your teen, since their bodies and common forms of sexual touch will be different:

> "Some of the inappropriate things a person may try to do to another person are actions or words that are sexual in nature. A person might try to touch your butt, your genitals, or your breasts or chest. They might try to do something else physical to you without your permission or make comments about your body in a gross way. A person might ask you for images of you naked or send images of themselves naked, and that would also not be okay. If a person were to touch you, try to convince you to touch them, do something inappropriate or sexual in front of you, or speak to you in an inappropriate way, I would always want you to come to me and tell me. It might be hard to say it out loud, so you could also write it down in a text or a note. You could also use a code word to signal to me that you need help. You don't need to live in fear of something like this happening; we can take some steps to prevent these things, such as hanging out with people in groups, keeping doors open when we are in a room with a person we are dating, and refraining from drinking alcohol or drugs. But if something like this were to happen, it is not your fault, no matter what. I will help you figure out what to do, okay?"

We want to strike a balance in these conversations, making sure that we're not overexposing a teen, but also ensuring that we're not failing to equip them for the brokenness of the world. It grieves me to have to explain these realities to teens. Yet I know full well that many teens, both guys and girls, have had an unwanted sexual experience, and they almost always wish someone had talked with them about this possibility before it happened. Use discernment in how much detail you will use based on what you know about your particular teen.

## COMMON RESPONSES TO UNWANTED SEXUAL EXPERIENCES

Teens can experience sexual assault from many different kinds of people, including peers, siblings, friends, romantic interests or partners, parents or caregivers, extended family members, teachers, spiritual leaders, or strangers. The teen's response will likely be different depending on who perpetrated the assault.

Regardless of whom the threat comes from, the brain of a teen will probably respond in one of a few ways. When we experience sexual trauma—or any kind of situation that incites significant fear—certain areas of the brain will go "offline." We tend to react in one (or more) of four ways: fight, flight, freeze, or fawn.[3]

1. *Fight*: The reflexive response of counterattack. This creative survival mechanism can take the form of physical efforts to push away advances, fight off an offender, or say, "Stop," or "No."

2. *Flight*: The reflexive response of running away or attempting to escape a situation. This creative survival mechanism can be done verbally in the buildup to a dangerous or uncomfortable situation, and it can be done physically through efforts to get away from someone.

3. *Freeze*: The reflexive response of paralysis. This creative survival mechanism is like an effort to "play dead" in a dangerous or uncomfortable situation. It shuts down the brain when the threat exceeds our capacity to cope.

4. *Fawn*: The reflexive response of attempting to placate or please the perpetrator. This creative survival mechanism, which is easily misunderstood by both victim and perpetrator as consent or desire to engage, can include saying flattering or kind things while trying to delay inevitable harm. It might also involve feigning pleasure to attempt to bring the experience to an end more quickly.

Our automatic responses can vary from experience to experience, but they are *automatic*. You cannot choose your fear response. So many survivors blame themselves for responding in one or more of these ways. But here's the truth: your trauma response, or your teen's trauma response, is as automatic as the reflex of a knee when a doctor hits it with a hammer. Just as we would never shame ourselves for this reflex, we want to remind ourselves and our teens not to shame ourselves for our automatic trauma responses, either in the moment or after. These are survival mechanisms, which we can honor as part of our body's design created by God to help us respond to crises, even as we grieve the brokenness of the world that causes us to need these mechanisms.

## UNDERSTANDING TRAUMA RESPONSES

Trauma comes back as a reaction, not a memory.

—Bessel van der Kolk

## RESPONDING TO DISCLOSURE VERSUS RESPONDING TO DISCOVERY

So how should you respond if you become aware that your teen has had an unwanted sexual experience? One dynamic that may shape your response is the difference between *disclosure* and *discovery*: Did your teen tell you about their experience, or did you discover their experience without them intending for you to know? When a teen discloses an unwanted sexual experience—telling you for themselves what occurred—your goal is to discern how best to receive your teen in that moment and respond in the aftermath.

## REGULATING YOUR EMOTIONS

It is important to work very hard to regulate your own emotions in the moment, regardless of whether it's a disclosure or discovery. If you are married and one of the spouses is better able to remain calm in the moment, or if you are a single parent and there is a close and trusted adult to have the conversation with you, it is best to let whoever can remain the most calm lead the conversation. While you will want to make clear that what happened to your teen was not okay, and that you are angry on your teen's behalf and sad that they had to experience that, there is a risk in allowing the intensity of your emotional reaction to lead your teen to regret either bringing this up or you finding out. There is the additional risk that, especially in the immediate conversations after, if your teen sees the emotional pain this causes you in a less contained way, your teen may move into emotional caregiving, worrying about you, and internally blaming themselves for "causing my parents pain." It's hard to fully appreciate just how much these experiences trigger self-blame, and parents who are understandably feeling a range of emotions can often unintentionally display this to an extent that the teen will carry shame for it.

## NAVIGATING A DISCLOSURE

1. *Thank your teen for their courage in telling you, and tell them you believe them*: Express admiration and pride in your teen for their courage. Remind them they are not in trouble and, if nothing else, make it clear that you believe them.

2. *Clarify what it is like for your teen to tell you by asking them about their feelings as they share*: Expect your teen to voice strong emotions such as fear, shame, disgust, embarrassment, sadness, and being overwhelmed.

3. *Validate and normalize the feelings that they share*: "I can understand that it feels [violating, overwhelming, frustrating] to share this. That makes a lot of sense that you would feel that. I think many people would feel that way."

4. *Challenge shame and self-blame*: Focus on the unwanted nature of the experience. Avoid the temptation to dwell on lost virginity, any deceit that may have been involved in events leading up to the offense (like a teen sneaking out), or anything else that directs blame for what happened toward your teen. Talk about how unfair and wrong the perpetrator's behavior was, calmly and clearly. Say clearly that you do not blame your teen for what happened.

5. *Refrain from asking a bunch of questions right away or going into problem-solving mode*: Set up another time to discuss the situation later, when you can discuss next steps. This first conversation's goal is emotional attunement to how your teen is processing what happened and validation of your child's experience. Keep the focus on them.

If you are a "fixer" when you are facing difficult moments in your life or others' lives, you will want to work extra hard to refrain from that impulse here.

6. *Offer to pray together*: Invite the Lord into this moment with your teen. Bring to him the feelings your teen is holding, and invite the consoling presence of the Holy Spirit. Highlight how precious your teen is to God, how he delights in them, and how nothing can ever change that. Keep the prayer brief, as this conversation can already be quite exhausting, but model that God is ready to meet us where we are in each moment. Here is a sample prayer:

> "Lord Jesus, we come to you with heavy hearts, in the pain of this unwanted sexual experience. Send your Holy Spirit upon us to console, release shame, and help _____ to see themselves through your loving and compassionate eyes. We know of your love for _____, and ask you to help _____ always to know how precious they are to you. Nothing can separate them from your love. Help us to know we can always bring anything and everything to you, and there is no condemnation in you. You know and see that _____ is not to blame for what happened, and they are precious and beloved in your eyes. Thank you for being with us here. We love you and ask for your guidance in this time. Amen."

## NAVIGATING A DISCOVERY

A parent's response will be a bit more complicated in a case of discovery. Parents often discover a teen's experience after first beginning to notice behavioral or emotional changes in their teen and becoming concerned. They may look into text messages, journals, or internet search histories in order to find evidence about what happened to change their teen's behavior. While this choice can open a parent's eyes to what is happening, it will likely feel like a betrayal and invasion of privacy to a teen.

For now, we won't get into the question of how much privacy teens ought to have from their parents at various ages, and whether this privacy should extend to things like text messages, notes on a teen's phone, or journal entries. On the one hand, parents are no less responsible for children's safety when they become teenagers; on the other hand, psychologically speaking, the need for privacy increases as children grow toward adulthood. Regardless, if a parent does choose to look into things that the teen believes are private—whether or not the parent agrees that these things are private—this can feel violating to teens and damage the trust in the parent-child relationship.

Let me offer an example of what a discovery situation can look like:

Marlene's mom, Jamey, went into Marlene's room to look around when Marlene was at soccer practice. Jamey had noticed Marlene being more irritable and distant, and she was concerned. Instead of talking to Marlene, assuming Marlene would not be honest, Jamey went through Marlene's journal and began to read a recent reflection. Marlene had written that she was "no longer a virgin." The journal entry went on, "It wasn't rape, but I definitely didn't want what happened." Jamey panicked and had no idea what to do. "If I tell Marlene," Jamey confided to a friend, "she will feel so betrayed. If I don't, what do I do with this knowledge?"

## REMEMBERING TO MANAGE YOUR EMOTIONS

If you find yourself in a situation like this, the first key is to give yourself time to process what happened before bringing this discovery to your teen. Unless your child is in immediate danger, and you must intervene right away to prevent future harm, give yourself permission to seek support for your initial reactions before talking with your child. Otherwise, your feelings can come out sideways onto your child, unintentionally making the situation worse.

Remember, if you do seek support from someone else before talking with your teen, the information you are sharing is your teen's private information. Typically, once you do talk with your teen, they will want to know who else knows about what happened. Keep the circle small and limited: it could ideally include just the teen's other parent (in a two-parent home) or one close confidant, such as a spiritual director, pastor, or best friend. Ensure that the person you tell will not disclose the information to anyone else (with the understanding that, if this is a mandatory reporting incident, that person will need to disclose the information to law enforcement). This allows you to protect your child's vulnerable information at a time when they are likely already feeling exposed.

Let's map out how Jamey responded to Marlene, which can serve as a model of how you could respond to your child in a similar situation:

Because Jamey went through Marlene's journal, she began the conversation by apologizing for invading Marlene's privacy. It was important for Jamey to take responsibility for this action and not lie about how she learned what happened to Marlene. Since Marlene already knew her privacy had been invaded, it helped for Jamey to do everything she could to rebuild trust, rather than keeping more secrets and giving Marlene more reasons to feel distrustful. By immediately apologizing for the betrayal of trust, Marlene was able to get to the important point of the conversation, which was to show up and care for Marlene.

Jamey was careful not to fixate on the "loss of virginity" or whatever sexual behavior had been discovered. Instead, she focused on the unwanted nature of Marlene's experience and actively said things to reduce shame.

Jamey also resisted the urge to go into detective mode. She told Marlene that she had additional questions, but she offered to come back to these questions later instead of asking everything all at once.

When the dust had settled a few days later, Jamey circled back with some follow-up questions. Before asking any questions, Jamey reminded Marlene to take her time: "If you aren't ready to tell me everything yet, that's okay." This allowed Marlene to regain a sense of choice and freedom after an experience that had evoked powerlessness and lack of freedom.

Jamey reminded Marlene, "This is your story to tell others." She wanted to make it clear that, while Jamey had already spoken confidentially with her spiritual director about what she found, for her own support, she would ask Marlene's permission for any other disclosures. This reminder also helped Marlene reclaim a sense of power and privacy.

Let's break this down further, slightly tweaking some of the steps from our conversation on disclosure:

1.  *Describe calmly what you found and how*: "I was in your room and saw your journal on your bed. I opened to a page that described an unwanted sexual experience you had recently."

2.  *Tell your teen that you believe them, and clarify what it is like for your teen to know you to have this information*: Expect your teen to voice strong emotions such as anger, fear, shame, disgust, embarrassment, sadness, and being overwhelmed.

3.  *Take responsibility for any invasion of privacy, rather than justifying why you did it, and validate the feelings that could be there*: "I can understand it likely feels [violating, overwhelming, frustrating] to know I looked through your personal items and [uncomfortable, embarrassing, scary] that I know what happened. That makes a lot of sense that you would feel that." You do not need to justify what you did, and you can take responsibility for the impact on your teen.

4.  *Challenge shame and self-blame*: Talk about the unwanted nature of the experience; don't discuss the "lost virginity," any deceit that may have been involved in events leading up to the offense (like a teen sneaking out), or anything that would seem to blame your teen for what happened. Say how unfair and wrong the perpetrator's behavior was. Say that you do not blame your teen for what happened. Thank them for having this conversation with you, and acknowledge how brave it is for them to do so.

5.  *Refrain from asking a bunch of questions right away or going into problem-solving mode*: Set up another time to discuss more later. As mentioned previously, be very careful not to go into "fix-it mode," especially if that is your impulse in difficult moments.

6.  *Offer to pray together*: Invite the Lord into this moment with your teen. Bring to him the feelings your teen is holding, and invite the consoling presence of the Holy Spirit. Highlight how precious your teen is to God, how he delights in them, and how nothing can ever change that. Keep the prayer brief, as this conversation can already be quite exhausting, but model that God is ready to meet us where we are in each moment.

## INVOLVING OTHER SUPPORTS

While this chapter can't cover all the nuances of how to respond after an unwanted experience, I want to name a few possible pathways for additional support. Remember, you do not want to disclose to anyone without first telling your teen that you will do so and, in some cases, without getting their permission. This maintains a semblance of power and control in your teen, who will need many opportunities to reestablish healthy autonomy and control after an unwanted sexual experience.

These supports could help your family problem-solve next steps, determine the process of including law enforcement, and so on:

- Licensed mental-health professionals trained in responding to crises. They can offer therapy and consultation on how to respond. Therapists are mandatory reporters of abuse and neglect of a minor, and they can assist you in making these reports to your state's reporting body when indicated.

- The other parent in a two-parent home, a spiritual guide, or a mentor or trusted support to your teen.

- A school guidance counselor.

- School administration, if the event happened on school premises or if the perpetrator was a teacher or fellow classmate.

- Local hospital and/or rape response team, if indicated.

- Law enforcement, which is especially important to consider if any criminal behavior occurred. If there is an imminent threat to your loved one, call 911; otherwise, call the nonemergency police line. It's important to note that unfortunately sometimes the way the system responds to sexual abuse further traumatizes a person, especially if it is a child.

## GIVING CHOICES WHENEVER POSSIBLE

In book 1 we spoke about how, with younger children, giving them choices is important. This is all the more important for your teen. If criminal behavior occurred that needs to be reported, give your teen the option of whether to be part of that call. Some teens will want to be involved, and others will prefer that you or a therapist report it on their behalf.

# FOLLOW-UP CONVERSATIONS

The impacts of unwanted sexual behavior will vary from person to person and will be shaped by a range of variables. I'd strongly discourage you from implying to your teen that they should be "over it by now." There is no timeline for grief; grief is part of the body's way of processing traumatic experiences. Remember, a trauma is anything that exceeds a person's capacity to cope.

## ESTABLISHING NORMALCY AGAIN

The most comforting thing for a child who has experienced trauma is feeling a sense of normalcy.

–Cindy Morgan

## INITIAL PRINCIPLES

Here are a few more follow-up principles that will allow you to support your teen in coping with an unwanted sexual experience:

- *Refrain from setting a timeline for healing or comparing their healing journey to that of others, even if meant to be encouraging*: "I know it can be confusing that you are still struggling with this, but you lived through something horrible, and there is no timeline on the impact. It's normal to carry the pain in different ways. I always want to hear about how it's impacting you, even if you feel frustrated that you aren't healed by now. Everyone is on their own timeline, and even if you know of others who have been through something similar who seem over it, that doesn't mean you are doing it wrong."

- *Initiate check-ins*: "I wanted to check in on how you are doing with the [assault/trauma] that you survived. I care about knowing what this is like now for you." (Make sure that you're also initiating lots of other conversations unrelated to this experience. The last thing you want is for your teen to feel as if this is the only part of their story you care about, or to be reminded of their trauma every time you strike up a one-on-one conversation with them.)

- *Remind them about the truths of what happened*: "It's normal sometimes to question, 'Was that real?' As time goes on, it can be very confusing because your memory can fade or feel spotty. Our memories fade and feel spotty to protect us from the pain of all the facts. Think of how painful it would be to remember all of it. God made your brain to protect you from some of that pain by leaving behind some of the details. Just because you don't remember everything or start to have questions, that doesn't mean it wasn't real. I still believe you."

- *Connect them to additional resources*: In some cases, a teen will not be ready to seek additional supports for themselves, such as therapy, immediately following a trauma. They may be more invested in reestablishing normalcy. However, in the months and years after an event, you can continue to offer opportunity for individual therapy, spiritual support, and group therapy support. This will help you identify—and, in some cases, buffer against—the delayed symptoms that can emerge in the aftermath of trauma, such as depression, anxiety, eating disorders, post-traumatic stress responses, substance abuse, or sexual acting out.

- *Help your teen access enjoyable or pleasurable experiences*: I often remind clients that healing from trauma is not merely learning to tolerate "painful emotions" such as grief, loss, sadness, anger, fear, or disgust. In fact, many survivors will say their biggest challenge is not tolerating these feelings, because their tolerance for them is likely great: they have endured and survived unimaginable pain. Much of healing from trauma involves helping a person safely tolerate pleasure again. In fact, some trauma survivors will have a fear response even to the word "pleasure" because of what it can symbolize. Helping your teen gradually identify and access safe forms of pleasure will be beneficial to their process of healing. To be clear, don't force your teen to engage in something you think could help them experience pleasure safely. Rather, create many opportunities for this: always invite, even if they say no every time. At some point, they may feel ready to say yes.

- *Continue to turn to Christ with the pain*: Time before the Blessed Sacrament can be a safe way for a young person to experience solitude with the Lord and honestly bring all their emotions to him (insofar as abuse happened outside of a religious context). It can be difficult in Mass or other public forums to externally process the pain of surviving abuse, but helping your teen find avenues to release these emotions in prayer can be helpful. Prayer journaling, art, and use of imaginative imagery can allow a person to experience the presence of Christ in their suffering. A common imagery exercise is imagining the grieving face of Christ (or the Blessed Mother or a female saint, if a female presence is more safe), who desires to protect your teen and is angry on your teen's behalf for the harm done to them. There are a range of ways to use imagery in a person's work in therapy to offer restoration in the midst of trauma processing.

## RESPONDING TO SELF-BLAME

One thing that often haunts survivors of trauma is the internalized message that "I wanted it." This can be a seed many perpetrators plant in the minds of those they abuse. This seed can grow into loathing, blame, and disgust when survivors turn their experiences inward on themselves. You may see a young person become more irritable, self-critical, perfectionistic, and rageful, possibly leading to self-harm or suicidal thoughts. If you see signs of these behaviors, seek mental-health support and recognize the importance of challenging the narrative that your teen "chose" what happened.

Because sexual stimulation of the genitals will usually lead to spontaneous pleasure responses regardless of a person's ability to consent, a teen's bodily pleasure during an unwanted sexual experience may confuse them and make them believe that they somehow were willing participants. This could not be further from the truth. You can help your teen understand that it's normal for a body to feel pleasure when sexually stimulated, even if they didn't choose or want what happened. You will also want to challenge the idea that, if your teen wanted behaviors (like kissing) that preceded their sexual experience, they must have also "wanted" what happened sexually. A person may consent to being kissed but not be open to genital touching or penetration. It will be easy for many teens to confuse these two kinds of "wanting," so help them understand the difference.

Here are a few things you can say to push back on harmful and shaming messages that emerge after trauma. Be direct, calm, and confident as you say these things:

> "You did not choose this. You also did not want this, even if your body responded with signs of pleasure. Stimulation leads to pleasure responses automatically, with or without our consent or desire. You are not to blame for your body's natural responses. I know it can be very confusing when that happens, and it may take time for you to believe what I am saying."

When you respond to a teen's disclosure of any kind of unwanted sexual experience, account for and speak to the possibility that a teen will blame themselves in the above ways. Acknowledging this can help your teen transform their blaming narrative into a narrative of resilience.

## THE HEALING PROCESS

To be clear, this chapter is not meant to be a treatment plan for sexual-abuse survivors, and it isn't comprehensive in its scope. But I want to conclude by describing how you can accompany a teen on their journey of healing and restoration. A central piece of the healing process occurs when someone integrates new meaning into their traumatic experience, establishing a sense of identity and purpose that accounts for their trauma but is not defined by it.

Some people think healing from sexual trauma means merely retelling and processing an unwanted sexual experience with others. I am convinced that mere retelling is not an end in itself—even if, for some, it is cathartic to share the details of what they survived. Healing after trauma involves transforming the meaning of an experience and discovering new meaning moving forward. Let's take the story of Tyler as an example.

Tyler remembers being sexually abused by a grandparent between the ages of ten and fourteen. For years, he blamed himself for this. "Why didn't I tell someone sooner?" he wondered. He was often told during these unwanted encounters that he "wanted" what happened; the sexual response of his body, combined with the pleasurable sensations he felt, left him believing this was true. He went on to cope with the pain of his experiences through pornography use and serial dating of women. The shame of his traumas compounded well into adulthood.

He initially came to therapy because of his compulsive pornography use, which had become increasingly problematic throughout his marriage. Extensive work to understand what pornography was "doing" for him led him to open up about the nature and extent of his experiences of sexual violation. As he processed these experiences in therapy, the meaning of his traumas and the ways he had learned to cope with them were being transformed. As therapy came to a close, he shared this:

> "It's starting to click for me now. The things I turned to for coping, like pornography, were actually efforts to soothe the pain and contain the many emotions I felt that had nowhere to go. I can be grateful that the patterns I developed helped me survive that time, even as I distance myself from those patterns now. I am proud of how I am finding new ways to manage my pain, and I feel a lot of compassion for the younger version of me who tried to control sexual experiences by viewing porn.
>
> "When I have memories or nightmares pop up, or sensory reminders of the trauma that bring up a strong fear response, I have started saying, 'That was then; this is now.' I tell myself things like, 'You are brave for surviving the unimaginable. You made it. You are free. That was real. That was wrong. And that's not happening anymore.'
>
> "For the first time in my whole life, I actually believe what I am saying. For a while, I said it but didn't believe it. Now, I actually believe it. I really am free. I can look those memories in the face and not be crushed by them. They are still horrible—don't get me wrong. I wouldn't wish what I survived on my worst enemy. But I am taking my power back. I am free."

While the journey may be long, your teen, like Tyler, can experience freedom after horrible evils. So much of the damage my clients have experienced after trauma involves the lack of ongoing support after an initial harmful event. Your family's response can be different. You can create maximum opportunity, from the very beginning, for your teen to find the same kind of healing and transformation that Tyler did. This is cause for rejoicing, even as you grieve the reality of harms that no child should endure.

# CHAPTER 12

# "HOW DO I NAVIGATE TECHNOLOGY ACCESS?"

## SETTING YOUR TEEN UP FOR SUCCESS IN A DIGITAL AGE

The average Christian parent has much less understanding of technology than their teen. Even if you have social media platforms, there are ever-evolving ways young people use and engage with social media that are different from the world we were raised in. Not only is social media unfamiliar territory for some parents, but you have much less time to learn and play catch-up. More American teens, ages thirteen to seventeen, than ever before have access to smartphones and a range of social media platforms. A recent Pew Research study found that 95 percent of teens have access to a smartphone and 45 percent report using it "almost constantly."[1] Sixty-five percent of parents express concern about their teen's media usage, and many of those parents report taking some steps to curb usage. At the same time, we know that parental involvement in their child's media usage is varied, and the more involved a parent is, the more likely a young person is to be protected from experiences of harm online.

Talking about technology, and in a particular way social media usage, is essential for healthy sexual formation of teens. Technology is often a primary gateway for a teen to be exposed to sexual content. One in five youth between the ages of nine and seventeen will view unwanted sexual material online. One in nine youth will experience a person attempting to solicit them for sexual favors online.[2] Christian teens I have worked with who did not have conversations about sexuality at home often turn to online platforms for guidance, which often only further confuses them. This magnifies the importance of weaving in conversations around appropriate use of technology and how it relates to sexuality with your teen.

As you read this chapter, I want you to understand where I'm coming from. After all the devastation I've seen from social media in the teens and families I work with, I encourage parents to avoid social media access as long as possible. I worry a great deal about what effects we are already seeing on mental health in teens and what we will discover with social development in the years after a generation has been raised by social media platforms. I use that language intentionally, because, in so many cases, it does seem like the most powerful internalized voice I hear from teens is the voice modeled to them by social media platforms, even beyond the voice of friends or parents. This voice flows into so many facets of life, and in a particular way shapes the expression, values, questions, and beliefs of young people around sexuality. Rather than blocking all access to social media (which is nearly impossible, especially as your teen grows up), we want to equip our teens to be able to critically engage media sources and platforms, as well as the sexual content and messaging therein.

## IDENTIFYING BARRIERS

There are so many potential barriers to parents being actively involved in teens' media usage. While many parents report being engaged, these same parents often do not feel effective in how they are engaging. Meanwhile, teens often feel misunderstood by their parents related to their media usage. These challenging dynamics must be accounted for if our goal is to help raise teens who can effectively navigate digital spaces.

Here are some of the most common barriers that keep parents from being effectively engaged:

- Time constraints
- Avoidance of conflict

- Being overwhelmed
- Awareness of similar challenges with media as your teen
- Lack of understanding of the reality and vastness of what is available to teens on social media
- Assuming a teen is better equipped than they actually are to manage social media

## REFLECTION QUESTIONS

- What are the barriers that keep you from being as involved in your child's technology use as you'd like to be?
- What would need to be different or put in place to open up space for you to be more effectively engaged?
- What is one effective strategy you have found for guiding your teen in social media or phone usage?
- What is one ineffective strategy you have tried? What has made it less effective for your family?

## MONITORING AND FILTERING SOFTWARE

### MANAGING EXPECTATIONS

If your teenager has a hard time managing their phone, remember, there wasn't a single time during your entire childhood where your parents gave you a fragile, pocket-sized, distraction casino worth $500-$1,000 and said, "Here, good luck."

—Jon Acuff

In the spirit of proactivity, if you purchase your teen a phone or they have access to another device (including your phone or iPad), immediately set up an application to monitor and filter media usage. Incorporating this permanently into your teen's technology use, discussing it openly, and explaining why it is a valuable part of equipping your teen to engage technology will all be important. Here's how you might introduce this:

> "One of the things many families do, including ours, is having software to monitor and filter content on the internet. As we have talked about, the internet is a blessing and also a bottomless pit of content, some that is helpful to see and a lot that is not going to be helpful. Either way, we want to hear about things you are seeing or reading on the internet, even when it's sexual content or information that you come across. We want to talk about this openly.
>
> "We also want to do our best to filter things that won't be helpful for you. It used to be that sexual content had to be gotten from a store, but now we have access to it at the click of a button. This is why we want to make sure we are making it easier for you to use a device well. If you find yourself still seeing things you don't want to see, bring it to me, even if you are afraid for getting in trouble. You will never get in as much trouble for anything that you are honest about."

## DISCUSSING SOCIAL MEDIA APPS

In addition to installing screen protections and filters, I want to offer some recommendations now for handling social media and other applications your teen may want to use once they have a device.

Many teens no longer text regularly, and they find a phone call archaic, which limits their contact with friends to social media platforms and apps. One mom shared with me, "None of my teen's friends call each other anymore or text. I am worried if I don't allow her to have Snapchat, she will be kept out of friendships in high school." This highlights the pressure many parents feel, as well as the reality that most teens will access social media platforms in the high-school years at some point.

This means it will become increasingly difficult to keep your teens off all media, even while knowing media sources have the potential to expose them to unhelpful messaging, including in the realm of sexuality.

When I talk with parents about monitoring technology use, most respond with the acknowledgment that they know way less than their teen about it all. I know that many of you aren't behind because you want to be. Life gets away from you. If you had endless hours in the day, surely you could do a research paper on technology platforms. But you are a limited person with limited resources and so many unique challenges that make this hard. There is no shame in acknowledging that you are not as involved as you might like to be, or that the strategies you have been using don't seem to be working.

Given how rapidly things change, I want to teach you how to have generalized conversations about all kinds of apps your teen might use, right at the onset of giving them a device:

> "Before you download any apps, we want to talk with you about what they're for and why they'll be helpful.
>
> "When you want to download a particular app, we will sit down with you and look through it, to learn about it together.
>
> "When you see things or read things on apps, whether they confuse you, disgust you, scare you, excite you, or invigorate you, we want to talk about those things.
>
> "Apps have so many cool things, and they also can be places that pull you in and make it hard to be present in daily life. We want to be aware of what we are viewing and for how long, so we don't get lost in it and miss out on in-person connections."

## BENEFITS AND DRAWBACKS OF SOCIAL MEDIA

Social media is not all bad. There are clear benefits that can come from accessing media platforms. This is especially important for parents to understand if you are skeptical of social media. If nothing else, understanding this allows you to better appreciate why social media might matter so much to your teen. Thirty-one percent of teens report that they find social media usage "mostly positive" in its impact on them.[3] Here are some reasons social media can be helpful:

1. It allows for people to connect outside of their immediate peer group. This is especially useful for people who struggle to connect socially in person because of communication barriers, developmental delays, social anxiety, or other challenges.

2.  It allows access to knowledge and building of practical skills. For example, a young person today can learn a skill through YouTube videos and online guides that might previously have required classes or a private tutor.

3.  It gives access to religious content through mediums teens are already using.

4.  It contains apps and information that promote mental health and reduce stigma around discussing complex topics.

5.  It raises awareness of social issues and other news or information that would otherwise be less accessible to youth.

6.  It provides a platform for self-expression, where many teens feel safe to speak freely and openly.

7.  It is a way to pass the time.

8.  It can help a person entertain themselves or keep their mood up.

There are also clear potential drawbacks related to social media usage for teens, and for all of us. Teens are particularly susceptible to a degree of manipulation and added vulnerability on social media and phones. Twenty-four percent of teens describe social media as "mostly negative in its impact."[4] Here are some possible sources of social media's negative impact:

1.  It facilitates cyberbullying and spreading of rumors, which can be more difficult to detect and more pervasive in their scope of impact when they occur online.

2.  It can diminish users' in-person social skills or contact.

3.  It paints an unrealistic image of other peoples' lives and relationships.

4.  It causes distractions and contains addictive elements.

5.  It is a likely platform for negative peer pressure.

6.  It can have many negative mental-health impacts. Teens are more likely to use social media when they feel lonely. In turn, as social media usage increases, subjective reports of loneliness increase. Social media use also often contributes to negative body image, specifically for young girls.

7.  It can increase relational drama in people's lives.

8.  It includes advertisements targeted to promote dissatisfaction and materialism.

9. Users are more likely to be exposed to pornography and other age-inappropriate content.

10. It encourages reliance on slang, which can diminish people's understanding of more formal language rules in other settings.

11. Users can be exposed to unsafe people.

12. Oversharing of personal information can result in identity theft or personal danger.

13. It interferes with sleep, appetite, and embodied human connection.

In the spirit of collaboration, in addition to knowing and looking through the platforms your teen is involved in, it's valuable to talk with your teen about what positive impacts and negative impacts they experience when they use social media. So many parents villainize social media, which makes a teen push back and deny any negative impact. This can become a verbal tug-of-war, which is frustrating for everyone. However, inviting teens to observe both what is helpful and what is unhelpful can encourage them to think in a more balanced way about social media use.

Here's how you could begin this conversation:

> "It's been great to get to learn more about social media and see what it's all about. As with anything else, social media can have some really good things about it and some things that aren't great. What are some of the things you really like about social media? What are some of the positive things that have come from your being on social media? How has it helped you?"

Anytime we want to invite more awareness, it can help to start by making space for a teen to share good things about an activity or situation. This will make them less likely to become defensive about their use of media. It also helps you understand what about social media is drawing your teen in.

After validating and honoring the cool things about social media, you can move to making space for some of the potentially harmful things a teen sees in their social media experience. I wouldn't recommend pushing the conversation too quickly in this direction, and I'd refrain from giving your own thoughts and concerns at first. This is a time to elevate the voice of your teen. You want to help them form an awareness of how every behavior has benefits and costs. Most importantly, when you help your teen discover and embrace ideas for themselves—such as the potential dangers of social media—these ideas will have much more influence in your teen's life than if you simply tell them what you want them to think. Here's a way you could shift the conversation toward the downside of social media:

> "I can see why all those good things we've talked about make you want to spend time on social media! Sometimes a thing that has good uses can also be unhealthy for us. Can you think of anything about social media that could be unhealthy? Have you seen it affect any of your friends, or other people you've heard about, in ways that aren't the best?
>
> "What would be signs that it is time to take a pause from social media? Or to delete a specific account?"

## PRINCIPLES FOR SOCIAL MEDIA USAGE

Forty-five percent of teens report that social media is neither absolutely positive nor absolutely negative in its impact on them.[5] It seems that, much of the time, social media can be used well or poorly, and the way we engage with it matters when it comes to impact.[6]

With that in mind, here are some principles I'd recommend for social media usage:

1. Social media usage is a privilege, not a right. If social media usage becomes a pathway for unhelpful content and exposure to unhealthy sexual information, its access will be reduced.[7]

2. When possible, do not punish for other unrelated behaviors by taking away social media. Reserve this punishment for when the offense is clearly tied to media usage whenever possible. Otherwise, media usage becomes more a place of conflict than it needs to be; asking a child to limit their social media use for any reason might come to feel like a punishment, even when they're not being punished. When a teen violates rules on social media and needs a social-media-related punishment, teach them appropriate engagement on media platforms and respect of boundaries, rather than simply cutting off their social media access temporarily and then allowing it again.

3. If your teen has shown they are not yet ready for the privilege of having their social media use restored after violating household expectations around social media, set a goal for how they might get there and what would need to change for that to be possible. For instance, if a teen is using social media outside of hours set for this, offer opportunities for them to use the device for a limited period of time (thirty minutes), with the expectation that they return the device right at the time limit and that searches are in keeping with appropriate content. When they do so three times, they can have the device back.

4. Set clear expectations for appropriate and inappropriate media use and what will lead to a pause from social media. Identify clearly some of the websites and types of content that are off limits (including sexting, nude photos), while explaining that, if these things come from others, you want to be told immediately.

5. If you are concerned about your teen not building social skills due to frequent media usage, rather than merely cutting off media (which is a place for some social engagement), challenge your teen to expand their live social engagement to counter media usage. (For instance, you could have them spend an hour of no-phone time with friends for every hour using media.)

6. When you notice social media is becoming a source of comparison and seeking out feedback, especially if it is impacting things such as body image or self-worth, talk with your teen about noticing the impact of social media on their sense of confidence and ask them to consider reducing time on screens. Explain the following to your teen: "When we use social media passively, absorbing content rather than connecting to others or contributing original content, it can lead to declined satisfaction with our own life. When social media usage is fostering comparison and looking for positive feedback, it can be harmful to your mental health."[8]

## SETTING CLEAR SCREEN BOUNDARIES

Briefly, I want to offer some clear screen boundary options that you could offer your teen upon getting them a device, flowing from conversations about the benefits and drawbacks of screen and social media usage.

One of the key approaches with teens is collaboration. Ask your teen, "How much time per day of screen time do you feel that you need?"[9] Their answer may surprise you. It will be important to negotiate this with them if they overshoot it!

Use your own discernment when it comes to establishing media boundaries based on your own family rules and approach. This list is a starting point for you toward that goal:[10]

1.  Carve out a minimum of one hour of "no devices" each day outside of school hours.

2.  Set the expectation that parents will check and monitor devices periodically. This will not be done by "snooping" but as an open check weekly or biweekly.

3.  Invest in hobbies and access to activities to engage in things that bring joy, peace, and calm. (Offer financial support, or invite this option for birthday gifts or just-because gifts from others.)

4.  Set time limits on apps. (Look at how much usage is had currently, and set a goal for reduced use that is gradual.)

5.  Set aside time to be outside daily.

6.  Do not use phones during meal times (for any family members).

7.  Identify events or activities where phones aren't necessary or appropriate, and set limits around these events (e.g., leaving phones in the car at church services, family gatherings, etc.). In a communal context, if you are on the phone, when possible name why so as not to be perceived as rude or disengaged. Keep phone usage in these contexts to a minimum.

8.  Keep devices out of bedrooms. If phone usage is disrupting sleep habits, set a new bedtime routine. Charge devices in common areas.[11]

9.  Identify inappropriate behaviors, such as mocking others, sharing personal information without permission, and gossiping, and invite sharing of this with parents when a teen sees it happening.

10. Discuss the impact of social media and have open dialogue about when and how to step back when it is draining (even if this means temporarily deleting an app).

11. Turn on privacy settings, and turn off location sharing.

12. Do not share first and last name, address, phone number, social security number, passwords, and bank or credit/debit card information on social media.

13. Do not get on virtual video chat without being in a part of the home where parents can monitor when talking with an online friend.

14. Do not send nude images or discuss sexual content with peers or strangers.

For some readers, setting these boundaries will mean changing an already set-in-place habit. I would recommend you do this collaboratively with your teen, especially when it involves scaling back usage. The process will need to be gradual for some, and others will prefer to scale back usage abruptly. Whereas with younger kids, it is less necessary to co-create boundaries, as they get older, we will be more effective when we collaborate on a workable plan.

## IDENTIFYING AND DISCUSSING RISKY SITUATIONS

One of the best resources available for identifying harm on the internet is the Child Rescue Coalition (CRC). I have cited them throughout this resource, but I also want to invite you to download their free and easy-to-read resource for parents.[12] They define and help you respond to everything from grooming to experiences of abuse, and they give a play-by-play on how to establish privacy settings on video games.

If you only do one thing from this whole chapter, read and apply the content from the CRC parent resource.

One of many things this document offers is a list to help identify grooming behaviors that some predators will use on children and teens, called the "7 P's of Grooming."[13] Let's consider how these grooming behaviors might look in a social media context:

1. *Praise*: Flattering a young person in online comments or video gaming chats

2. *Precocious conversation*: Asking about personal information, including clothing, dating history, and sexual behavior

3. *Photo sharing*: Sharing revealing photos and making requests for images as well

4. *Privacy*: Requesting secrecy or deletion of content

5. *Pressure*: Blackmailing or making threats if a child stops sending images or videos or money, such as threatening to tell parents or police

6. *Presents*: Sending gifts, gift cards, or gaming-platform currency such as "Robux"

7. *Pulling away to control / possessiveness*: Threatening to end the relationship if the child doesn't pull away from others and make more time for them

When your teen begins using a phone, whether it's theirs or yours, initiate a conversation about how grooming can occur online. Try something like this:

> "Being online, in games or chats, can be a great way to connect with friends and feel seen and known. It can feel really good to meet people who like similar things and take an interest in us. Sometimes, people who get online try to take advantage of that feeling by gradually leading us to believe they can be trusted when they can't be. We call this grooming. Usually a person who grooms wants to make you feel uniquely special, and they will flatter you by telling you lots of nice things about yourself. Then, they will gradually ask you for personal information about yourself or your family, eventually asking things that are more sensitive, such as about your history of dating. They may try to share photos of themselves or ask for you to send photos or videos of yourself. Some people will even ask for naked photos or ask to text about sexual content. Have you ever heard of this being done?"

## IS CHECKING TEENS' DEVICES A VIOLATION OF PRIVACY?

Some teens and parents may worry that a parent checking a teen's device is a violation of the teen's privacy. The key is transparency and open conversation. I recommend making a rule that when a teen in your house owns a device, having a parent check it regularly is part of what the teen agrees to when they use the device. This way, you're not breaking trust and surprising a teen by telling them that you monitor their device only after you find something you're concerned about.

While it can help for teens to have some privacy as they begin to differentiate into adulthood, you can make it clear to them from the beginning that devices are not private spaces in your family.

Specialists in identifying child predators strongly challenge the idea that looking at your teenager's phone is snooping. One writer explains, "Think about it this way—would you be happy for your child to meet a 43-year-old strange man in a park while you stood only 10 or 15 yards away? Why should it be any different when your child is in their bedroom meeting a potential child predator online?" The writer goes on, "It is 100% YOUR right to check your child's devices. Please do it, and be proactive, positive and a part of the solution."[14]

## PROACTIVELY DISCUSSING NUDITY AND SEXUAL CONTENT

In chapter 5, we talked about introducing sexual behavior to your preteen and teen. Here's how you could have a conversation about nude photos and sexting, both relevant to device usage:

> "Some teens will talk about different sexual activities that aren't sexual intercourse. Two of these are nude photos and sexting. If you ever hear about these things, we can talk about them more so you understand them more. For now, I want you to know that people sometimes will ask for someone to send them a naked photo of themselves or a photo revealing parts of their private areas. Some people will try to send sexual information or talk about doing sexual activity in a text, on the phone, or in a video or anime, and sometimes they will do so without asking first. What would you want to do if someone asked to engage in those with you?
>
> "You can always tell your parents if that were to happen. Even if someone tells you you'll get in trouble for telling me, or they threaten to ruin your reputation or spread a lie about you, you will never get in trouble for telling the truth, okay?"

## WHEN YOU HAVEN'T HAD THE EARLIER CONVERSATIONS

This next section is especially for parents who haven't had the opportunity to have these earlier conversations when your teen first received a device. If your teen is already using apps that you don't fully understand and haven't vetted, I'd recommend asking your teen to temporarily pause their use of these apps until you've had a chance to learn more. Here's how you could move in this direction now:

> "We want to talk a bit about screen usage. We are taking some time to learn about social media, since we've realized we don't know enough about it and really haven't talked much about it with you. That means that we are going to need you to take a temporary pause from social media until we can learn a bit about how these platforms work. I know that is really frustrating, and it may be hard to pause. What do you think is a realistic amount of time for you to pause, to give us time to catch up and learn how this works?"

Once you set a time frame for you to get on these apps and see what they are about, invite your teen to show you around the application. This can be a bonding time of fun and play, while also being an informational time that doesn't require that you do a ton of research on your own.

## "THE HOUR CHALLENGE"

"The Hour Challenge" is putting aside your phone for the first hour after school or work. It means that you set a timer (on the kitchen oven or on your phone) and put the phone far away from your reach. Then do, well, anything else for an hour. (This is a great challenge to do with your teen!)

The goal of this challenge is to prepare your teen for the emotions they will experience when they stop using their phone. The first few days, they will likely feel more anxiety, loneliness, irritability. Eventually, they will likely begin to feel relief.[15]

What are some options to do with the time?

- Lie down and shut your eyes. It's not even important if you are able to sleep, but simply that you are engaging in intentional "rest" time.
- Return to a hobby you haven't picked up in a while.
- Learn a new hobby that is tech-free and requires low energy (paint by number, knitting, crafting).
- Pick something to learn how to build.

- Play solitary games such as Legos or solitaire.
- Sit in silence and mindfully do something (drink water, eat a snack, pray).
- Engage in mindful movement (stretch on the floor, go for a walk, throw a football with a friend or sibling).
- Do free drawing. Take a piece of paper and, using whatever medium you are drawn to, take some time to "contain" whatever comes up from the day onto the paper. Maybe you are feeling agitated and annoyed. Pick a color that captures that to you, and "show" the feelings on the page. Let yourself get lost in the act of getting it out. Keep these drawings, and look back on them later.

## RESPONDING TO CHALLENGING SITUATIONS AROUND MEDIA USAGE

Before this chapter comes to a close, I want to offer some common scenarios that can too often come up with families. We will look at a story where a teen was exchanging sexually explicit images with a girlfriend and at a situation where a teen received explicit images and content they did not ask for from others.

### SENDING SEXUALLY EXPLICIT IMAGES

Marcus, a fifteen-year-old, has been dating his girlfriend, Dori, the same age, for about six months. Marcus's dad, Hank, in checking through social media messages in the monthly check-in, came across a conversation between Marcus and Dori where Marcus asked Dori, "Can I get another picture?" The context for the exchange and a picture that had been sent made it clear that Marcus had figured out how to pass sexually explicit images with Dori on his social media without it getting caught in filters set on his device. What is the best way for Hank to address this type of situation?

1. *Describe the situation calmly*: "I saw that you and Dori have been exchanging photos on your app that are not appropriate, and it appears that you asked her for it. I want to talk with you about it and want to ask you to be as honest as possible about it."

2. *Validate the difficult emotions that can come up in this conversation and your goal for having it*: "I know this can be a difficult moment and conversation. You may feel embarrassed, defensive, and angry. I want you to know that I am not here to shame you, but to help you learn and move forward."

3. *Honor what might have prompted your child to make this request of some- one, and be curious about what contributed to it*: "I know you really like Dori, and it is normal to be curious about the body of the person you are dating, and even to wish to see them naked. There are lots of rea- sons why some people might ask for a picture, whether it's because we heard other friends doing it or saw it in movies or media, among other reasons. What contributed to you asking her?"

4. *Acknowledge the seriousness of this, and hold both the understandable desire and the importance of learning self-mastery over desire*: "It is very dangerous and serious to ask that of someone and is not ever an appropriate ask. Dori's body isn't an object to be used. As her boy- friend, it's actually your job to honor her body and show her by your behavior how worthy she is of being protected from use or harm. So, even while you may be curious about her body and wish to see her naked, it is important instead to refrain from asking for things that are not yours to receive. Even if a girl says she is comfortable with that, it is not okay to use her in that way."

5. *Check in with your teen*: "What are you learning as we talk about it? What are you willing to commit to when it comes to making changes in how you treat Dori?"

6. *Discuss next steps*: "What would you be willing to do to make amends to Dori? Because this happened, we will want to take a break from social media for two weeks, to help you focus on other things and get some space from that. Then, we can reevaluate."

## RECEIVING EXPLICIT CONTENT

Another scenario that is sadly all too common is when a teen receives unwanted images from someone or is pressured into sending explicit images. Many times, sexually explicit images received by a teen are actually *not* requested by the receiver. This is important to keep in mind, since it will allow you to stay curious and not assume that, because you see inappropriate sexual content on your teen's device, they requested it.

Trey's mom, Shaundell, was doing a monthly run-through of social media usage on her teen's phone. She came across some concerning messages Trey had been getting on one of the accounts he has.

Shaundell couldn't tell from the context of the discussion whether Trey had asked for these images and conversations or not. Trey had just moved to a new school and had been trying to make friends, but struggled to feel connected to his new community, so he had been spending a lot more time online recently. How should Shaundell address this situation?

1. *Describe the situation calmly*: "I saw there were some inappropriate images and comments coming through on your social media account from ___. I want to talk with you about it and want to ask you to be as honest as possible about it."

2. *Validate the difficult emotions that can come up in this conversation and your goal for having it*: "I know this can be a difficult moment and conversation. You may feel embarrassed, defensive, angry, and protective of the person who sent them. I want you to know that I am not here to shame you, but to help you learn and move forward."

3. *Clarify the situation, and prompt for whether the image was requested or not*: "Can you tell me what happened? Did they send this without your permission?"

4. *Acknowledge the seriousness of this, and hold both the understandable confusion, embarrassment, and shame around this and the importance of learning to set boundaries and cease contact with people engaging in these behaviors*: "It is very dangerous and serious for that person to send those images and say those things to you. That is not ever an appropriate behavior, and anytime anyone asks for images from you or sends images, know that it is not your fault and you can always tell me. You will never get in trouble if you let me know what is going on. I will help you figure out what to do."

5. *Check in with your teen*: "What are you learning as we talk about it? What are you feeling now?"

6. *Discuss next steps*: "It's important to block people who are engaging inappropriately online. Are you willing to do that now, and do you have concerns about doing that? If this ever were to happen again,

what could you do to make sure you have support and don't have to go through it alone?"

## CULTIVATING VIRTUE IN SOCIAL MEDIA USE

You will want to circle back after each of the above scenarios and continuously be active in your awareness of your teen's media usage in order to protect them from these difficulties, to the degree possible. Left to their own devices, teens will find themselves in precarious situations. With your help and active involvement, they can develop the skills needed to more effectively use media and technology into adulthood.

Social media is a place that doesn't demand anything of us other than passive reception of its content. It's an escape, a great dissociative device, and a way to numb discomfort. It is also an access point to a world of information, entertainment, and community. These factors, among many others, make it incredibly difficult for many of us to step away from it. As we raise kids with screens in such close proximity to them, we must be careful not to expect from them a degree of self-discipline that we have not yet helped them cultivate. Like the cultivation of all virtue, this is an area for guidance, practice, and patience along the way.

If you're intimidated by the magnitude of this task, take courage! God is not surprised by our media age. He will help us find a way forward, both for us and for our children. With proactive conversations when possible, responsive conversations when necessary, and active involvement in our teens' lives, we can help our teens develop into adulthood with less shame, more confidence, and protection from some of the harms that can come through media sources.

# EPILOGUE

The primary goal of being a parent is to raise saints. The path to sanctity, or holiness, is oriented toward Christlikeness. Equipping our children for a life of holiness does not mean we can shield them from suffering or promise them a life of ease. Yet it does mean obeying Christ's command to protect the "little ones" from stumbling. In doing so, we open up opportunities for the Lord to enter in. His love covers a multitude of sins, to be sure, but he is also clear in saying, "Whoever causes one of these little ones who believe in me to sin, it would be better for him to have a great millstone fastened round his neck and to be drowned in the depth of the sea" (Matthew 18:6).

Raising teens to become saints involves everything from initiating proactive conversations to responding in moments when the unpredictable happens. When I think about the sacred task of raising teens, I remember the lives of so many saints who died in or soon after their teen years. We must not underestimate the capacity of our teens for holiness, a life infused with spiritual gifts, and wisdom beyond their years. The fruits of the Spirit that flow from the Sacraments of Initiation allow our teens to live in love, joy, peace, forbearance, kindness, goodness, faithfulness, gentleness, and self-control (see Galatians 5:22–23). Forming teens to effectively radiate these fruits by their lives is no small task. It is your most important parental work.

Our faith offers us rich guidance in how to become saints in every area of our lives, include our sex and sexuality. While this book is meant to help you guide your teens on this journey, it is also—like every book—incomplete. You are leaving with some questions answered (I hope) and many others, no doubt, unanswered. This, I hope, can be a reminder that we have need for the Lord to guide us. We have need for him to send his Spirit upon us as we seek to raise teens. There is none other than Christ who can save us, and he promised to send his Holy Spirit among us to be with us always, wherever life takes us and our children (see John 14:16).

Fear not, for Christ is with us always and is not scandalized by the current age. I write these final words on the Feast of Pentecost, which feels fitting. Parenting out of fear can be its own "upper room" that feels safe initially but can stifle the Spirit's work. Stepping out in trust in the provision of God gives way to miracles. With this in mind, we bring our reflections to a close and invite the Holy Spirit to infuse us with greater courage, understanding, and clarity to navigate all that is to come as we raise the next generation.

I pray that the words of Pope Benedict XVI on Pentecost can be our prayer:

> The Holy Spirit overcomes fear. We know that the disciples sought shelter in the Upper Room after the arrest of their Lord and that they remained isolated for fear of suffering the same fate. After Jesus' Resurrection their fear was not suddenly dispelled. But here at Pentecost, when the Holy Spirit rested upon them, those men emerged fearless and began to proclaim the Good News of the crucified and risen Christ to all. They were not afraid because they felt they were in the hands of the strongest One. Yes, wherever the Spirit of God enters he puts fear to flight; he makes us know and feel that we are in the hands of an Omnipotence of love. His infinite love does not abandon us. It is demonstrated by the witness of martyrs, the courage of confessors of the faith, the undaunted zeal of missionaries, the frankness of preachers, and the example of all the saints, even some who were adolescents and children. It is demonstrated by the very existences of the Church, which despite the limitations and sins of men and women continues to cross the ocean of

history, blown by the breath of God and enlivened by his purifying fire. With this faith and joyful hope let us repeat today, through the intercession of Mary: *"Send forth your Spirit, O Lord, and renew the face of the earth."*[1]

Come, Holy Spirit! Fill our hearts with your love, and infuse us with supernatural graces to love well those entrusted to our care.

Deuteronomy offers a final word of encouragement for us as well: "Only take heed, and keep your soul diligently, lest you forget the things which your eyes have seen, and lest they depart from your heart all the days of your life; make them known to your children and your children's children" (Deuteronomy 4:9).

May we teach all that we have learned together to our children and have the privilege of seeing our children's children. May all of us lean into the call to hold fast to the faith, savor the truths of the Gospel, and share them with peace, joy, and hope as long as we live.

# ACKNOWLEDGMENTS

This book flowed from countless conversations with dear friends, family, and clients who trusted me with questions and musings about raising healthy and holy teens. In this book you will find my reflections alongside the wisdom of too many people to name who have blessed me with the opportunity to journey with them through this life. All names and stories included in this book have been changed and significant details have been tweaked to respect the confidentiality of all people who have entrusted their stories to me. Many of the stories are a synthesis of several stories of people I have known or met with clinically, to honor confidentiality and privacy of friends, family, and clients.

As I wrap up this project, I owe particular thanks to my mentor, colleague, and friend—Dr. Mark Yarhouse. Thank you for being a reliable guide and encouragement to me over the years and for the intangible and tangible ways you have invested in me. (My iceberg drawings improve with each passing day!) Without your support, I would not be who and where I am as a psychologist and as a Christian.

Thank you to all the friends, colleagues, and family who instilled hope in me and were patient with me as I brought this project to completion. In a particular way, thank you to Anna Heling, LCSW; Lauren Accolla, LMFT; Jason Evert; and Dr. Lexie Hammerquist for taking time to mull through these pages and offer your insights. Thank you also to Maggie Spooner, who worked diligently to help with the formatting of this manuscript. Dr. Gregory Coles was there for me as an editor and friend all along the way, making my musings into comprehensible prose when it counted, as usual!

Working with Ave Maria Press yet again has been a blessing in every sense of the word. Kristi McDonald, Karey Circosta, and their team managed to turn what was once intended to be a single book into a two-book series. Kristi's belief in me and willingness to think through the nitty-gritty details gave me stamina throughout.

Finally, I want to thank the teen clients and families whom I have had the privilege to walk with over these years. I often feel unworthy to be in the presence of so many lights in what can feel like a dark world. I feel grateful for the countless moments of healing that you have courageously invited me into. I pray God infuses you with the experience of his gaze as you enter more deeply into the knowledge of his love for you. We need only to let ourselves be loved by him.[1] On behalf of all who have failed to reflect his love to you, I am sorry. We need more Christians like you.

# APPENDIX

## RESOURCES REGARDING MENTAL HEALTH, COPING, AND BOUNDARIES

### BOOKS ON MINDFULNESS

Gregory Bottaro, *The Mindful Catholic: Finding God One Moment at a Time.*

### BOOKS ON TEACHING COPING FOR TEENS

Sissy Goff, *Braver, Stronger, Smarter: A Girl's Guide to Overcoming Worry and Anxiety.*

### BOOKS ON TEACHING COPING AND SETTING BOUNDARIES FOR PARENTS

Sissy Goff, *The Worry-Free Parent: Living in Confidence So Your Kids Can Too.*
Lysa Terkeurst, *Good Boundaries and Goodbyes: Loving Others Without Losing the Best of Who You Are.*

## RESOURCES REGARDING TRAUMA AND PROCESSING

### BOOKS

Aundi Kolber, *Try Softer: A Fresh Approach to Move Us out of Anxiety, Stress, and Survival Mode—and into a Life of Connection and Joy.*
Bessel van der Kolk, *The Body Keeps the Score: Brain, Mind, and Body in the Healing of Trauma.*
Allison Cook, *The Best of You: Break Free from Painful Patterns, Mend Your Past, and Discover Your True Self in God.*

Pete Walker, *Complex PTSD: From Surviving to Thriving*.

Lindsay C. Gibson, *Adult Children of Emotionally Immature Parents: How to Heal from Distant, Rejecting, or Self-Involved Parents; Recovering from Emotionally Immature Parents: Practical Tools to Establish Boundaries and Reclaim Your Emotional Autonomy*.

Aundi Kolber, *Strong Like Water*.

Mark Wolynn, *It Didn't Start with You: How Inherited Family Trauma Shapes Who We Are and How to End the Cycle*.

Richard Schwartz, *No Bad Parts: Healing Trauma and Restoring Wholeness with the Internal Family Systems Model*.

## PODCASTS
*The Place We Find Ourselves*
*Matthias J. Barker Podcast*

## RESOURCES REGARDING SHAME AND VULNERABILITY
Curt Thompson, *The Soul of Shame*.

Brene Brown, *The Power of Vulnerability: Teachings of Authenticity, Connection, and Courage; The Gifts of Imperfection*.

## RESOURCES REGARDING PORNOGRAPHY / SEXUAL SELF-HATRED / COMPULSIVE SEXUAL BEHAVIORS
### BOOKS
Jay Stringer, *Unwanted: How Sexual Brokenness Reveals Our Way to Healing*.

Patrick Carnes, *Out of the Shadows; Facing the Shadow; Sexual Anorexia; In the Shadows of the Net; Contrary to Love: Helping the Sex Addict*.

### BOOKS FOR WOMEN SPECIFICALLY
Marnie Ferree, *No Stones: Women Redeemed from Sexual Addiction*.

Rachael Killackey, *Love in Recovery: One Woman's Story of Breaking Free from Shame and Healing from Pornography Addiction*.

## RESOURCES REGARDING TECHNOLOGY USE/ PROTECTING TEENS FROM INAPPROPRIATE ONLINE CONTENT
Common Sense Media
Child Rescue Coalition
Andy Crouch, *The Tech-Wise Family*

## RESOURCES REGARDING TALKING WITH YOUR TEEN ABOUT SEXUALITY

Conversations about L.I.F.E. Program (GetFamiliesTalking.org)
GivingtheTalk.com

## RESOURCES REGARDING GENDER

Mark Yarhouse, *Understanding Gender Dysphoria.*
Mark Yarhouse and Julia Sadusky, *Emerging Gender Identities: Understanding the Diverse Experiences of Today's Youth.*
Mark Yarhouse and Julia Sadusky, *Gender Identity and Faith: Clinical Postures, Tools, and Case Studies for Client-Centered Care.*
Abigail Favale, *The Genesis of Gender.*

## RESOURCES REGARDING SAME-SEX SEXUALITY

### ORGANIZATIONS

Eden Invitation
Revoice
Center for Faith, Sexuality and Gender
Posture Shift
Kaleidoscope
EQUIP

### BOOKS

Eve Tushnet, *Gay and Catholic; Tenderness.*
Greg Coles, *Single, Gay and Christian; No Longer Strangers.*
Greg Johnson, *Still Time to Care: What We Can Learn from the Church's Failed Attempt to Cure Homosexuality.*
Wesley Hill, *Washed and Waiting; Spiritual Friendship.*
Matt and Laurie Krieg, *An Impossible Marriage.*
Caleb Kaltenbach, *Messy Grace; Messy Truth.*
Mark Yarhouse and Olya Zaporozhets, *Costly Obedience; When Children Come Out.*
Mark Yarhouse, *Understanding Sexual Identity.*
Mark Yarhouse, Janet Dean, Michael Lastoria, and Stephen Stratton, *Listening to Sexual Minorities.*

### PODCASTS

*Dear Alana,*
*Life on Side B*

# NOTES

## INTRODUCTION

1. "The family, a natural society, exists prior to the State or any other community, and possesses inherent rights which are inalienable; the family constitutes, much more than a mere juridical, social and economic unit, a community of love and solidarity, which is uniquely suited to teach and transmit cultural, ethical, social, spiritual and religious values, essential for the development and well-being of its own members and of society; the family is the place where different generations come together and help one another to grow in human wisdom and to harmonize the rights of individuals with other demands of social life; the family and society, which are mutually linked by vital and organic bonds, have a complementary function in the defense and advancement of the good of every person and of humanity." Holy See, *Charter of the Rights of the Family*, October 22, 1983, https://www.vatican.va/roman_curia/pontifical_councils/family/documents/rc_pc_family_doc_19831022_family-rights_en.html.

2. "Leaving Catholicism," Pew Research, April 26, 2022, https://www.pewresearch.org/religion/2009/04/27/faith-in-flux3/;

"Most Teenagers Drop Out of Church When They Become Young Adults," Lifeway Research, August 11, 2021, https://research.lifeway.com/2019/01/15/most-teenagers-drop-out-of-church-as-young-adults/.

3. Pope Paul VI, *Gaudium et Spes* [Pastoral Constitution on the Church in the Modern World], December 7, 1965, no. 24, https://www.vatican.va/archive/hist_councils/ii_vatican_council/documents/vat-ii_const_19651207_gaudium-et-spes_en.html.

## 1. "WHY AM I HAVING SUCH A HARD TIME STARTING THE CONVERSATION?"

1. Adam Young, host, "Why It's So Important to Understand Your Story," *The Place We Find Ourselves* (podcast), October 2022, https://open.spotify.com/episode/1LenL11OvDI4mxWRWSJeJZ?si=60c9ea0064194d02.

2. Jay Stringer and Adam Young, hosts, "How Your Story Affects Your Sexuality," *The Place We Find Ourselves* (podcast), March 23, 2023, https://open.spotify.com/episode/2x2HJKNpx8WLG1EusfA6zY?si=9b5237becbef4ad6.

3. This approach, called Narrative Therapy, is a way to integrate one's life experience into a coherent narrative and externalize various experiences to gain perspective and glean new wisdom from them.

4. All names included in this book have been changed and significant details have been tweaked to respect the confidentiality of all people who have entrusted their stories to me. Many of the stories are a synthesis of several stories of people I have known or met with clinically, in order to honor confidentiality and privacy of friends, family, and clients.

5. This quote is adapted from a talk by Fr. Boniface Hicks to priests, given at Mundelein Seminary. "Ravished Sacred Heart Prayer," FatherBoniface.org, August 23, 2022, https://fatherboniface.org/audio/2022/22-08-21%20Mundelein%20Seminary%20Retreat%20On%20The%20Heart/20220823%204%20Conf%20Ravished%20Sacred%20Heart%20Prayer.m4a.

## 2. "WHAT IS HAPPENING TO MY SON'S BODY?"

1. Deborah Guardado, "The Male Reproductive System," ThingLink, accessed May 7, 2023, https://www.thinglink.com/scene/896477526635839489.

2. Abvie, "Normal Puberty Development," PubertyTooSoon.com, accessed May 7, 2023, https://www.pubertytoosoon.com/about-cpp/normal-puberty-development?cid=ppc_ppd_msft_CPP_DA_Do_I_Have_puberty_in_girls_before_age_Phrase_US-LUPR-210569&&msclkid=c10fdb08e0f211f856bcb89c35c2c954&gclid=COLe5ZHc7_sCFWOyxQIds7IP8w&gclsrc=ds.

## 3. "WHAT IS HAPPENING TO MY DAUGHTER'S BODY?"

1. "Normal Puberty Development," PubertyTooSoon.com, accessed May 7, 2023, https://www.pubertytoosoon.com/about-cpp/normal-puberty-development?cid=ppc_ppd_msft_CPP_DA_Do_I_Have_puberty_in_girls_before_age_Phrase_US-LUPR-210569&&msclkid=c10fdb08e0f211f856bcb89c35c2c954&gclid=COLe5ZHc7_sCFWOyxQIds7IP8w&gclsrc=ds.

2. David Austen, *Young People, Pornography & Age-Verification* (Revealing Reality, 2020), https://revealingreality.co.uk/wp-content/uploads/2020/01/BBFC-Young-people-and-pornography-Final-report-2401.pdf.

3. Antonia Pérez Villa, "What Happens in Female Reproductive System?," HelpUandfun, January 24, 2017, https://helpuandfun.blogspot.com/2017/01/what-happens-in-female-reproductive.html.

4. Some young women may prefer to figure out how to use tampons, pads, or other items on their own out of a sense of independence or may prefer to

have a medical professional help with explaining the process further. For those teens who have a history of sexual trauma, it will be important to attune to this and consider utilizing the support of a therapist to help your daughter work towards building her comfort level with menstruation and bodily changes, as these changes can trigger feelings of powerlessness, loss of control, and fear.

## 5. "HOW DO I ACTUALLY HAVE THE SEX TALK?"

1. "Talking with Your Teens about Sex," CDC, November 21, 2019, https://www.cdc.gov/healthyyouth/protective/factsheets/talking_teens.htm.

2. Birds & Bees, Instagram post, June 3, 2022, https://www.instagram.com/birds__bees/.

3. Thank you to Jason Evert for your contributions in this chapter and specifically for your language here.

## 6. "WHAT ABOUT MASTURBATION?"

1. "Masturbation and Young Children," Mott Children, November 2020, https://www.mottchildren.org/posts/your-child/masturbation-and-young-children.

2. Cynthia Robbins, Vanessa Schick, Reece Michael, Debra Herbenick, Stephanie Sanders, Brian Dodge, and J. Dennis Fortenberry, "Prevalence, Frequency, and Associations of Masturbation with Partnered Sexual Behaviors among US Adolescents," *Archives of Pediatrics & Adolescent Medicine* (December 2011): 1087–93.

3. Some messages about chastity too often overpromise that if you "follow the rules," you are guaranteed a meaningful marriage. This "prosperity gospel" model of faith contrasts the reality of the Christian life. We can follow the commands of God and still suffer in this world. We are not guaranteed a robust sex life by virtue of living chastely, even if we can also know that chastity does help us discover the meaning of our bodies more fully. There is still work to be done in marriage to help a couple foster the sexual life that is rich and meaningful.

4. Speak with your physician about warning signs for testicular cancer and be sure to discuss this in a way that does not cause undue fear. Regular physicals will also allow for monitoring of this.

## 7. "WHAT ABOUT PORNOGRAPHY?"

1. David Austen, *Young People, Pornography & Age-Verification* (Revealing Reality, 2020), https://revealingreality.co.uk/wp-content/uploads/2020/01/BBFC-Young-people-and-pornography-Final-report-2401.pdf.

2. Austen, *Young People, Pornography & Age-Verification.*

3. This table provides a summary of findings from a 2020 report on pornography use in youth: Austen, *Young People, Pornography & Age-Verification.*

4. Apps include Bark, Aura, Qustodio, and Accountable2You. See Bark, https://www.bark.us/learn/ps-block-adult-content/?msclkid=86636e ae97f21dac0a990d552055170f&utm_source=bing&utm_medium=cpc&utm_campaign=Search+US+%7C+Catch+All&utm_term=accountability+ap

p&utm_content=Accountability+%7C+General. Aura, "Protect Your Kids Online with Parental Controls," accessed May 14, 2023, https://buy.aura.com/parental-controls-2?irclickid=2xBVPyyBBxyNWceRwL37OzQZU kAUy10lL0TYx80&iradname=Gtwy-PC+-+PC+Family+Bundle+Dedicat ed-+no+price&iradid=1555907&irgwc=1&c1=34020&camp=12398&utm_ source=top10&utm_medium=ir_affiliate&mktp=IR_Affiliates&sharedid=&utm_ gateway=parental-controls. Qustodio, https://www.qustodio.com/en/ premium/. Scot Chadwick, "Overcome Pornography through Accountabili- ty," Accountable2You,December 7, 2021, https://accountable2you.com/blog/ overcome-pornography/.

5. Fight the New Drug is one significant resource taking the lead in research- ing pornography, talking about its impacts, and discussing the responsibility we have to one another in reducing the demand for porn. They are a secular organization that elevates important information in this space. They have a documentary series, *Brain, Heart, World*, that would be helpful to share with teens to springboard conversations in this area.

## 8. "HOW DO WE RESPOND TO CRUSHES AND DATING?"

1. "Basics of Teen Romantic Relationships," Pew Research, Octo- ber 1, 2015, https://www.pewresearch.org/internet/2015/10/01/ basics-of-teen-romantic-relationships/.

2. Through the Sacraments of Initiation, all are called to "holiness and to the mission of evangelizing the world . . . as pilgrims on the march towards the homeland." *Catechism of the Catholic Church*, 2nd ed. (Washington, DC: United States Catholic Conference, 2011), 1533, accessed May 13, 2023, https://www. usccb.org/sites/default/files/flipbooks/catechism/.

3. No matter your particular vocation, "Christ is the center of all Christian life. The bond with him takes precedence over all other bonds, familial or social." Whether we find ourselves discerning permanent singleness, in a state of single- ness, or discerning marriage or religious orders, the meaning of these callings is found in Christ. The *Catechism* is clear that "esteem of virginity for the sake of the kingdom and the Christian understanding of marriage are inseparable, and they reinforce each other." *Catechism of the Catholic Church*, 1618, 1620.

4. This mirrors the wedding vows said on a person's wedding day in a Cath- olic marriage ceremony. Long before a young person who is called to marriage enters it, you can begin to plant seeds about its purpose.

5. It is important to note that age ranges provided here are general recom- mendations, and the specific age that is appropriate for your teen will vary. Age-appropriateness can depend on many factors, including your teen's devel- opmental level, exposure to sexual content, degree of social media use, and other factors. Adjustments also may need to be made for neurodivergent youth.

6. Susan Sprecher, Lucia F. O'Sullivan, Michelle Drouin, Julie Verette- Lindenbaum, and Marion C. Willetts, "Perhaps It Was Too Soon: College Stu- dents' Reflections on the Timing of Their Sexual Debut," *Journal of Sex Research* 59, no. 1 (March 2021): 39–52.

7. "Over Half of U.S. Teens Have Had Sexual Intercourse by Age 18, New Report Shows," CDC, June 22, 2018, https://www.cdc.gov/nchs/pressroom/nchs_press_releases/2017/201706_NSFG.htm.

## 9. "HOW DO I TALK WITH MY CHILD ABOUT GAY PEOPLE?"

1. In this chapter, I will use "experience same-sex attraction," "same sex desire," and "experience same-sex sexuality" intermittently, to account for a range of ways people may use language to communicate their attraction patterns.

2. Casey Copen, Anjani Chandra, and Isaedmarie Febo-Vazquez, *Sexual Behavior, Sexual Attraction, and Sexual Orientation among Adults Aged 18–44 in the United States: Data from the 2011–2013 National Survey of Family Growth* (National Health Statistics Reports, 2016), 1–13.

3. The most recent Gallup Poll study (2022) indicated that 1% of US adults identify as lesbian, 1.4% as gay, and 4.2% as bisexual, which means that 6.6% of US adults in 2022 identified as LGB. Jeffrey M. Jones, "U.S. LGBT Identification Steady at 7.2%," *Gallup*, February 22, 2023, https://news.gallup.com/poll/470708/lgbt-identification-steady.aspx.

4. J. L. Stewart, Leigh A. Spivey, Laura Widman, Sophia Choukas-Bradley, and Mitchell J. Prinstein, "Developmental Patterns of Sexual Identity, Romantic Attraction, and Sexual Behavior among Adolescents over Three Years." *Journal of Adolescence* 77 (December 2019): 90–97.

5. There have been steady increases in the percentage of Americans who identify as LGBT. In 2022, the percentage of Americans identifying as LGBT was 7.2%. This had doubled since 2012, when the percentage was 3.5%. Jones, "U.S. LGBT Identification Steady at 7.2%."

6. The *Spiritual Friendship* blog has wrestled with this robustly and for many years. They have an entire section of their blog that attends to the language debate. Eve Tushnet also addresses this in her book *Gay and Catholic: Accepting My Sexuality, Finding Community, Living My Faith* (Notre Dame, IN: Ave Maria Press, 2014). Daniel Mattson, once a figure with some prominence who was involved with Courage, wrote a 2012 article and a 2017 book called, *Why I Don't Call Myself Gay: How I Reclaimed My Sexual Reality and Found Peace* (San Francisco, CA: Ignatius Press, 2017). Mattson is no longer being cited as an exemplar in these spaces and has since parted ways with Courage. Ron Belgau, a respected voice in this conversation, responded to Courage's approach on language in the following article: "Why I Don't Call Myself a Gay Christian," *First Things*, July 27, 2012, https://www.firstthings.com/web-exclusives/2012/07/why-i-dont-call-myself-a-gay-christian. See also Ron Belgau, "A Note on Courage and Language," June 17, 2019, https://spiritualfriendship.org/2019/05/24/a-note-on-courage-and-language/#more-9698.

7. *Catechism of the Catholic Church*, 2nd ed. (Washington, DC: United States Catholic Conference, 2011), 2357, accessed May 13, 2023, https://www.usccb.org/sites/default/files/flipbooks/catechism/.

8. The following article reflects on the breadth of research on sexual orientation causal theories up to that time. While I do not agree with every conclusion drawn in the review by the authors, it offers a helpful summation of the range of research available regarding causal theories. Michael J. Bailey, Paul L. Vasey, Lisa M. Diamond, S. Marc Breedlove, Eric Vilain, and Marc Epprecht, "Sexual Orientation, Controversy, and Science," *Psychological Science in the Public Interest* (October 2016): 45–101.

9. I first heard the analogy of moving from coast to coast in the realm of causal arguments from Mark Yarhouse in talks and trainings around this conversation.

10. This is especially helpful since well-meaning adult supports, including priests, religious, and trusted adults, can be less helpful when they try to talk with minors in spiritual direction, Confession, or other avenues about the causal pathways related to sexual orientation. Helping your teen know how to handle these moments will be important, since many teens have been negatively impacted by conversations that focus on causal questions at the expense of helping support a teen in virtuous living in the midst of their experience, regardless of how it came to be.

11. If you are interested in learning about the research on sexual orientation change, there is a book by Mark Yarhouse that reviews a line of research around ministry groups that looked at sexual orientation change in their members. Stanton Jones and Mark Yarhouse, *Ex-Gays?: An Extended Longitudinal Study of Attempted Religiously Mediated Change in Sexual Orientation* (Downers Grove, IL: Intervarsity Press Academic, 2007), 1–11.

12. Greg Johnson, *Still Time to Care: What We Can Learn from the Church's Failed Attempt to Cure Homosexuality* (Grand Rapids, MI: Zondervan, 2021).

13. Research by Lisa Diamond accounts for the notion of fluidity in women when it comes to sexual attraction: Lisa Diamond, *Sexual Fluidity: Understanding Women's Love and Desire* (Cambridge, MA: Harvard University Press, 2009)

14. Jones and Yarhouse, *Ex-Gays?*, 1–11.

15. Sexual orientation change efforts (SOCE) are illegal therapeutic practices in a range of states and are strongly discouraged by the bodies that license mental-health professionals. While I am generally not a proponent of legislation around therapeutic practices, I can appreciate why the SOCE legislation has been introduced. I have worked with a range of clients who were harmed by SOCE, particularly when they entered into these programs as minors. There are competent therapists who can support your teen in exploring their values and experiences to live with sexual desires in a value-congruent way. Mark Yarhouse's Sexual Identity Therapy is a model that is a third option distinct from gay-affirmative care and distinct from SOCE. There are organizations within Catholic circles that unfortunately still promote a model for therapy and pastoral care that assumes sexual minorities ought to be healed of their attractions in order to glorify God more fully. This frames heterosexuality as a sign of greater virtue or holiness, which is certainly not the case. It seems advantageous to make the focus of pastoral care around virtuous living, not attraction shifts, per se. See the *Dear Alana*, podcast series for thoughtful reflections on the impact of sexual

orientation change efforts on the mental health of Christians who identify as LGB. Simon Kent Fung, *Dear Alana,*. Tenderfoot TV, August 13, 2023.

16. Courage International has been known to take a strong stance that identity language is unhelpful and recommends using "same-sex attracted" or "struggling with same-sex attraction." Individuals within the Catholic Church have advocated for this perspective as well. Others, like Eden Invitation, do not prescribe language to those involved in their ministry, while being faithful to Church teaching that reminds us that none of us can be reduced to our sexual orientation alone. *Spiritual Friendship* has housed significant conversations about the use of labels as well. Helpful dialogues exist where people such as Greg Coles and Rachel Gilson reflect on the importance of language and how they hold the use of language differently in their own experiences of same-sex desire.

17. Abigail Favale explores the preservation of the good in feminism in much greater depth in her book, *The Genesis of Gender: A Christian Theory* (San Francisco, CA: Ignatius Press, 2022).

18. In the Vatican's 1986 document on the pastoral care for homosexual persons, the language used was "homosexual persons," since "homosexual" was a common term at the time. While "homosexual" is not often used in common vernacular, it has been replaced with terms such as "gay person," "lesbian person," or "bisexual person." We have not seen magisterium documents emerge that address the language debate as of yet. See Congregation for the Doctrine of the Faith, "Letter to the Bishops of the Catholic Church on the Pastoral Care of Homosexual Persons," Vatican.va, October 1, 1986, https://www.vatican.va/roman_curia/congregations/cfaith/documents/rc_con_cfaith_doc_19861001_homosexual-persons_en.html.

19. From this multifaceted approach there are numerous advantages to be gained, not the least of which is the realization that a homosexual person, as every human being, deeply needs to be nourished at many different levels simultaneously. The human person, made in the image and likeness of God, can hardly be adequately described by a reductionist reference to his or her sexual orientation. Everyone living on the face of the earth has personal problems and difficulties, but challenges to growth, strengths, talents, and gifts as well. Today, the Church provides a badly needed context for the care of the human person when she refuses to consider the person solely as a "heterosexual" or a "homosexual" and insists that every person has a fundamental identity: the creature of God, and by grace, his child and heir to eternal life. See "Letter to the Bishops of the Catholic Church on the Pastoral Care of Homosexual Persons."

20. St. Thomas Aquinas. *Summa Theologiae*, I-II, Question 26, Article 4, Retrieved from https://www.newadvent.org/summa/2026.htm.

21. See John 15:13.

22. This insight incorporates a quote displayed later on in this chapter from Jean Coles, a Christian mother who recounts how she responded when her son came out as gay, which is displayed in the following resource: Mark Yarhouse and Olya Zaporozhets, *When Children Come Out: A Guide for Christian Parents* (Downers Grove, IL: IVP Academic, 2022), 10.

23. If you are not Catholic, you could consider the following to be a "biblical" understanding or a Christian understanding of sexual morality more broadly, although certain explanations of Church teaching are not shared by all Christian traditions, which is why I distinguish a Catholic ethic by name here.

24. This quote is a quote from Jean Coles, a Christian mother who recounts how she responded when her son came out as gay. Yarhouse and Zaporozhets, *When Children Come Out*, 10.

25. The most helpful book I have found on spirituality for sexual minorities is Eve Tushnet's *Tenderness*. Eden Invitation is a Catholic faith community that helps LGB-identified and same-sex-attracted Catholics grow in community, intimacy, and spiritual maturity. They have many resources on their website: "Resources," Eden Invitation, accessed May 12, 2023, https://www.edeninvitation.com/resources.

26. This reference to "beneath the surface" comes from an idea that was initially developed by Mark Yarhouse, which involves using an iceberg metaphor for understanding the deeper questions of sexual minority youth. The "tip of the iceberg," what we usually see, includes the questions, behaviors, and labels of sexual minority youth. What lies "beneath the surface" are a person's spiritual questions about belonging, identity, community, purpose, and intimacy. We want to focus relationships and ministry on answering the questions beneath the surface, even when teens may not be explicitly asking those questions of us.

27. There are many Christians who provide helpful models to Christian sexual minorities. Henri Nouwen is one writer who experienced same-sex attraction and was faithful to the Lord in his vocation. More modern writers and speakers include Eve Tushnet, Greg Coles, Wesley Hill, Nate Collins, Laurie Krieg, Meg Batz, and *Life on Side B* podcast hosts, among others. They offer a variety of models for young people who can begin to envision a life in the Church through the witness of fellow Christians.

28. *Catechism of the Catholic Church*, 2359.

29. One of the most helpful books for parents looking for guidance on how to respond when you become aware of your child's sexual orientation is *When Children Come Out* by Mark Yarhouse and Olya Zaporozhets. Informed by extensive research with Christian parents and families, it will be a deep dive into how to process this news as parents. Another helpful resource is *Guiding Families*, from Posture Shift, which is targeted more toward a Protestant readership. *Guiding Families of LGBT Loved Ones: For Every Pastor and Parent and All Who Care*, (Houston, TX: Posture Shift Books, 2023).

30. This is a quote by Greg and Lynn McDonald who founded Embracing the Journey, a Protestant ministry for parents after a loved one comes out as gay or transgender. For more on their ministry, follow them at www.embracingthejourney.org.

31. This information comes from Mark Yarhouse and Olya Zaporozhets's book *When Children Come Out*. This book flows from a line of research looking at the experiences of Christian parents following a disclosure of same-sex sexuality by their child. See Yarhouse and Zaporozhets, *When Children Come Out*, 6.

## 10. "HOW DO I TALK WITH MY CHILD ABOUT TRANSGENDER PEOPLE?"

1. Leanna Mah, Yvonne Y. Chan, and Jennifer H. Yang, "Gender Identity in Disorders of Sex Development," *Principles of Gender-Specific Medicine* (2017): 27–43.

2. Abigail Favale coins this phrase in *The Genesis of Gender* to describe the theory of gender that is widely ascribed to in American society today. The gender paradigm asserts that gender is a social construction alone, and that there are no essential male/female differences. Within this paradigm, gender is fluid, and thus there are and could be endless gender identities and endless sexual orientations as a result. Abigail Favale, *The Genesis of Gender: A Christian Theory* (San Francisco, CA: Ignatius Press, 2022)

3. Mark Yarhouse and Julia Sadusky, *Emerging Gender Identities: Understanding the Diverse Experiences of Today's Youth* (Grand Rapids, MI: Brazos Press, 2020).

4. Deb is a pseudonym, but I use "they/them" pronouns here because that is what Deb requested during our conversations during the brief consultation.

5. I use "he/him" pronouns here because Jacob and I agreed to use these pronouns in our conversations as he was using "he/him" pronouns in nearly all contexts throughout therapy, while exploring various labels and language.

## 11. "WHAT IF THEY TELL ME SOMETHING BAD HAPPENED TO THEM?"

1. "Children and Teens: Statistics," Rainn, accessed May 12, 2023, https://www.rainn.org/statistics/children-and-teens.

2. Marjorie Sable, Fran Danis, Denise Mauzy, and Sarah Gallagher, "Barriers to Reporting Sexual Assault for Women and Men: Perspectives of College Students," *Journal of American College Health* 55, no. 3 (November–December 2006): 157–62.

3. Aundi Kolber, *Try Softer: A Fresh Approach to Move Us out of Anxiety, Stress, and Survival Mode—And into a Life of Connection and Joy* (Carol Stream, IL: Tyndale Refresh, 2020): 25-29; Allison Cook, *The Best of You: Break Free from Painful Patterns, Mend Your Past, and Discover Your True Self in God* (Nashville, TN: Nelson Books, 2022): 26–32.

## 12. "HOW DO I NAVIGATE TECHNOLOGY ACCESS?"

1. "Teens, Social Media, and Technology," Pew Research, May 31, 2018, https://www.pewresearch.org/internet/2018/05/31/teens-social-media-technology-2018/#vast-majority-of-teens-have-access-to-a-home-computer-or-smartphone.

2. Sheri Madigan, Vanessa Villani, Corry Azzopardi, Danae Laut, Tanya Smith, Jeff R. Temple, Dillon Browne, and Gina Dimitropoulos, "The Prevalence of Unwanted Online Sexual Exposure and Solicitation Among Youth: A Meta-Analysis," *Journal of Adolescent Health* 63, no. 2 (August 2018): 133–41.

3. Much of the list of positives below is adapted from clinical experience and draws from the 2018 Pew Research study findings in "Teens, Social Media, and Technology," where teens reported the positive reasons for their understanding that social media has a mostly positive effect.

4. "Teens, Social Media, and Technology."

5. "Teens, Social Media, and Technology."

6. In a health advisory on social media use in adolescence, the American Psychological Association (APA) recently offered important guidelines for media usage with teens. See "APA Panel Issues Recommendations for Adolescent Social Media Use," APA.org, May 9, 2023, https://www.apa.org/news/press/releases/2023/05/adolescent-social-media-use-recommendations#:~:text=Limit%20social%20media%20use%20so,%2D%20or%20appearance%2Drelated%20content. Additionally, the *New York Times* came out with a valuable article on the subject that offers additional prompts and questions that can be useful to incorporate in your conversations with your teens. See Catherine Pearson, "How Parents Can Help Teens Navigate Social Media," *New York Times*, May 15, 2023, https://www.nytimes.com/2023/05/15/well/family/kids-social-media.html.

7. "Why Parents Need to C.R.A.M. & Learn Internet Safety," Child Rescue Coalition, accessed August 5, 2022, https://childrescuecoalition.org/educations/why-parents-need-to-c-r-a-m-learn-internet-safety/.

8. "Teens and Social Media Use: What's the Impact?," Mayo Clinic, February 26, 2022, https://www.mayoclinic.org/healthy-lifestyle/tween-and-teen-health/in-depth/teens-and-social-media-use/art-20474437.

9. "5 Healthy Tech Habits for the New Year," Child Rescue Coalition, 2022, https://childrescuecoalition.org/educations/5-healthy-tech-habits-for-the-new-year/.

10. Sample boundaries are adapted in part from "Teens and Social Media Use: What's the Impact?"; "5 Healthy Tech Habits for the New Year"; and "Social Media and Teens," AACAP.org, March 2018, https://www.aacap.org/AACAP/Families_and_Youth/Facts_for_Families/FFF-Guide/Social-Media-and-Teens-100.aspx.

11. Carley Yoost and Moe McClanahan, *C.R.A.M.: A Parent's Study Guide to Managing Kids and Technology* (eBook, Child Rescue Coalition and Safe Surfin' Foundation, accessed May 13, 2023), https://drive.google.com/drive/folders/1OQRFj6z9yi7vpqeSdUoxYLLkIrh-Xjyc.

12. Yoost and McClanahan, *C.R.A.M.: A Parent's Study Guide to Managing Kids and Technology.*

13. Yoost and McClanahan, *C.R.A.M.: A Parent's Study Guide to Managing Kids and Technology.*

14. "Why Parents Need to C.R.A.M & Learn Internet Safety."

15. Stats listed below this statement are drawn directly from Jingjing Jiang, "How Teens and Parents Navigate Screen Time and Device Distractions," Pew Research, August 14, 2020, https://www.pewresearch.org/internet/2018/08/22/how-teens-and-parents-navigate-screen-time-and-device-distractions/.

## EPILOGUE

1. Benedict XVI, "Homily of His Holiness Benedict XVI: Eucharistic Celebration on the Solemnity of Pentecost," Vatican.va, May 31, 2009, emphasis original, https://www.vatican.va/content/benedict-xvi/en/homilies/2009/documents/hf_ben-xvi_hom_20090531_pentecoste.html#:~:text=This%20pure%2C%20essential%20and%20personal%20%22fire%22%2C%20the%20fire,of%20the%20Apostles%3A%20the%20Holy%20Spirit%20overcomes%20fear.

## ACKNOWLEDGMENTS

1. This is adapted from a quote by Henri Nouwen: "For most of my life I have struggled to find God, to know God, to love God. I have tried hard to follow the guidelines of the spiritual life—pray always, work for others, read the Scriptures—and to avoid the many temptations to dissipate myself. I have failed many times but always tried again, even when I was close to despair. Now I wonder whether I have sufficiently realized that during all this time God has been trying to find me, to know me, and to love me. The question is not 'How am I to find God?' but 'How am I to let myself be found by him?' The question is not 'How am I to know God?' but 'How am I to let myself be known by God?' And, finally, the question is not 'How am I to love God?' but 'How am I to let myself be loved by God?' God is looking into the distance for me, trying to find me, and longing to bring me home." Henri J. M. Nouwen, *The Return of the Prodigal Son: A Story of Homecoming*. New York: Bantam Doubleday Dell, 1994, 106.

# BIBLIOGRAPHY

AACAP. "Social Media and Teens." AACAP.org, March 2018. https://www.aacap.org/AACAP/Families_and_Youth/Facts_for_Families/FFF-Guide/Social-Media-and-Teens-100.aspx.

Abbvie. "Normal Puberty Development." PubertyTooSoon.com. Accessed May 7, 2023. https://www.pubertytoosoon.com/about-cpp/normal-puberty-development?cid=ppc_ppd_msft_CPP_DA_Do_I_Have_puberty_in_girls_before_age_Phrase_US-LUPR-210569&&msclkid=c10fdb08e0f211f856bcb89c35c2c954&gclid=COLe5ZHc7_sCFWOyxQIds7IP8w&gclsrc=ds.

American Psychological Association. "APA Panel Issues Recommendations for Adolescent Social Media Use." APA.org, May 9, 2023. https://www.apa.org/news/press/releases/2023/05/adolescent-social-media-use-recommendations#:~:text=Limit%20social%20media%20use%20so,%2D%20or%20appearance%2Drelated%20content. Aura. "Protect Your Kids Online with Parental Controls." Accessed May 14, 2023. https://buy.aura.com/parental-controls-2?irclickid=2xBVPyyBBxyNWceRwL37OzQZUkAUy10lL0TYx80&iradname=Gtwy-PC+-+PC+Family+Bundle+Dedicated-+no+-price&iradid=1555907&irgwc=1&c1=34020&camp=12398&utm_source=top10&utm_medium=ir_affiliate&mktp=IR_Affiliates&sharedid=&utm_gateway=parental-controls.

Anderson, Monica, and JingJing Jiang. "Teens, Social Media and Technology 2018." Pew Research Center: Internet, Science & Tech, May 31,

2018. https://www.pewresearch.org/internet/2018/05/31/teens-social-media-technology-2018/#vast-majority-of-teens-have-access-to-a-home-computer-or-smartphone.

Austen, David. Rep. *Young People, Pornography & Age-Verification*. Revealing Reality, January 2020. https://revealingreality.co.uk/wp-content/uploads/2020/01/BBFC-Young-people-and-pornography-Final-report-2401.pdf.

Bailey, J. Michael, Paul L. Vasey, Lisa M. Diamond, S. Marc Breedlove, Eric Vilain, and Marc Epprecht. "Sexual Orientation, Controversy, and Science." *Psychological Science in the Public Interest* 17, no. 2 (2016): 45–101.

Bark. Accessed January 11, 2023. https://www.bark.us/learn/ps-block-adult-content/?msclkid=86636eae97f21dac0a990d-552055170f&utm_source=bing&utm_medium=cpc&utm_campaign=Search+US+%7C+Catch+All&utm_term=accountability+app&utm_content=Accountability+%7C+General.

Belgau, Ron. "A Note on Courage and Language." *Spiritual Friendship*, June 17, 2019. https://spiritualfriendship.org/2019/05/24/a-note-on-courage-and-language/#more-9698.

Benedict XVI. "Homily of His Holiness Benedict XVI: Eucharistic Celebration on the Solemnity of Pentecost." Vatican.va, May 31, 2009. https://www.vatican.va/content/benedict-xvi/en/homilies/2009/documents/hf_ben-xvi_hom_20090531_pentecoste.html#:~:text=This%20pure%2C%20essential%20and%20personal%20%22fire%22%2C%20the%20fire,of%20the%20Apostles%3A%20the%20Holy%20Spirit%20overcomes%20fear

Birds & Bees. Instagram. Accessed May 13, 2023. https://www.instagram.com/birds__bees/.

*Catechism of the Catholic Church*. 2nd ed. Washington, DC: United States Catholic Conference, 2011. https://www.usccb.org/sites/default/files/flipbooks/catechism/.

Centers for Disease Control and Prevention. "Over Half of U.S. Teens Have Had Sexual Intercourse by Age 18, New Report Shows." CDC, June 22, 2018. https://www.cdc.gov/nchs/pressroom/nchs_press_releases/2017/201706_NSFG.htm.

———. "Talking with Your Teens about Sex." CDC, November 21, 2019. https://www.cdc.gov/healthyyouth/protective/factsheets/talking_teens.htm.

Chadwick, Scot. "Overcome Pornography through Accountability." Accountable2You, December 7, 2021. https://accountable2you.com/blog/overcome-pornography/.

Child Rescue Coalition. "Why Parents Need to C.R.A.M. & Learn Internet Safety." Accessed August 5, 2022. https://childrescuecoalition. org/educations/why-parents-need-to-c-r-a-m-learn internet-safety/.

Congregation for the Doctrine of the Faith. "Letter to the Bishops of the Catholic Church on the Pastoral Care of Homosexual Persons." Vatican.va, October 1, 1986. https://www.vatican.va/roman_curia/congregations/cfaith/documents/rc_con_cfaith_doc_19861001_homosexual-persons_en.html.

Cook, Allison. *The Best of You: Break Free from Painful Patterns, Mend Your Past, and Discover Your True Self in God*. Nashville, TN: Nelson Books, 2022.

Copen, Casey, Anjani Chandra, and Isaedmarie Febo-Vazquez. "Sexual Behavior, Sexual Attraction, and Sexual Orientation among Adults Aged 18–44 in the United States: Data from the 2011–2013 National Survey of Family Growth." National Health Statistics Reports 88 (January 27, 2016): 1–13.

Diamond, Lisa M. *Sexual Fluidity: Understanding Women's Love and Desire*. Cambridge, MA: Harvard University Press, 2009.

Earls, Aaron. "Most Teenagers Drop Out of Church When They Become Young Adults." Lifeway Research, August 11, 2021. https://research.lifeway.com/2019/01/15/most-teenagers-drop-out-of-church-as-young-adults/.

Eden Invitation. "Resources." Accessed May 12, 2023. https://www.edeninvitation.com/resources.

Favale, Abigail. *The Genesis of Gender: A Christian Theory*. San Francisco, CA: Ignatius Press, 2022.

Fung, Simon Kent. *Dear Alana*, (podcast). Tenderfoot TV: August 13, 2023.

Hewitt, Kristen. "5 Healthy Tech Habits for the New Year." Child Rescue Coalition, 2022. https://childrescuecoalition.org/educations/5-healthy-tech-habits-for-the-new-year/.

Hicks, Fr. Boniface. "Ravished Sacred Heart Prayer." FatherBoniface. org, August 23, 2022. https://fatherboniface.org/audio/2022/22-08-21%20Mundelein%20Seminary%20Retreat%20On%20The%20Heart/20220823%204%20Conf%20Ravished%20Sacred%20Heart%20Prayer.m4a.

Jiang, Jingjing. "How Teens and Parents Navigate Screen Time and Device Distractions." Pew Research Center: Internet, Science & Tech, August 14, 2020. https://www.pewresearch.org/internet/2018/08/22/how-teens-and-parents-navigate-screen-time-and-device-distractions/.

Jones, Jeffrey M. "U.S. LGBT Identification Steady at 7.2%." *Gallup*, February 17, 2023. https://news.gallup.com/poll/470708/lgbt-identification-steady.aspx.

Jones, Stanton, and Mark Yarhouse. *Ex-Gays?: An Extended Longitudinal Study of Attempted Religiously Mediated Change in Sexual Orientation.* Downers Grove, IL: Intervarsity Press Academic, 2007.

Kolber, Aundi. *Try Softer: A Fresh Approach to Move Us out of Anxiety, Stress, and Survival Mode—And into a Life of Connection and Joy.* Carol Stream, IL: Tyndale Refresh, 2020.

Laure, Sara. "Masturbation and Young Children." MottChildren.org, November 2020. https://www.mottchildren.org/posts/your-child/masturbation-and-young-children.

Lenhart, Amanda, Monica Anderson, and Aaron Smith. "Basics of Teen Romantic Relationships." Pew Research Center: Internet, Science & Tech, October 1, 2015. https://www.pewresearch.org/internet/2015/10/01/basics-of-teen-romantic-relationships/.

Madigan, Sheri, Vanessa Villani, Corry Azzopardi, Danae Laut, Tanya Smith, Jeff R. Temple, Dillon Browne, and Gina Dimitropoulos. "The Prevalence of Unwanted Online Sexual Exposure and Solicitation among Youth: A Meta-Analysis." *Journal of Adolescent Health* 63, no. 2 (August 2018): 133–41. https://doi.org/10.1016/j.jadohealth.2018.03.012.

Mah, Leanna W., Yvonne Y. Chan, and Jennifer H. Yang. "Gender Identity in Disorders of Sex Development." *In Principles of Gender-Specific Medicine*, 27–43. Cambridge, MA: Academic Press, 2017.

Mattson, Daniel. "Why I Don't Call Myself a Gay Christian." *First Things*, July 27, 2012. https://www.firstthings.com/web-exclusives/2012/07/why-i-dont-call-myself-a-gay-christian.

———. *Why I Don't Call Myself Gay: How I Reclaimed My Sexual Reality and Found Peace.* San Francisco, CA: Ignatius Press, 2017.

Mayo Clinic Staff. "Teens and Social Media Use: What's the Impact?" Mayo Clinic, February 26, 2022. https://www.mayoclinic.org/healthy-lifestyle/tween-and-teen-health/in-depth/teens-and-social-media-use/art-20474437.

Nouwen, Henri J. M. *The Return of the Prodigal Son: A Story of Homecoming.* New York, NY: Bantam Doubleday Dell, 1994.

Pearson, Catherine. "How Parents Can Help Teens Navigate Social Media." *New York Times,* May 15, 2023. https://www.nytimes.com/2023/05/15/well/family/kids-social-media.html.

Pew Research Center. "Leaving Catholicism." Pew Research Center: Religion & Public Life Project, April 4, 2009. https://www.pewresearch.org/religion/2009/04/27/faith-in-flux3/.

Posture Shift Ministries. *Guiding Families of LGBT Loved Ones: For Every Pastor and Parent and All Who Care,* Fifth Edition. Houston, TX: Posture Shift Books, 2023.

Qustodio. Accessed April 18, 2023. https://www.qustodio.com/en/premium/.

RAINN. "Children and Teens: Statistics." Accessed May 12, 2023. https://www.rainn.org/statistics/children-and-teens.

Robbins, Cynthia L., Vanessa Schick, Michael Reece, Debra Herbenick, Stephanie A. Sanders, Brian Dodge, and J. Dennis Fortenberry. "Prevalence, Frequency, and Associations of Masturbation with Partnered Sexual Behaviors among US Adolescents." *Archives of Pediatrics & Adolescent Medicine* 165, no. 12 (December 2011): 1087–93.

Sable, Marjorie, Fran Danis, Denise Mauzy, and Sarah Gallagher. "Barriers to Reporting Sexual Assault for Women and Men: Perspectives of College Students." *Journal of American College Health* 55, no. 3 (November–December 2006): 157–62. https://doi.org/DOI: 10.3200/JACH.55.3.157-162.

Sprecher, Susan, Lucia F. O'Sullivan, Michelle Drouin, Julie Verette-Lindenbaum, and Marion C. Willetts. "Perhaps It Was Too Soon: College Students' Reflections on the Timing of Their Sexual Debut." *Journal of Sex Research* 59, no. 1 (March 2021): 39–52.

Stewart, J. L., Leigh A. Spivey, Laura Widman, Sophia Choukas-Bradley, and Mitchell J. Prinstein. "Developmental Patterns of Sexual Identity, Romantic Attraction, and Sexual Behavior among Adolescents over Three Years." *Journal of Adolescence* 77 (December 2019): 90–97.

Stringer, Jay, and Young, Adam, hosts. "How Your Story Affects Your Sexuality." *The Place We Find Ourselves* (podcast), March 23, 2023. https://open.spotify.com/episode/2x2HJKNpx8WLG1EusfA6zY?si=9b5237bec-bef4ad6.

ThingLink. "The Male Reproductive System." Accessed May 7, 2023. https://www.thinglink.com/scene/896477526635839489.

Tushnet, Eve. *Gay and Catholic: Accepting My Sexuality, Finding Community, Living My Faith.* Notre Dame, IN: Ave Maria Press, 2014.

Villa, Antonia Pérez. "What Happens in Female Reproductive System?" HelpUandfun, January 24, 2017. https://helpuandfun.blogspot.com/2017/01/what-happens-in-female-reproductive.html.

Yarhouse, Mark A., and Olya Zaporozhets. *When Children Come Out: A Guide for Christian Parents.* Downers Grove, IL: IVP Academic, 2022.

Yarhouse, Mark A., and Julia Sadusky. *Emerging Gender Identities: Understanding the Diverse Experiences of Today's Youth.* Grand Rapids, MI: Brazos Press, 2020.

Yoost, Carley, and Moe McClanahan. C.R.A.M.: A Parent's Study Guide to Managing Kids and Technology (eBook). Child Rescue Coalition and Safe Surfin' Foundation. Accessed May 13, 2023. https://drive.google.com/drive/folders/1OQRFj6z9yi7vpqeSdUoxYLLkIrh-Xjyc.

Young, Adam. "Why It's So Important to Understand Your Story." *The Place We Find Ourselves* (podcast), October 2022. https://open.spotify.com/episode/1LenL11OvDI4mxWRWSJeJZ?si=60c9ea0064194d02.

# INDEX

**Julia Sadusky** is a licensed clinical psychologist and the owner of Lux Counseling and Consulting. She is the author of *Start Talking to Your Kids about Sex* and is a consultant, speaker, and adjunct professor. Sadusky has done extensive research in sexual development and specializes in trauma-informed care.

She earned a bachelor's degree from Ave Maria University and a master's degree and doctorate in clinical psychology from Regent University. Sadusky is an affiliate member of the American Psychological Association.

Her clinical practice is in Littleton, Colorado.

www.juliasadusky.com
Instagram: drsadusky
Linktree: linktr.ee/drjuliasadusky
Facebook: www.facebook.com/drsadusky
YouTube: @dr.juliasadusky5716

# Don't Miss the Book for Parents of Younger Children

## Start Talking to Your Kids about Sex
### A PRACTICAL GUIDE FOR CATHOLICS

While it is crucial to talk to teenagers about sex, boundaries, and their changings bodies, having similar conversations with your elementary-age kids are just as important. That is why Julia Sadusky also wrote *Start Talking to Your Kids about Sex* in order to give parents—or anyone who educates or takes care of children— practical advice and Q&A sections to help you have these talks with younger children in an age-appropriate way.

This go-to resource is structured around the most frequently asked questions Sadusky receives in her clinical practice, including

- When do I start talking to my kids about these topics?
- What is healthy body exploration?
- Should I make my kids hug strangers?
- How can I help my kids learn to say no when I'm not around?
- What are good "house rules," and how do I justify them to other adults?
- What do I do if my kids say they had an unwanted sexual experience?
- How should I respond to invitations to sleepovers and overnight trips?

While the book is geared toward parents, extended family members, caregivers, mentors, mental health professionals, and educators also will find the information helpful.

## "Timely and important work!"
—Jackie and Bobby Angel
Catholic authors and speakers

Look for this title wherever books and eBooks are sold.
Visit **avemariapress.com** for more information.